P. J. COLE.

A GREAT ESTATE AT WORK
The Holkham estate and its inhabitants in the nineteenth century

A GREAT ESTATE AT WORK

The Holkham estate and its inhabitants in the nineteenth century

SUSANNA WADE MARTINS

CAMBRIDGE UNIVERSITY PRESS
CAMBRIDGE
LONDON · NEW YORK · NEW ROCHELLE
MELBOURNE · SYDNEY

Published by the Press Syndicate of the University of Cambridge
The Pitt Building, Trumpington Street, Cambridge CB2 1RP
32 East 57th Street, New York, NY 10022, USA
296 Beaconsfield Parade, Middle Park, Melbourne 3206, Australia

© Cambridge University Press 1980

First published 1980

Printed in Great Britain at the University Press, Cambridge

Library of Congress Cataloguing in Publication Data
Martins, Susanna Wade, 1946–
A great estate at work.
Bibliography: p. 000
Includes index.
1. Holkham Hall. I. Title.
DA664.H643M37   942.6'1   79-51827
ISBN 0 521 22696 1

Contents

List of figures	page vi
List of tables	x
Preface	xi
Acknowledgements	xiii
Abbreviations	xiv

1	The Holkham estate in its setting	1
2	The landlords	39
3	The running of the estate	67
4	The tenant farmer and his farm	105
5	The landlord and the labourer	187
6	Some conclusions: the landlord, the tenant and the landscape	249

Appendix 1
Agricultural statistics for the county of Norfolk in 1854 — 259

Appendix 2
Investments of the first two Earls of Leicester, 1811–1891 — 267

Appendix 3
The amount of rent collected, the sum in arrears and the amount spent on repairs on the Holkham estate, 1790–1900 — 270

Appendix 4
Size of farms and expenditure on them, 1790–1900 — 273

Appendix 5
Condition of cottages on the Holkham estates, 1851 — 275

Select bibliography — 283
Index — 285

Figures

1.1	The Norfolk estates of the Coke family c. 1850. From Holkham MSS, H. W. Keary, 'Survey of the estates of the Earl of Leicester' (1851).	*page* 2
1.2	Norfolk estates over 3,000 acres in 1873. From J. Bateman, *The Great Landowners of Great Britain and Ireland* (London, 1883).	8
1.3	The price of a quarter of wheat in Norwich, 1790–1900. From the *Norfolk Chronicle* market reports.	12
1.4	Proportion of land in each Norfolk Poor Law Union under various crops in 1854. Based on appendix 1.	20
1.5	Proportion of land in each Norfolk Poor Law Union under various grain crops within the total grain acreage. Based on appendix 1.	21
1.6	Proportion of land in each Norfolk Poor Law Union under root, peas and beans. Based on appendix 1.	23
1.7	Number of animals per acre within each Norfolk Poor Law Union. Based on appendix 1.	24
2.1	Family tree of the Cokes of Norfolk, 1776–1909. From C. W. James, *Chief Justice Coke, his Family and Descendants at Holkham* (London, 1929).	41
2.2	Thomas William Coke, owner of Holkham 1776–1842.	43
2.3	Thomas Coke, second Earl of Leicester and owner of Holkham 1842–1909.	53
3.1	Francis Blaikie, agent to the Holkham estates 1816–32.	68
3.2	The home farm at Longlands.	82
3.3	Arrears in rents, rents collected and the amount spent on improvements, 1790–1900. From Holkham MSS, audit books.	86
3.4	Percentage of income from rents invested in improvements. From Holkham MSS, audit books.	94

Figures

4.1	John Hudson, tenant of Lodge Farm, Castle Acre, 1822–69.	115
4.2	Rents on the farms tenanted by the Hudson family. From Holkham MSS, audit books.	117
4.3	John Hastings, tenant of Longham Hall Farm, 1869–84.	123
4.4	Rents on Longham Farm. From Holkham MSS, audit books.	124
4.5	Longham before and after enclosure. From Holkham MSS, estate maps.	128
4.6	Weasenham farms, c. 1850. Holkham MSS, estate maps.	129
4.7	Tittleshall farms, c. 1850. Holkham MSS, estate maps.	130
4.8	Types of improvement work undertaken on the Holkham estates, 1790–1900. From Holkham MSS, audit books.	132
4.9	The Great Barn at Holkham.	135
4.10	A farm of Great Massingham c. 1800.	136
4.11	Model farm plan by Waistell. From C. Waistell, *Designs for Agricultural Buildings* (London, 1827).	141
4.12	Round house at Wheycurd Farm, Wighton.	142
4.13	Waterden farm premises from the north-east.	144
4.14	Plan of Waterden Farm. From Holkham MSS, 'Holkham estate farm premises and cottages 1856–'.	144
4.15	Plan of Grenstein farm, Tittleshall. From Holkham MSS, 'Holkham estate farm premises and cottages 1856–'.	145
4.16	Plan of Panworth Hall Farm, Ashill. From Holkham MSS, 'Holkham estate farm premises and cottages 1856–'.	146
4.17	Farm houses on the Holkham estate designed by Samuel Wyatt. (a) Kempstone Lodge. (b) Lodge Farm, Castle Acre. (c) Wicken Farm, Castle Acre.	148
4.18	Barn, Wicken Farm, Castle Acre.	151
4.19	Barn, Leicester Square Farm, South Creake.	151
4.20	Plan of Leicester Square Farm, South Creake. From a modern survey.	152
4.21	Plan of the Great Barn, Holkham. From R. N. Bacon, *Agriculture of Norfolk* (London, 1844).	154
4.22	Barn, Manor Farm, Tittleshall.	157
4.23	Stable and horse yard, High House Farm, Weasenham.	159
4.24	John Hudson's model farm plan. From J. Hudson. 'On the construction of farm buildings', *J.R.A.S.E.*, vol. 11 (1850), p. 282.	167

viii *Figures*

4.25 Farm premises, Egmere Farm. (a) Cattle sheds, interior of northwest yard, looking north. (b) Cattle sheds, exterior, looking south. (c) Loose boxes, interior. 170
4.26 Plan of Egmere Farm. Holkham MSS, 'Holkham estate farm premises and cottages 1856–'. 171
4.27 Number of buildings on the Holkham farms at the time of Keary's report. From Holkham MSS, H. W. Keary, 'Survey of the estates of the Earl of Leicester' (1851). 175
4.28 Plan of Hall Farm, Wighton. From Holkham MSS, 'Holkham estate farm premises and cottages 1856–'. 179
4.29 Farm premises, Sparham. (a) Loose boxes. (b) Cattle sheds. 181
4.30 Concrete sheds, Wicken Farm, Tittleshall. 182
5.1 Holkham reading room. 195
5.2 Cottages on the Houghton estate, c. 1800. From Houghton MSS, Samuel Hill, 'A survey of the Norfolk estates of the Marquis of Cholmondeley' (c. 1800). 209
5.3 Cottages at High House farm, Weasenham. 211
5.4 New cottages built at Holkham by Thomas William Coke. From *Annals of Agriculture*, vol. 20 (1793) 213
5.5 Rose cottages, Holkham. 214
5.6 Cottages, Holkham Staithe. 214
5.7 Cottages, Flitcham, 1833. 215
5.8 Cottage plans published on the *Norfolk News* (8 Oct. 1863). 220
5.9 Cottages, Great Bircham. (a) Unimproved cottage. (b) Late-nineteenth-century cottages. 223
5.10 Cottages, Harpley Dam, Flitcham. 226
5.11 Cottage plans 1850–70. From Holkham MSS, 'Holkham estate, farm premises and cottages, 1856–'. 227
5.12 Cottage plans, 1870s. From Holkham MSS, 'Holkham estate, farm premises and cottages, 1856–'. 230
5.13 Cottages, Sparham. 231
5.14 Cottages, Holkham Staithe. 231
5.15 Improvements to cottages in the 1880s. From cottage plans in the muniment room at Holkham. 233
5.16 Addition of a second floor to cottages at Mileham, 1890. From cottage plans in the muniment room at Holkham. 234

Figures

6.1 Aerial view of estate landscape. (a) Coastal area between Holkham and Wells, showing 1856 drainage dyke, Holkham branch of the Wells and Fakenham railway, and the woodland belt around the park. Note the large regular fields of planned enclosure. (b) Holkham park and house. 250

6.2 Plan of Holkham park. From Holkham MSS, estate maps. 252

Tables

1.1	Agriculture statistics for Norfolk, 1871–91	31
2.1	Total decennial net income of the Holkham estate, 1850–99	60
2.2	Total investments per decade by the second Earl of Leicester	64
3.1	Ten-yearly statistics for the home farm, 1843–1907	80
3.2	Amounts spent on repairs and percentage return in rent increases, 1790–1899	101
3.3	Rent and expenditure on five Holkham farms, 1790–1900	102
4.1	Tenant stability on Holkham farms, 1790–1890	112
4.2	Farms with two phases of building, one before 1850 and one 1860–83	178
5.1	Holkham Almshouses accounts for 1854, from account book, 1804–90	205
5.2	Expenditure and number of date stones for ten-year periods, 1850–80	225

Preface

The main aim of this book is to present one of the nineteenth century's greatest agricultural estates, showing the physical and institutional fabric it created and sustained. New farms were laid out, suited to changing agricultural practice, and the park altered to please changing tastes. A social conscience, as well as expediency, in the period 1860–1914 resulted in the building of most of the estate cottages that survive today. The structure of estate administration also changed during the period and all these factors directly affected tenant farmers and cottagers. Although it has not proved possible to explore in depth the multivarious lives of estate inhabitants, fascinating though this would be, an attempt has been made to describe their way of life in so far as it was influenced by the landlord and his agent.

One of the reasons why the Holkham estate was chosen for such a study was the great variety of both documentary and architectural evidence available. Such is the wealth of both types of material that it is possible to wander over about seventy farmsteads which have remained often unaltered since the 1880s and substantially unchanged since the 1830s, knowing the names and relative success of the tenants who held them, when different buildings were built, why and how much they cost, and what difference, if any, these improvements made to rents. We can follow estate correspondence with tenants and often know why tenants finally decided to leave. Estate descriptions of both farms and cottages tell us what they were like at different periods and many of the cottages as well as the farms survive for study.

This is not the first piece of research to use the Holkham archives, but it is the only one to use the building evidence extensively, and to combine the evidence from both sources to provide something approaching a complete picture of estate life.

Mrs A. M. W. Stirling was the first to use the Holkham documents. As a relation of the Cokes, she was able to consult many family memories, as well as personal papers which are now lost, to produce her biography of Thomas William Coke published in 1908. Although this book is invaluable in many ways, it has been shown to contain many inaccuracies and, in common with many biographies of its period, is full of political and family detail but frustratingly lacking in social and economic evidence.

Most of the inaccuracies have been corrected and many gaps filled by Dr R. A. C. Parker's recent book on the financial and economic affairs of the Cokes from 1707 to 1842. However, this study is again limited to seeing things from the landlord's viewpoint and there is little attempt to analyse the wider effects of the estate on the community over which it exercised so much control. Dr Parker's work ends in 1842 and does not cover the fascinating period of boom and depression which dominates the agricultural history of the second half of the nineteenth century.

The post-1880 depression was in many ways revolutionary in the way it changed the landlord–tenant relationship, while reducing rents by half to the level of seventy years before. This can all be followed in surprising detail through the estate papers. To survive, many landlords were investing more outside their estates, in business, usually through the stock exchange. This transfer of capital from agriculture to commerce after 1870 can be followed through the Holkham archives.

This book has been written in the belief that such a total study of a great estate at work is of value to students of nineteenth-century social, economic and agricultural history as well as to local historians.

Acknowledgements

Most of the work for this book was originally carried out for a Ph.D. thesis at the University of East Anglia, which was completed in 1975. My tutor, Dr R. G. Wilson, gave freely of his time to help me and I owe much to the informed advice and encouragement he gave me.

There have been many different lines of enquiry to be followed, all of which have relied heavily on the help of other people. Firstly there was the work in the estate office and muniment room at Holkham Hall, the home of the Earl of Leicester. Without the late Earl's permission to use the documents there, this research would have been impossible. The estate archivist, Dr W. O. Hassall, has not only guided me through the extensive estate archives, but has always shown a great interest in what I have been doing, and his enthusiasm has always been an encouragement. The agent, Mr Ian Whitworth, and the estate office staff, in particular Mr R. D. Bunting, have been very patient and allowed me to visit many estate buildings and also to work in the office.

Other sources have been consulted, mainly housed in the Norfolk Record Office and the Norfolk Local Studies Library, and I have much appreciated the help and guidance given to me by the staff.

Thirdly this research has involved visiting the many farms erected by the estate during the period being studied and everywhere I was greeted with kindness and cooperation. The owners and tenants I met gave all the help they could and some went to great lengths to look out documents for me and gave up time to pass on much useful information.

Finally the constant interest taken in my research by my husband has been an enormous encouragement and I am sure that without him this work would never have been completed.

Photographs are reproduced by kind permission of the following: The Courtauld Institute of Art, University of London, for figs. 2.2 and 3.1

Major R. L. Coke for fig. 2.3, photographer Hallam Ashley F.R.P.S.

The Royal Agricultural Society of England for fig. 4.1, photographer Hallam Ashley F.R.P.S.
Mr Peter Hastings for fig. 4.3
Lady Cholmondeley for fig. 4.10, photographer David Yaxley
Air Photographs Index of the Norfolk Archaeological Unit for fig. 6.1, photographer Derek A. Edwards

ABBREVIATIONS

J.R.A.S.E. *The Journal of the Royal Agricultural Society of England*
N.R.O. Norfolk Record Office
V.C.H. *Victoria County History*

I
The Holkham estate in its setting

> The fairest where many are fair.
> (Arthur Young 1804)[1]

The intensive agriculture of north-west Norfolk in the middle of the Napoleonic War boom must certainly have appeared very 'fair' to the eyes of an agricultural commentator; and this area, developed under the influence of large estates, the biggest of which was Holkham, still has an atmosphere of prosperity today. But Holkham's fame was not based only on its size. Thomas William Coke, created Earl of Leicester of Holkham in 1837, was the owner from 1776 to 1842. He built up a very high reputation for estate management and agricultural improvement and also pursued an active political career. Holkham was quoted as a model of estate administration and his tireless efforts at promoting publicity for new techniques brought him renown on both sides of the Atlantic. His annual sheep shearings between 1778 and 1821 were virtually private agricultural shows and these attracted dignitaries from Britain, Europe and America.

All the glory that surrounds the legend of Thomas William Coke makes it very easy to forget the work of his ancestors, the importance of the part played by the tenants and also the general atmosphere of improvement which prevailed in Norfolk at the time. Recent studies have put his work into the context of his predecessors, and many of the more extravagent claims of the Holkham legend have been shown to be unfounded.[2] However, a solid core of evidence remains to demonstrate the importance of the Holkham estate to the development of English agriculture in general and that of Norfolk in particular. The reputation of the estate remained high throughout the later part of the century and the first earl's son, another Thomas, kept up the tradition of good management, even through the depression at the end of the period.

---

[1] A. Young, *A General View of the Agriculture of the County of Norfolk* (London, 1804), p. 32.
[2] R. A. C. Parker, *Coke of Norfolk, a Financial and Agricultural Study, 1707–1842* (Oxford, 1975).

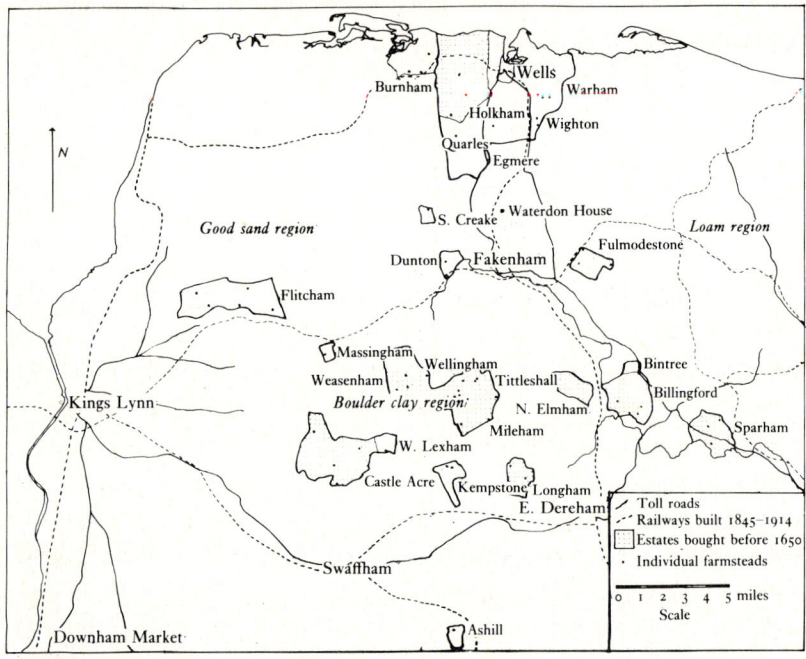

1.1 The Norfolk estates of the Coke family, c. 1850.

The accumulation of the Holkham estates

The purchase of the Holkham estates was begun by Chief Justice Edward Coke in the seventeenth century, at a time when other families who were to remain important county landowners throughout the nineteenth century were also amassing their possessions. Edward Coke was born in 1550 at the family home of Burghwood Hall, Mileham. In 1576 he bought Godwick Manor in the neighbouring parish of Tittleshall and it was there that he made his home. By 1600, the nearby manors of Wellingham, Weasenham and Elmham had been added to form the basis of his mid-Norfolk estates. In 1606, Billingford was purchased, in 1610, Longham and in 1612, Sparham. Castle Acre was added in 1616 (fig. 1.1).

In 1610, the manor of Holkham was bought. It was the first to be purchased in the north-west of the county, and in 1653 became the home of the Chief Justice's son, who lived in the old manor house of Hill Hall.

This remained a residence of the Cokes until about 1750 when it was replaced by the new Holkham Hall.[3]

The Chief Justice died in 1634 and must by then have spent at least £100,000 on purchasing land.[4] This mony came both from his two wives and from his lucrative career. Income from rents would have contributed a small proportion. Expansion in the north-west was continued by the Cokes throughout the eighteenth century with the acquisition of the Burnhams in 1756 and 1757, Wighton in 1750 and Warham in 1785. The soils in this area are very different to those further south. They are much lighter and need careful farming if they are to be productive. Most of the coastal strip was saltmarsh. In 1660 John Coke reclaimed 350 acres of marsh and in 1772 Thomas Coke reclaimed a further 400.[5]

There were no new parishes added to the estates after 1785. Instead small pieces of land were brought within the parishes already mainly controlled by the Cokes. By 1851, the estate included seventy farms as well as small holdings and cottages. It was by far the largest estate in Norfolk (42,000 acres), being over twice the size of its two nearest rivals at Raynham (19,679 acres) and Houghton (16,995 acres).[6]

The topography of the Holkham estates

The seventy farms of the Holkham estate were divided among twenty-six parishes across central and north-west Norfolk. These parishes varied in size, population and appearance. They ranged from the depopulated parishes of Quarles, Waterden, Kempstone and Egmere, to the populous villages of Tittleshall and Castle Acre. Waterden, Kempstone and Egmere were all the sites of medieval villages, as earthworks and ruined churches show. By 1800 Waterden, Egmere and Quarles contained one farm each and Kempstone two. The population of Quarles in 1851 was only twenty. Waterden, with an acreage of 763, contained four houses and thirty-nine people. Kempstone's 809 acres contained twelve houses and fifty-eight people and the larger parish of Egmere (1,200 acres) nine

---

[3] C. W. James, *Chief Justice Coke, his Family and Descendants at Holkham* (London, 1929), p. 93.
[4] *Ibid.*, p. 306.
[5] A. M. W. Stirling, *Coke of Norfolk and his Friends*, 2 vols. (London, 1908), vol. 1, p. 248.
[6] J. Bateman, *The Great Landowners of Great Britain and Ireland* (London, 1883), pp. 78 and 415.

houses and fifty-four people. In these parishes all the land and houses were owned by the Holkham estate.

At the other extreme, the population of Castle Acre was 1,567. Most of the land (3,250 acres), but only a few of the houses, were owned by the Coke family. Castle Acre was a small market town laid out in the Middle Ages with a market place, priory and castle. Fairs were held here in August and May until the end of the nineteenth century.

Tittleshall parish covered a similar acreage and had a population of 615, mostly living in the nucleated village near the church. In common with other Holkham estate parishes, the farms were mostly outside the village in the centre of their fields, frequently with a couple of cottages beside them. All the mid-Norfolk parishes are mainly on boulder clay where there is very little building stone available, and both farms and cottages are built of brick or flint and brick. They are typical estate villages dominated by nineteenth-century cottage architecture. The countryside is well wooded and undulating and much of the land heavy and difficult to work.

The westernmost parish owned by the Cokes in the nineteenth century was Flitcham (4,108 acres and 486 inhabitants). Here the land is lighter and better, and carstone was available as a building stone. Consequently this parish looks very different from other estate villages.

The northern part of the estate adjoining Holkham Park is all on light chalky soil. Again there is no building stone, and flint and brick buildings predominate. In some villages near Holkham the yellow brick manufactured at the Holkham brick kilns was used for building, especially for the farm houses and some cottages. The countryside is more open, the fields tend to be larger and the average farm size is also greater.

Communications across such a widely dispersed estate must have been difficult. A few toll roads crossed the area linking Wells to Fakenham and Wells to Norwich. Coaches travelled west from Wells to Hunstanton. Otherwise the area was covered by a network of lanes which were in a better state of repair in the well drained chalky areas than in the wet clay areas. Different parts of the estate would have looked towards the market towns of East Dereham, Swaffham, Fakenham or Wells, while for larger centres some would have turned to Norwich and others Kings Lynn. The coming of the railways helped to improve communication, both within the county and to London. The line from Dereham to

Fakenham was opened in 1844 and a continuation to Wells was promoted by the Cokes and opened in 1856. This made it much easier for the agent to visit the mid-Norfolk estates. References to his spending the night at Tittleshall stop after this date. Instead he made requests to be met off the train at the nearby village of North Elmham. The coming of the railway also helped open up the area to the London market and we hear of Holkham farmers sending their livestock and dairy produce to London by rail.

By 1850, the population of the parishes mostly owned by the Coke family was somewhere near eight and a half thousand. Although by no means all these people were living in estate cottages or farms or were dependent on the estate for their livelihood, they were all in some way affected by it and in 1776 there was already a good tradition of estate management to be maintained. It was the work of men like Coke that was quoted in support of the landlord–tenant system, and certainly at Holkham this could be seen working at its best.

The role of the landlord in the development of improved agriculture

One of the most important developments of nineteenth-century farming was the great increase in demand for fixed and working capital, and by the late eighteenth century the system of financing agriculture was becoming better defined. The tenant was usually responsible for providing his working capital and the landlord the fixed capital. Landlords were suspicious of tenants who could not afford to buy their own seed or implements and it was rare to find a landlord helping a tenant in this way. Although ways in which a landlord could influence the farming on his estate included the example set by the home farm, the terms laid down in the lease, and the personal interest of the landlord and his agent, his most valuable contribution to improvement was the provision of fixed capital.[7] It was unusual for a tenant to be responsible for new buildings on his farm, although sometimes he had to cart materials and provide labour. The extent to which he had to pay for repairs, drainage and hedging also varied. On less well run estates, the tenant might be driven to carry out improvements himself, because of

---

[7] H. J. Habakkuk, 'The economic functions of English Landowners in the seventeenth and eighteenth centuries', *Explorations in Entreprenurial History*, vol. 6 (December 1953), pp. 92–102.

the landowner's lack of interest.[8] The Hare estate, centred on Stow Bardolph, Norfolk, is an example of one where the cost of centrally planned improvements was largely borne by the tenant.[9]

Working capital included money for seed, stock, machines and artificial fertilisers. Better strains of seed and stock were being developed from the late eighteenth century. The stationary threshing machine was being introduced in the 1790s and the first portable one was invented in Norfolk and shown at the Woburn Agricultural meeting in 1803.[10] It was one of the first of a long list of different and increasingly specialised implements needed for intensive farming. Farm sale catalogues for Holkham farms in the late nineteenth century show the great variety of implements needed by them. In 1877 at Lodge Farm, Castle Acre, there were 120 lots of farm machinery. These included the ploughs, harrows, scarifiers, cultivators and rollers which prepared the soil, and a variety of seed drills to plant the crops. Harvesting machinery consisted of reaping and mowing machines, binders, a threshing drum and two elevators with horse gearing. Several Gardener's turnip cutters prepared the root crops for animal feed. As well as the cost of machinery and improved strains of seed and livestock, artificial fertilisers were also beginning to be used. In the early nineteenth century bone meals, guano and nitrates began to supplement farmyard manures. If the land was to be kept in good shape, landlords wanted to attract tenants with capital for working their farms.

Ideally, the owners of the land had to provide the necessary buildings to house the animals and the crop, and cottages for the labourers. They also had to lay out the farms and often had to drain the land as well. Usually the tenant was responsible for keeping the buildings in repair. During the nineteenth century, the number and variety of farm buildings increased. As livestock husbandry intensified, cattle sheds and loose boxes became more important than barns. More specialised implements needed shelter. Barn machinery became more complex and steam engine houses were often required. Animal foodstuffs needed more preparation, and special rooms, often with boilers, had to be built. If tenants with capital were to be attracted to farms, then the farm itself needed to be highly capitalised. The developments on the Holkham estate during this

[8] G. E. Mingay, *English Landed Society in the Eighteenth Century* (London, 1963), chapter 7.
[9] Hare MS, N.R.O.
[10] G. E. Fussell, *The Farmers' Tools* (London, 1952), p. 161.

period are significant, and the study of them helps answer general questions about how much capital was needed to provide the type of farm suitable for intensive farming, how far the improvements made were really needed by progressive farmers and whether farming was in fact over-capitalised by the 1870s.

Throughout the period the estate was held by landlords intensely interested in agricultural improvement. They were prepared to invest capital in the estate on a large scale, and gave practical encouragement to good farming by granting long leases. The second earl was prepared to modify husbandry covenants to allow for experiment and progressive farming. Both earls employed able agents who could advise tenants on farming practice and make sensible assessments of where landlord's capital was needed. The home farm was always well run as an example to the tenantry. The size of many of the farms meant that men of capital were needed to farm them, and though there can never have been many people with both enough capital and of the right calibre to take on a Holkham farm, there was never a shortage of applicants in the first half of the nineteenth century. The importance of progressive tenants to the development of Holkham agriculture must not be overlooked. It was their farms, as well as the land within Holkham park itself, that were inspected and admired at sheep shearings. The result was an estate of intensive farms whose example was respected for nearly a century by many European and American as well as British farmers and landowners.

The origins of Norfolk agriculture

North-west Norfolk, in contrast to the areas to the south and east, was dominated by great estates (fig. 1.2). Much of the area was controlled by Houghton (the Walpoles), Raynham (the Townshends) and Melton Constable (the Astleys), all of which were estates over 12,000 acres. To the east there were few estates over 6,000 acres. Much of this had been enclosed at an early date and was farmed by owner-occupiers. Their numbers seem to have been declining by the end of the eighteenth century as 'numerous little places of the yeomanry have fallen into the hands of men of fortune'.[11] Nathaniel Kent, the journalist and land agent, noted the change with anxiety. The decline of small farmers meant

---

[11] W. Marshall, *Rural Economy of Norfolk*, 2 vols., (London, 1787), vol. 1, pp. 6–8.

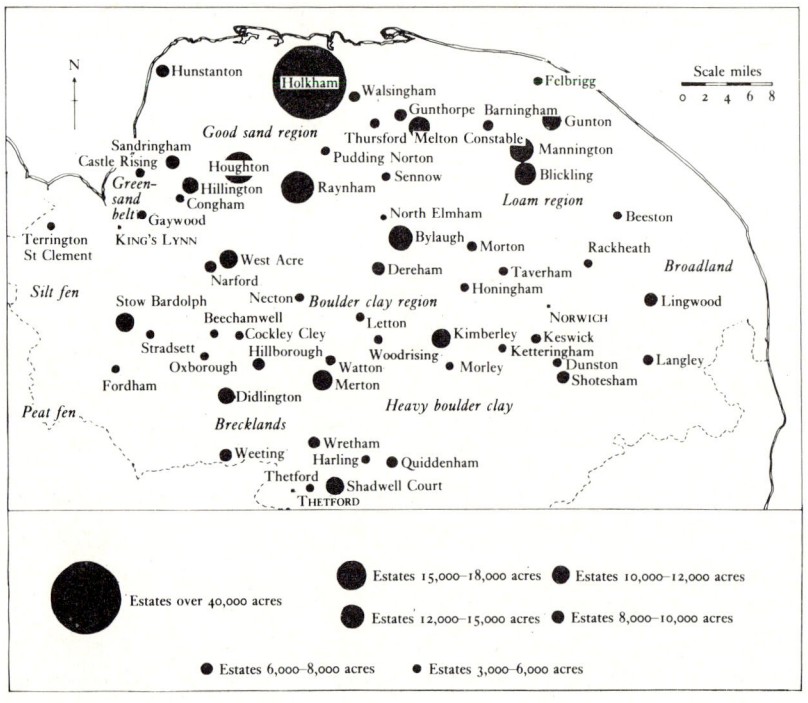

1.2 Norfolk estates over 3,000 acres in 1873.

a decrease in the produce they traditionally provided, such as hogs, poultry and dairy goods.[12] However, the small owner-occupier farmers remained an important part of the Norfolk farming economy throughout the nineteenth century.

The contrast between the north-west and the east of the county was not simply one of freehold and leasehold. the Suffolk farmer and agricultural writer, Arthur Young, in his survey of Norfolk, divided the country into the wet and the dry'.[13] Large farms were mainly concentrated on large estates, and those on the dry sandy soils were sometimes over 1,000 acres; Young quoted Egmere and 'another farm near Holkham' as examples. The number of larger farms at Holkham increased between the two estate surveys of 1780 and 1850, not so much as a result of the amalgamation of farms as through the buying of new land. In 1780 there were four Holkham farms over 1,000 acres and

[12] N. Kent, *A General Survey of the Agriculture of the County of Suffolk* (London, 1796), p. 132.
[13] Young, *The Agriculture of Norfolk*, p. 17.

fourteen between 500 and 1,000 acres. By 1850 there were six over 1,000 and twenty-eight between 500 and 1,000 acres. The number of farms below 100 acres remained fairly static while the number between 100 and 300 declined from twenty-three to nineteen. Holkham farms were on average far larger than in the county as a whole. Farms over 1,000 acres made up nearly 8% of the Holkham estate, but 1.8% of Norfolk as a whole. But 58% of Norfolk farms were under 100 acres while only 8% of the Holkham estate was composed of these smaller farms. About a quarter of both Norfolk and the Holkham estate was made up of medium-sized farms of between 100 and 300 acres.

If the farms of the dry sandy soils were large, those on the 'moderate soils' varied between 400 and 600 acres, and on the very heavy soils south of Norwich and over mid-Norfolk they were often much smaller. These were the areas dominated by owner-occupiers, and over half the Norfolk farms under 100 acres were freehold. On these farms techniques tended to remain primitive and here Norfolk farming was seen at its worst; 'for perhaps no other county presents greater contrasts between the best and the worst farming'.[14] Heavy soils needed draining and the small farmers had not the capital. Where the lands were heaviest and most difficult to work the farms and fields were small and badly arranged. Where the land was tenanted the rents were often disproportionately high.[15]

The richest soils were to be found in the north-east of the county, where much of the land was well farmed by owner-occupiers on small or medium sized farms. William Marshall, author of several contemporary agricultural surveys, claimed that this was the original home of 'Norfolk husbandry'. 'In east Norfolk alone we are to look for that regular and long established system of practice which has raised deservedly the name of Norfolk husbandmen: and which in a principal part of this district, remains unadulterated to the present time.'[16] It seems likely that new farming methods began on good soils; then when they proved successful they would be adopted on the poorer sandy soils to the west, where the great estates dominated and where more capital was available for the investment needed to make the poorer soils productive.[17]

[14] J. Caird, *English Agriculture in 1850–51* (London, 1851), p. 161.
[15] C. S. Read, 'Agriculture of Norfolk', in W. White, *Norfolk Directory* (London, 1883), p. 70.
[16] Marshall, *Rural Economy*, vol. 1, p. 2.
[17] For further discussion on the origins of 'Norfolk agriculture', see H. W. Saunders, 'Estate management at Raynham in the years 1661–1686, and 1706', *Norfolk Archaeology*, vol. 19, no.

Arthur Young, writing in 1771, thought that there were seven different types of improvement which added up to the Norfolk system:
1. Enclosure, with or without the assistance of Parliament.
2. The use of marl and clay.
3. The proper rotation of crops.
4. The cultivation of turnips, hand hoed.
5. The cultivation of clover and artificial grasses.
6. Long leases.
7. Large farms.[18]

All these features are certainly typical of the agriculture of some areas of the county in the late eighteenth century. Turnips were being grown as part of crop rotations and fed to cattle and sheep in the field by the late seventeenth century.[19]

Enclosure, long leases and large farms create a favourable environment for the practice of improved agriculture, while marling, and rotations including turnips, clover and artificial grasses, are all developments in husbandry techniques. Where a landlord–tenant system was dominant, the landlord was more likely to be responsible for providing suitable conditions for agricultural improvement than for introducing the new techniques themselves. This would be up to the tenant.

Other factors which influenced the development of improved farming in Norfolk were out of the control of both landlords and farmers. Geographical features such as the county's long coastline and many small ports meant there was easy access to export markets. Proximity and trading connections with Holland, the home of intensive agriculture, meant that technical knowledge could easily be acquired. By the eighteenth century the expanding city of London was looking beyond the traditional food-producing counties of Kent and Essex, as far as Suffolk and Norfolk. Industrialisation, coupled with population increase, meant that by 1800 agriculture was expected to feed more people with a labour force which was to decline in numbers throughout the

---

1 (1916), pp. 39–66; J. H. Plumb, 'Sir Robert Walpole and Norfolk husbandry', *Economic History Review*, second series, vol. 5 (1952), pp. 86–9; E. Kerridge, 'Turnip husbandry in high Suffolk', *Economic History Review*, second series, vol. 8 (1955–6), pp. 390–2; Daniel Defoe, *A Tour through the Eastern Counties* (1722); Marshall, *Rural Economy;* A. Young, 'A minute on the husbandry of Thomas William Coke, Esq.', *Annals of Agriculture*, vol. 2 (1784), p. 353, and 'A week in Norfolk', *Annals of Agriculture*, vol. 14 (1793), p. 456; and Parker, *Coke of Norfolk*, chapter 1.

[18] A. Young, *A Farmer's Tour*, 2 vols. (London, 1771), vol. 2, p. 150.

[19] Kerridge, 'Turnip husbandry', pp. 390–2.

nineteenth century. The Napoleonic Wars provided an added stimulus to the home production of food.[20]

When Thomas William Coke inherited Holkham in 1776, he was taking over at a time when experimentation and interest in improving techniques was running very high. The good land to the east of his estates was being expertly farmed. His neighbours, the Townshends, had for some time been encouraging new methods. 'Turnip' Townshend had retired to his estates in 1730 and devoted himself to improvements. The letters of John Wrott, steward to Sir Robert Walpole, show that by 1701 marling, the growing of artificial grasses, turnips and crop rotations were well established practices at Houghton. Cattle and sheep were being fattened on the turnip fields.[21] Nor had Coke's predecessors at Holkham been idle. The estate had been well managed, and long leases stipulating crop rotations were not his innovation. The insertion of husbandry clauses in Holkham leases began in the early eighteenth century, although until the 1780s leases allowed the tenant the alternative of a six- or a four-course rotation and only rarely prevented him growing two corn crops in succession. Similarly, long leases of up to twenty years are to be found in the eighteenth century, while in the early nineteenth century shorter leases of eight to twelve years were common.[22] Thus the Holkham estate in 1776 was not only surrounded by others where landlords were encouraging intensive farming techniques already pioneered in other parts of the county, but was also one where there was a tradition of progressive management.

Norfolk agriculture in the nineteenth century

Agricultural fortunes in Norfolk, as elsewhere, were increasingly influenced by international factors and this is reflected by the price of wheat in Norwich, which certainly followed national trends (fig. 1.3). Farming prospered during the Napoleonic Wars. Wartime conditions and particularly the continental blockades meant that little wheat was imported. Poor harvests at home produced famine conditions in several years and wheat prices reached their highest for the century. In 1802 the price in Norwich was over 130 shillings a quarter. In 1796 the figure was between

[20] N. Riches, *The Agricultural Revolution in Norfolk* (London, 1967 reprint), pp. 24–32.
[21] Plumb, 'Sir Robert Walpole', pp. 86–9.
[22] Parker, *Coke of Norfolk*, pp. 66–8.

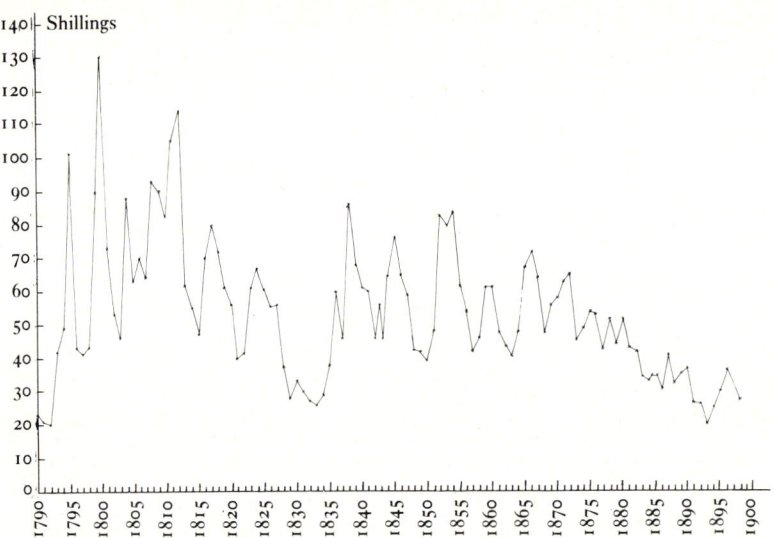

1.3 The price of a quarter of wheat in Norwich, 1790–1900.

100 and 110 shillings and in 1811 between 110 and 120 shillings. These high prices stimulated confidence in farming and investment by both tenant and landlord. Income from rents at Holkham rose from £19,000 to £30,000 over the war period. Improved methods had meant that the output of grain in Norfolk had increased greatly during the last years of the eighteenth century. Kent wrote that in a good year the four main Norfolk ports (Yarmouth, Lynn, Wells and Blakeney/Cley) exported as much grain as the rest of England.[23] Some enterprising farmers even thought that it was worth owning ships themselves for transporting their grain out of the county. Mr Overman of Burnham and Mr Money Hill of Waterden, both Holkham tenants, 'kept their sloops constantly employed in taking corn to London and bringing rape cake manure from Holland, London or Hull, wherever it could be procured at the best and cheapest rate'.[24]

However, there was already criticism of Norfolk farming. High grain yields could partly be explained by the fact that much land was newly enclosed and had been used for grain for less than a century. Secondly, the area relied heavily on imported cattle. 'Although 20,000 fattened cattle left the county every year, only a quarter of them had been bred

[23] N. Kent, *A General Survey of the Agriculture of the County of Norfolk* (London, 1796), p. 144.
[24] Young, *The Agriculture of Norfolk*, p. 490.

locally. The other three quarters came from Scotland or Ireland. It was high time the occupiers or rather the proprietors of Norfolk turned their attention towards the breeding of the whole of their fatting stock.'[25]

Arthur Young also commented on both the bad management of pasture, which was in such contrast to the arable land, and the lack of good breeding cattle.[26] The Norfolk breed of cattle had little to recommend it, and at Holkham Coke was encouraging the introduction of Devon Longhorn. However, Norfolk sheep were held in higher esteem and were thought well suited to the area, but Southdowns were growing in popularity. Especially when they were crossed with Norfolks, they produced both more wool and more meat. By 1804, the Southdowns already dominated the area between Swaffham and Holkham, although there were still many Norfolks between Brandon and Swaffham.[27]

Even the famous four-course system had its critics. By the 1790s, the land was already becoming sick from the too frequent planting of turnips. Kent wrote, 'The land does not relish them so well as formerly, so that great care is necessary in raising them and more seed is required, and after all it is a teasing and precarious crop and admits of no certain rules to ensure absolute success.'[28] It was also found that clover could not be grown continuously in a four-course system. It was more successful when the clover seed was mixed with trefoil and rye-grass and planted in a six-course rotation.

Although both contemporary writers and those who followed them often refer to the 'Norfolk system', there were many types of improved husbandry adapted to local needs. Except for the good lands of the Flegg district, Norfolk was not suited to the cultivation of wheat, and barley was usually the most important cereal crop. It was only in the good soils of the north-east and near Norwich and Yarmouth, where manure could be bought, that a four-course system based on a wheat, roots, barley, grass rotation was commonly adopted. Elsewhere, six-course shifts, in which a white grain crop was grown less often, were more successful.[29]

If the high grain prices of the Napoleonic Wars coupled with population increase encouraged the production of grain, the increased prosperity of the farmers was offset by the distress the high prices caused the low paid labourers. The level of poor rates is an indication of their

---

[25] Kent, *The Agriculture of Norfolk*, p. 150.
[26] Young, *The Agriculture of Norfolk*, p. 445.
[27] *Ibid.*, p. 448.
[28] Kent, *The Agriculture of Norfolk*, p. 52.
[29] *Ibid.*, p. 56.

plight, and these were very high throughout the war years. 'Poor rates, which no longer back than twenty years were so light that a farmer, when he went to a farm, hardly thought it worth while to enquire the amount of them; but now it has become the first question he must ask.'[30] That the war was not entirely to blame has been shown by the evidence gathered by Young. In many parishes, the poor rate had doubled between 1752 and 1792 while wages had altered very little.[31] It was against this background of hardship that agriculture prospered; and farmers became gentlemen while rents and the value of land doubled.

The end of the Napoleonic Wars brought a slump in grain prices which was not accompanied by a fall in poor rates or rents. In 1815, the price of wheat in Norwich had dropped to between 40 and 50 shillings a quarter and it continued to fall. Many tenant farmers were unable to pay their rent out of yearly income, but land continued to be improved in spite of falling profits. From 1820 onwards, bone dust and rape cake were applied to the land as fertilisers. The growing of mangolds was also introduced and these replaced turnips in many areas where the latter had become unsatisfactory. Marling continued on the light soils.[32] Mr Wright, a land agent in Norwich, reported to the select committee on agriculture in 1833 that in spite of the fact that farming profits had dropped by between 10% and 6% the land was 'in as good a state as ever I knew it'. It was well cultivated and as well stocked.[33] The most important development of this period was the increased emphasis on cattle grazing and yard feeding, and the number of cattle grazed trebled between 1815 and 1843. Norfolk agriculture became a completely mixed farming system, but most of the improvements were still being carried out in the west of the county. Holkham tenants such as John Hudson of Castle Acre and Mr Garwood of West Lexham were noted for the amount of marling they were doing, while the much-needed draining in the south of the county was lagging behind.[34] The rich farms of the east continued to be farmed much as before, and Bacon refers to the 'wealthy occupiers of Tunstead and Happing'.[35]

By the 1840s, the farmers were again optimistic. Grain prices never

[30] *Ibid.*, p. 156.
[31] Young, *The Agriculture of Norfolk*, facing p. 492.
[32] R. N. Bacon, *Agriculture of Norfolk*, (London, 1844), p. 90.
[33] Parliamentary Papers (1833), (612v), *Select Committee on Agriculture*, minutes of evidence, p. 98.
[34] Barugh Almack, 'Norfolk Agriculture', *J.R.A.S.E.*, vol. 5 (1845), p. 310.
[35] Bacon, *Agriculture of Norfolk*, p. 192.

again reached the famine levels of the war, but they were well above the low figures of the early 1830s. However, by this period farm income was not so dependent on grain prices. Livestock was playing a far more important role. As urban standards of living slowly improved, meat became a more normal part of the diet, and the coming of the railway to Norfolk in the 1840s provided a less wasteful way of getting livestock to the London market. In February 1844 between one third and one half of the cattle at Smithfield had been fattened in Norfolk. John Hudson said that, before the railway, several days were occupied in driving stock to London. Sheep lost an average of seven pounds weight on the way, and a bullock lost twenty-eight pounds. This meant a loss of £600 a year to Hudson. After the opening of the railway stock was able to reach London within a day with virtually no loss of weight.[36]

Agricultural techniques continued to develop and this period saw the adoption of many improvements in Norfolk. 'Norfolk husbandry' made farms self-sufficient units. They provided their own manure for the land and grew their own foodstuffs, but more grain and meat could be produced by the buying of fertilisers and foodstuffs, and the increase in their use can be seen in the expanding number of agricultural feed and fertiliser merchants. This eventually meant that it was possible to abandon the strict rotation system and grow two white grain crops in succession, but high farming needed capital and thus the disparity between the large and the small farmers increased. Only farms of over 300 acres were really suited to high farming.[37] In 1855 John Hudson asked Lord Leicester whether he could depart from the terms of his lease and grow barley instead of roots in several fields. This request was repeated in 1856 and permission was again granted. In 1857, Lord Leicester's agent wrote to him, 'As your last second white crop, oats after wheat, was so extremely good, I have no hesitation in agreeing to your request to sow oats after wheat in field 32.' In 1868 Hudson was finally given permission to crop in any way he though fit, so long as he brought the land back into the four-course shift before his lease ran out. At the same date similar requests were being made by other tenants and they were always granted.[38]

The growing of two white crops in succession had been made possible

---

[36] Caird, *English Agriculture*, p. 170.
[37] F. M. L. Thompson, 'The second agricultural revolution', *Economic History Review*, second series, vol. 21 (1968), pp. 62–73.
[38] Holkham MSS, letter books.

by the extensive use of fertilisers. John Hastings used yard manure as far as it would go, but by far the greatest part of the land was fertilised by artificials. These included rape cake, nitrate of soda and potash.[39] By 1844, when R. N. Bacon published his report on Norfolk agriculture, it is clear that fertilisers were used very generally. 'Since the return of comparative prosperity, the principal improvement has been the increased use of artificial manures, principally bone dust, oil cake, nitrate of soda and salt petre, and by a more liberal use of rape cake indeed to an almost infinite extent.'[40]

Artificial foods were being used widely by 1844. These not only produced a bigger beast more quickly, but also enriched the manure. Swedes, cut hay, bean and barley meal were supplemented by oil cake. The quantity varied from four to ten pounds a day for cattle and half a pound a day for sheep. Cattle were yard fed and on some of the large farms stall fed, while sheep were nearly all fed in the open fields. John Hudson wrote, 'The greatest improvement that I know of in farming is the consuming of linseed cake on the land by sheep and having the turnip sliced by Gardener's cutter. I have grown a third more grain since I adopted that plan.' Hudson fed half a pound of linseed cake a day to his sheep and seven to ten pounds to his cattle. 'By this which may appear a large amount, I am able to graze double the quantity of both sheep and cattle.'[41]

Bacon summarised the replies to his questionnaires on the subject of manures, fertilisers and artificial feed stuffs by saying, 'The effect [of rape cake used as feed] has been to enhance the quality of farm yard manure from 20 to 40% at least, while the system of feeding sheep on the land with oil cake has increased the value of the tilth and brought the land more rapidly into a much higher state of cultivation.' Norfolk farmers had increased the number of sheep and cattle grazed so that the county had become an exporter rather than an importer of sheep within a few years. 'A vast increase in the number of cattle grazed has taken place, the staple crop of her husbandry rendered more certain, while quality had been improved and quantity increased.'[42]

Even with the use of more fertilisers, crop rotations were not abandoned. On the light lands, six-course shifts were normal. This meant that sheep could be folded on the land before each crop of corn. On the

[39] Bacon, *Agriculture of Norfolk*, p. 111.
[40] Bacon MS 4363, N.R.O.
[41] Ibid.
[42] Bacon, *Agriculture of Norfolk*, p. 111.

very poor land, oats and peas were sometimes substituted for wheat. The problem of land sickening from clover was overcome by not planting it more than every eight or twelve years, and substituting trefoil, white clover, rye-grass and cow grass in the rotation.[43]

By the 1840s the advantages of mechanisation were cautiously accepted by the minority of progressive farmers. All of them used drills although many dibbled some of their wheat because they found that less seed was wasted. Bacon was constantly surprised by the meanness of farmers who would buy a cheaper type of machine rather than the original and stronger version and then complain of its shoddiness. All possessed threshing machines, although many preferred to flail some of the crop. On one farm, presumably to create work, threshing machines were used only in the summer and flails in the winter. On another a little barley was flailed 'for convenience'. In contrast, another found flailing too expensive, when the costs of carting and stacking were taken into account. Most Norfolk threshing machines seem to have been horse driven, although a few steam engine houses survive. On a farm at Costessey labour was so abundant and cheap that the machine was hand powered, 'which costs as much as to flail – we are too many men so I do not use horse power'.

On most farms the change had been made from reaping the corn harvest with a sickle to mowing with scythes fitted with iron cradles to gather the corn and lay it in regular swaithes across the field for the binders. One farmer underlined his answer to this question in Bacon's questionaire: 'I mow wheat *and have done so since 1799.*' Some were not sure of the advantages. Many said that the stubble was more difficult to plough in after mowing than reaping and thus mowing was injurious to the following year's crop. John Hudson of Castle Acre provided a description of harvest on his farm in 1850.

> The crop on this farm is generally 300 acres of wheat and 300 of barley for which 100 to 120 men, women, girls and boys are engaged. 34 men mow the wheat and in order to lay it evenly their scythes are fitted with cradles made of iron rods. These men are each followed by two women, or one woman and a boy or girl to gather up the corn into small sheaves. Eight team men belonging to the farm follow to shock up the sheaves of which they place ten in a shock. As the sheaves are shocked, the stubble is horse racked. The rackings are tied up and carted and placed separately. 300 acres of wheat are usually cut in six days. The carting took another eight days...when conditions are at all favourable the harvest is completed in 18 to 20 days.

[43] *Ibid.*

This description confirms the fact that the nineteenth-century harvest field of the 'high farmer', before the introduction of the mechanical reaper, was a crowded, labour-intensive place. But labour was cheap and, as with threshing, there was often as yet little incentive to replace men by horse power.

On many farms, both horses and oxen were used, the oxen mainly for ploughing on heavy land. Where the motive power was entirely horse the average was about one horse to every thirty acres. On large farms the ratio was lower. On John Hudson's 1,300 acres there were forty horses, or one horse to every 37.5 acres. On small farms it was higher – Mr Harvey with 135 acres had six horses (one horse to 23 acres).

The size of the workforce could vary greatly. Lord Leicester in the 1880s thought that if all the labour was to be housed locally, then one cottage for every fifty acres of cultivated acreage should be provided. A household might supply, as well as one male labourer, a full time boy and seasonal female and child workers. The average work-force seems to have been about one man for every thirty acres. Twelve men were employed on a 360 acre farm at Tittleshall in 1851. However, particularly up to the 1870s, female and child labour was very important as well, and gangs also performed many seasonal tasks. Labour costs per acre were higher on smaller farms. The higher horse per acre ratio would automatically increase the number of teamsmen, and the farms were also often less efficiently run. Mr Harvey's medium soil farm cost about 40 shillings an acre in labour, while Mr Clowes' 184 acres at Hemsby cost 43 shillings. John Hudson's bill was between 20 and 30 shillings per acre. By 1868 it had risen to £2, when his labour bill was £2,000, which included the wages of a bailiff, blacksmith, carpenter and wheelwright. This is less than the sum spent on cattle food and rent (both £3,000), but twice as much as that on artificial manures. Hudson was famous for the amount of cattle cake and artificials he used, so for most farmers, in spite of the fact that manpower was cheap, the labour bill must have been their largest outgoing.

Wages for day labour were fairly uniform at 10 shillings a week, with 2 shillings extra for teamsmen. Nearly all farmers preferred to use gangs. All used women and children extensively and they were paid between 2 and 5 shillings a week.

Bacon's survey only covers eighty farms and these included the most progressive in the county. There must have been many where the old-fashioned sickle continued to be used, and where drills and threshing machines were never seen. Even on the large farms a machine had to be well proven before it would be bought. Where a job could be as well done by hand there was little incentive to change. If gangs could be hired, then the responsibility of finding the labour was no longer the farmers', and so he could afford to be wary of new methods. High farming in Norfolk did not involve increased mechanisation so much as the use of fertilisers and foodstuffs to increase yields and improve stock.

We are very fortunate in that, in 1854, Norfolk was chosen, along with Hampshire, as one of the two counties in which a pioneer method for the collection of agricultural statistics was tried. This involved the setting up of statistical committees in each poor law union within the county. These consisted of a small body of leading agriculturalists with the chairman of the board of guardians as chairman of the committee. A classifier or enumerator was appointed for each parish and he was responsible for the delivery and collection of the schedule from every occupier of over two acres. This questionnaire asked how much land was under the cultivation of various crops and also the type and number of livestock kept. As a result, the agricultural statistics produced were for the separate Poor Law Unions within the county.[44] This enables us to compare the proportions of the types of crops grown in different areas of the county in a way which no other set of statistics allow. Figs. 1.4–1.7 are drawn from these statistics, which are given in appendix 1.

Fig. 1.4 shows the proportions of land in each union under various crops in 1854. In every area a system of mixed farming predominated. Except for the Breckland area of the Thetford union, where grain only accounted for 6.35% of land, grain crops took up the majority of the land. Very often they took up about the same area as that under roots and artificial grasses put together. This situation can be seen clearly in Aylsham and Docking. The only unions that do not follow this pattern are Blofield and Downham. Rather than growing grass, Blofield seems to have relied on the permanent meadow and pasture of broadland for animal feed. In the very fertile and often recently cultivated fenland area of Downham, 45.6% of the land was under grain – the highest percentage for any of the Norfolk unions. Except in these two unions, the percentage of various crops grown would seem to show that crop rotations were

[44] Parliamentary Papers (1854), (1761), LXV, *The Agricultural Statistics for Norfolk and Hampshire*, Sir John Walsham and Mr Hawley, pp. 290–300.

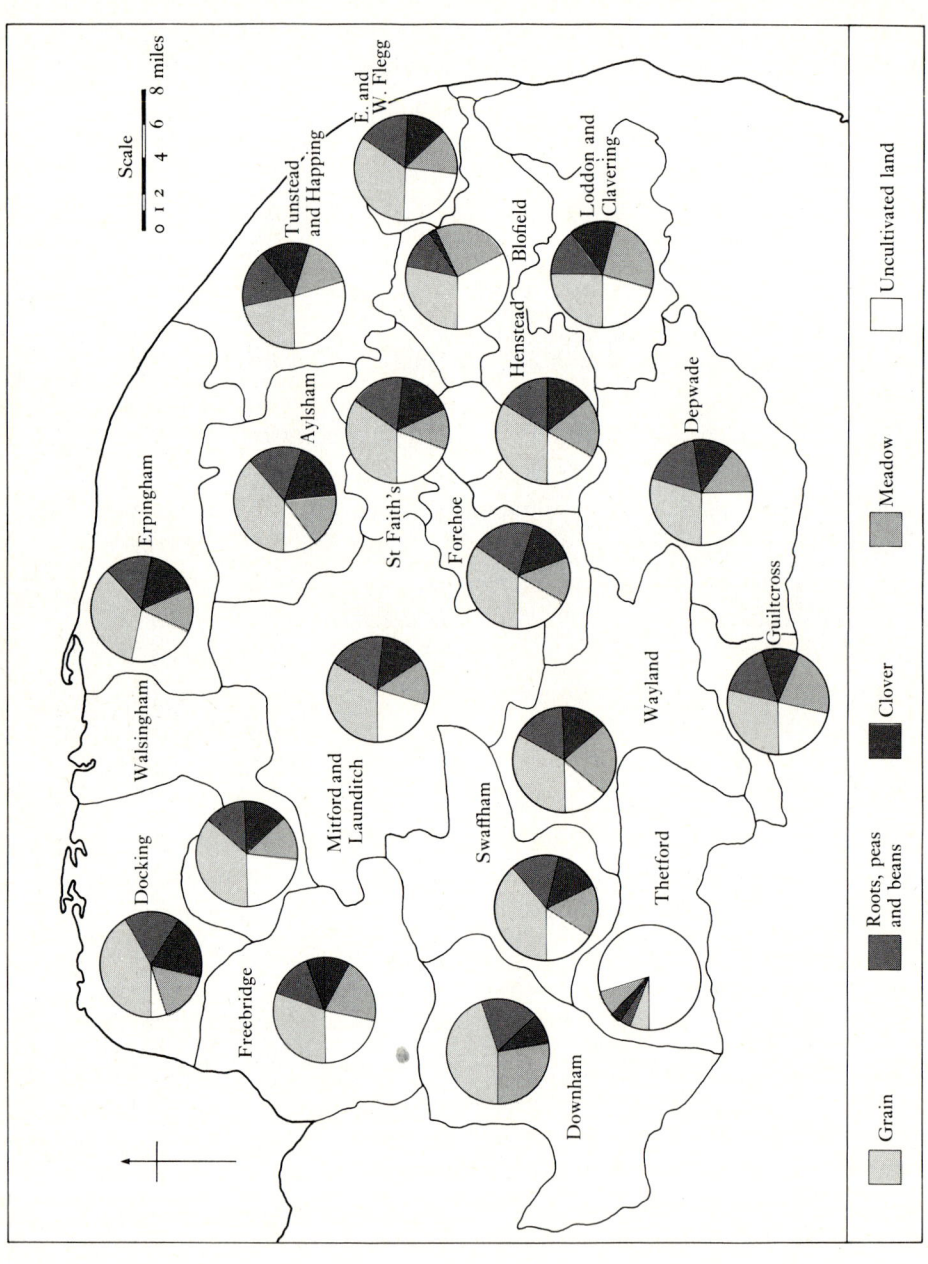

1.4 Proportion of land in each Norfolk Poor Law Union under various crops in 1854.

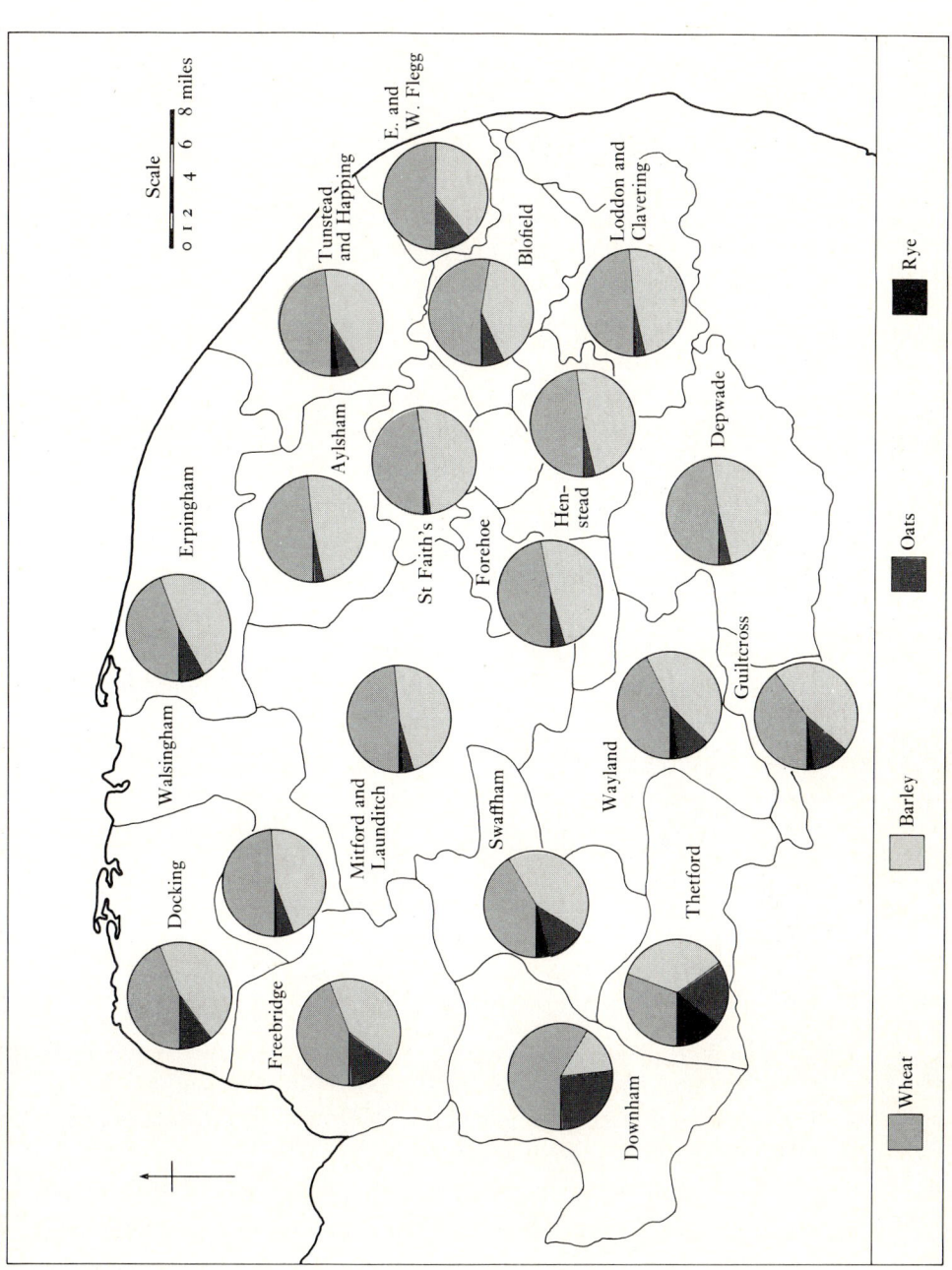

1.5 Proportion of land in each Norfolk Poor Law Union under various grain crops within the total grain acreage. Based on appendix 1.

generally being followed. The four-course shift allowed for twice as much grain as turnips to be grown. In the poorer lands where five- or six-course rotations were more usual grain crops did not take such precedence. (Docking and Walsingham in the west grew grain on 39.2% and 36% of their land while the heavy soils of Guiltcross, Wayland and Depwade in the south planted only 31%, 33% and 32% of their land in grain.) Other than Thetford union the broadland unions of Loddon and Clavering and Tunstead and Happing have the lowest percentage of total acreage under grain. Not surprisingly, there is a much higher proportion of meadow in both these areas. A quarter of the Blofield union, much of which is marshland, was meadow, as was 29% of the fenland union of Downham.

Fig. 1.5 shows the types of grain being grown. Wheat, although the most profitable grain crop, was not ideally suited to Norfolk soils. Instead Norfolk was famous as a barley county. Oats and rye were grown on the poorest soils. The largest areas of wheat were planted in the fertile fens and the rich loams of the Blofield region. As a result of careful farming, the light sandy soils of Docking and Walsingham unions were also producing large wheat crops. In only the very light Breckland soils of the Thetford union and the very heavy soils of Guiltcross was less than 40% of the arable land used for wheat. The fact that many of the other heavy land areas were planting more than 40% of their land in wheat suggests that there must have been considerable drainage of the clays by 1854. It would be more valuable to know the grain *yields* as well as the acreages for small areas, rather than the figures for the county as a whole, so that an assessment could be made of the suitability of the land to the crop, but these are not available.

More barley than wheat was grown in most of the heavy south Norfolk unions and on the light sandy soils of Docking and Erpingham in the north. In most areas little rye was grown. It was to be found mainly in the poor soils of Thetford union. Oats was a rather more important crop, especially in the west of the county, with Downham growing the most (26.3% of grain crop) and Thetford 20%.

Various crops could be grown after wheat in a crop rotation to restore the soils as well as to provide a fodder crop onto which livestock could be folded in the fields. These included the root crops, turnips, mangolds, and carrots as well as peas and beans which were particularly suited to the heavier soils. It is extraordinary that even though by the 1850s many

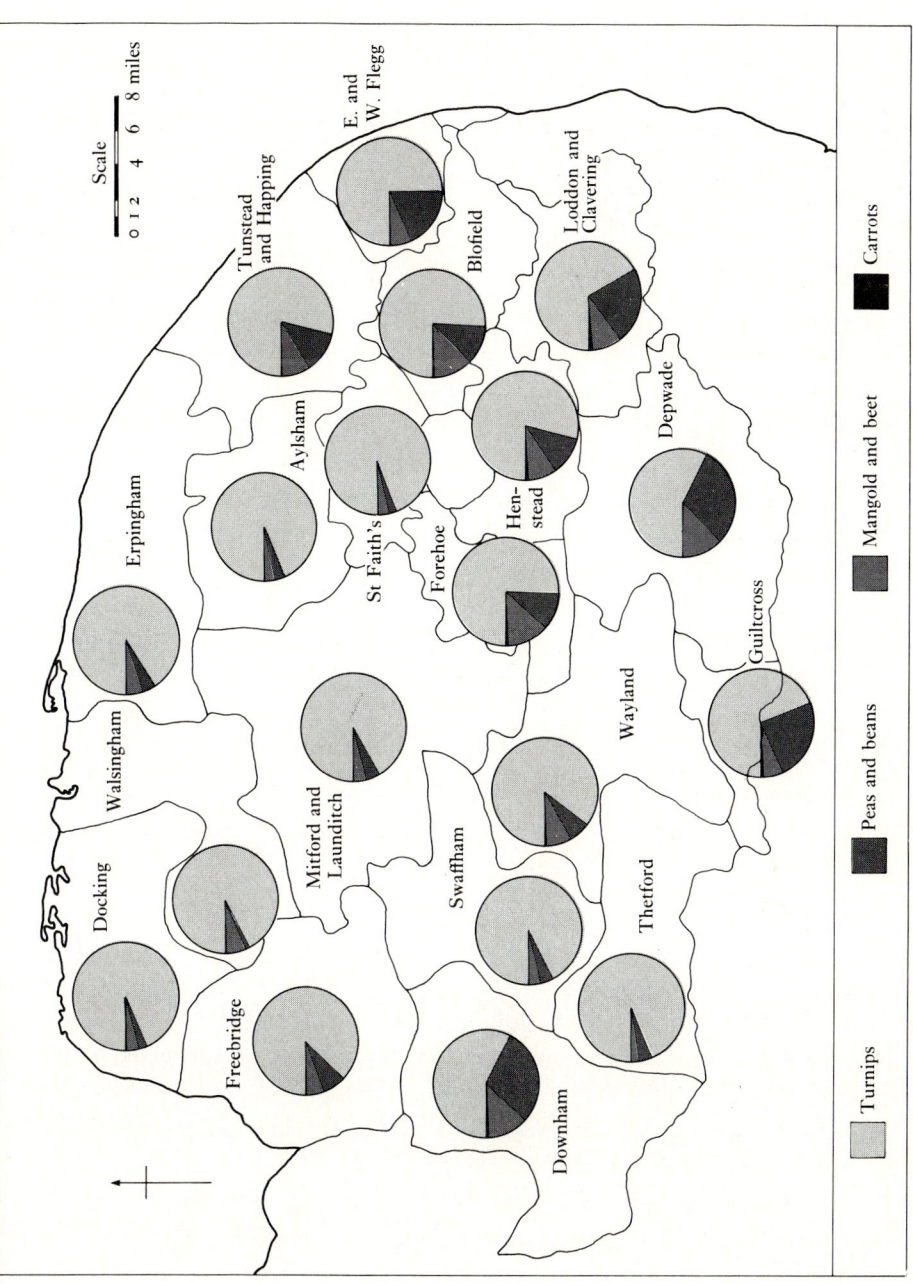

1.6 Proportion of land in each Norfolk Poor Law Union under root, peas and beans. Based on appendix 1.

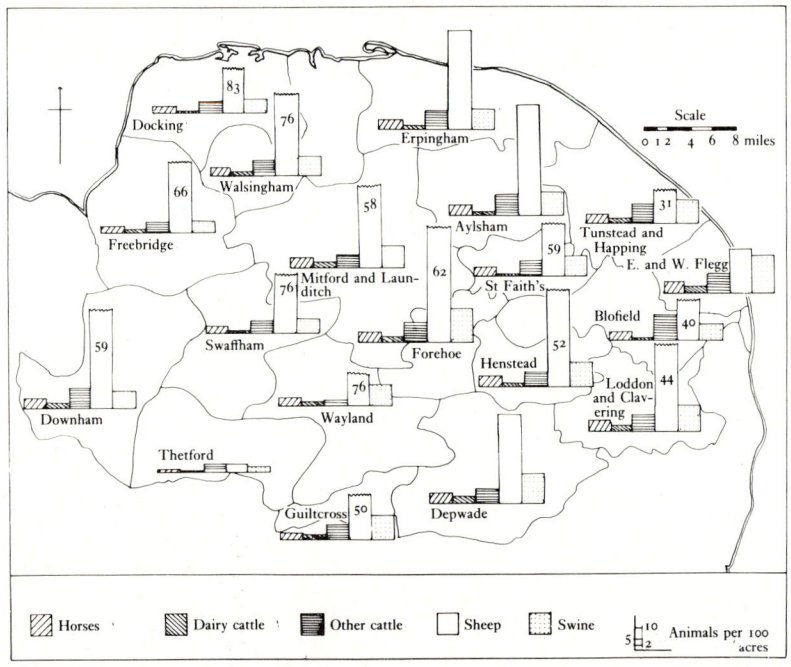

1.7 Number of animals per acre within each Norfolk Poor Law Union. Based on appendix 1.

farmers realised the superior food value of mangolds over turnips, in all unions these formed only a small proportion of the root crop. Only in Forehoe, Downham and Depwade is the area under mangolds more than 12% of the root crop. Very few carrots were grown and so turnips still dominated the root crop, making up over 90% of the crop in Aylsham, Docking, Erpingham and Walsingham unions. Peas and beans were of little importance here and were only grown in any quantity in the heavy southern unions. Fig. 1.6 shows that in spite of the ravages of finger and toe disease among turnip crops and the acknowledged fact that mangolds were better food value, farmers still preferred to grow turnips, and only on the heavy lands were peas and beans replacing the root crops within the rotation pattern. Bacon went so far as to say 'The prosperity of the Norfolk farmer depends principally on his successful cultivation of the turnip, and consequently on no other crop is so large an outlay made, either in manure or labour or so much care or attention bestowed.'

Fig. 1.7 shows the intensity of livestock husbandry in Norfolk. The number of horses kept gives some indication of the types of agriculture in an area and the amount of machinery used; although it also reflects the heaviness of the soil as heavier soil will need more horse power to work it. Forehoe, Henstead, Loddon and Clavering and East and West Flegg had the most horses for their acreage with one horse for between nineteen and twenty acres. The light lands of the north-west, although intensely farmed, needed fewer horses. Guiltcross union, covering much heavy land, had only one horse for every twenty-eight acres, which suggests a low level of cultivation and mechanisation. The little farmed Breckland unions of Thetford and Swaffham had only one horse for every fifty-nine and thirty-two acres.

Even with the coming of the railway, dairy cattle were still of little importance in 1854. The most were kept near Norwich and in the Forehoe union from where milk could easily be sold in the city. The high percentage of meadow and pasture within the area meant that in the broadland unions of East and West Flegg, and Loddon and Clavering, the number of dairy cattle was greater than elsewhere. Even in these areas the number kept was far lower than in Lancashire in the 1870s, where one cow for every seven acres was kept and where Liverpool provided a large market.[45]

Sheep were particularly valuable on light soils where it was claimed that the folding of them on the turnip crop had made the land strong enough for wheat cultivation. It is not surprising therefore that the most sheep were kept in Docking and Walsingham unions. Sheep were also widely kept on the light soils bordering on Breckland in Wayland and Swaffham unions. Pigs did not usually form a very important part of the farming economy. A few were kept for domestic use and they were therefore predominantly in the areas of small farms in the heavy soil areas. Depwade and Forehoe kept the most pigs in 1854, while the small farmers of East and West Flegg also kept one pig to about seven acres. As these statistics were only collected from occupiers of two or more acres, cottagers' pigs were not included.

These statistics highlight some of the regional differences to be found across the county. The most striking is the poorness of the Thetford region, with very little grain grown and a third of that oats and rye. Very few horses were kept to work this under-utilised region, and livestock

[45] T. W. Fletcher, 'Lancashire livestock farming during the Great Depression', *Agricultural History Review*, vol. 9 (1961), p. 20.

was also unimportant. In contrast the fens were very fertile and intensively farmed with a high percentage of the land under grain and a high proportion of that being wheat. On the light lands we see a careful rotation system depending on the folding of sheep on the turnip fields. The grain nearly always makes up about the same areas as under both roots and grasses, suggesting a four-course system. On the heavier lands of the south, more barley was grown than wheat, and peas and beans replaced turnips in the rotation, but otherwise there was little difference in the farming system. On the marshland areas permanent pasture was more important and more dairy cattle were kept, but the fertility of the higher land allowed a high percentage of wheat to be grown. The average yield of wheat over the county was thirty bushels per acre. Sir John Walsham thought this a high yield, considering that only a small proportion of Norfolk soil was naturally suited to its cultivation. Barley was a more important crop and it gave better yields (thirty-four bushels per acre). Oats grew mainly in the poor regions and produced a relatively low yield (forty-six bushels per acre). Although mangolds were a nutritious crop, they were slow to take over from the turnip, which was still dominant in most areas, particularly in the north-west, where it provided the main food for the large flocks of sheep. It is a pity that none of the later statistics are broken down into regions within the county, as there is nothing with which to compare the 1854 statistics and we are unable to identify regional changes in agricultural practice.

In 1858 Clare Sewell Read published his first report on Norfolk agriculture and, as he was a Norfolk farmer himself, his reports are probably accurate. Like others, he tended to concentrate on the more progressive farms, but he did not hesitate to condemn some of the practices of the smaller and less conscientious estates. 'In the east there is hardly one estate of any great size... The lesser proprietors of east Norfolk farm much of the land themselves and let their farms at high rents... to the east the enclosures are small, the hedgerow timber abundant, and most of the land not calculated for sheep.'[46] Read thought that in contrast improvements were continuing to be made in the west. A quarter more wheat was grown per acre than fifteen years previously, largely as a result of artificial manures, especially guano. Fertilisers were making it possible to grow more wheat instead of barley. The amount of steam threshing equipment was also increasing. There were very few

---

[46] C. S. Read, 'Recent improvements in Norfolk farming' *J.R.A.S.E.*, vol. 19 (1858), pp. 265–311.

stationary engines, but the convenient portable engines which could be used at field barns were more numerous.

Read noted that the four-course rotation was no longer being strictly adherred to and by the 1850s there was much feeling among farmers that restrictive husbandry clauses were necessary for bad and not good farmers. 'The less a good farmer is interfered with the better.' There is no suggestion in Read's report that Norfolk farming was in any way dropping back. Improvements both on the heavy and the light soils were continuing. Almack in 1845 had noted that much drainage had been carried out. 'Almost every variety of drainage may be found in Norfolk and there are few places to be named from whence you can go many miles without finding drains of some sort.'[47]

We have little other evidence for Norfolk as a whole for the period before 1873. Farmers continued to prosper and rents on the great estates rose. It seems likely, especially on the great estates, that more cattle were kept in the later part of the period. Certainly the number of cattle grazed in the marshes was increasing. Norfolk remained an important food producer for the rest of industrialised Britain, and while there was no foreign competition her position remained secure.

In the 1870s the years of high grain prices, which English farmers had come to regard as normal, came to an end. Foreign grain from the recently opened up prairies of North America was finding its way on to the British market and had the effect of reducing the price of English wheat. The price of grain on the Norwich market fell from about 65 shillings a quarter in 1872 to below 55 shillings for the rest of the century. The lowest price was 25 shillings in 1894.

From 1873 farmers were also suffering from bad harvests. In 1894 C. S. Read stated that in Norfolk there had not been an 'all-round good crop of farm produce since 1874'. 1879 had been a particularly disastrous year, while 1891–2 was cold and miserably wet. In contrast, 1893 was a year of drought, which had resulted in a poor wheat and barley harvest, a hay harvest a third of the usual size and half the normal turnip crop. The light soils of much of Norfolk needed rain as well as heat to produce a good crop.[48] After the many years of prosperity, farmers could not understand this change in fortune. They assumed that it was purely the

---

[47] Almack, 'Norfolk Agriculture', p. 308.
[48] Parliamentary Papers (1894), (c.7400–1), XVI, *Royal Commission on Agriculture*, first report, minutes of evidence, part 2, question 15952.

result of bad seasons, and that given a good harvest all would be well again. Many did not realise that the long term problem was one of foreign competition and that if farming were to remain profitable there must be a change in the emphasis of production.

Bad harvests, the low price of wheat, and the unsaleable state of much of the barley produced meant that farming profits from grain were very low indeed. Only those farmers with livestock to sell fared better. Development in Australia meant that the price of wool was falling after 1864, while the price of store sheep fluctuated.[49] In 1833, Norfolk sheep were selling at 'extravagent prices'[50] and Henry Overman, giving evidence in 1881 to the enquiry into agriculture, said that he could not grumble about the price sheep fetched although there was no profit in wool.[51]

Read said that in Norfolk the farmers with stock were faring best, but that in the 1890s they too had suffered. Norfolk cattle were badly hit by pleuro-pneumonia.[52] From 1891 refrigerated ships meant that the price for mutton as well as wool was falling steadily. Cattle plague, foot and mouth disease and liver fluke had also devastated livestock.[53]

Many farmers saw the rise in agricultural wages as a cause of the depression. Read said that the main increase in farming costs was the labour bill. In the 1840s, rents had been twice the labour bill. Now it was the other way round.[54] (This was the result of decreased rents as well as increased wages.) Between 1872 and 1881 Overman said that the cost of labour had gone up by 5 shillings an acre. In 1879 his labour bill was £2,450 to work a farm of 1,100 acres. This was an increase of £300 over the annual average for the years 1866–9.[55] When asked who were the best off, the landlords, the tenant or the labourers, Overman replied that it was the labourers who 'lived in affluence'.[56] Other sources show that in the 1870s wages did rise from the 10 shilling average of the 1850s to nearly 14 shillings in 1880 and that as food prices declined the standard of living of farm labourers did improve, although there was

[49] E. H. Whetham, 'Livestock prices in Britain, 1851–93', *Agricultural History Review*, vol. 11 (1963), pp. 102–19.
[50] Read, 'Agriculture of Norfolk'.
[51] Parliamentary Papers (1881), (c.3096), XVII, *Royal Commission on Agriculture*, minutes of evidence, part 2, pp. 735–48.
[52] Parliamentary Papers (1894), *Royal Commission on Agriculture*, question 16621.
[53] Whetham, 'Livestock prices'.
[54] Parliamentary Papers (1894), *Royal Commission on Agriculture*, question 16060.
[55] Parliamentary Papers (1881), *Royal Commission on Agriculture*, question 51781.
[56] *Ibid.*, question 51919.

still a long way to go before they could really be described as affluent. Farmers not only complained about the price of labour but also its standard. Both Overman and Read reported on the poor work of the younger men. Overman blamed this on 'agitators in the villages who have corrupted the younger men'. He said, 'I believe that on every farm there is one man appointed to look and see that there is not too much work done. Whenever I find out that man he always goes: I never tell him what for, but he always goes.'[57] Read complained that all the brightest and most intelligent labour had left the land, and that there was little juvenile labour as boys were all at school.[58] Census returns for 1871 and 1901 show that in fact the number of young men working on the land declined in the same proportion as other age groups and no faster. The total male workforce declined from 41,269 to 33,498, while those between the ages of twenty and thirty-five years of age declined from 10,507 to 9,215. The number of those over fifty-five declined more steeply from 8,651 to 1,367. It was therefore not true to talk, as many farmers did, of an ageing population of farm labourers. Juvenile labour had declined. No children under ten appear in the 1901 return, and only 210 were listed in 1871. The number between ten and fifteen years of age had halved from 4,711 to 2,139. The Royal Commission received complaints about labour from all over England, but E. H. Hunt has recently calculated that both wage rates and productivity in Norfolk were among the lowest in England.[59]

Although the causes of the depression were not fully understood by farmers, who tended to blame the bad harvests and the rising wage bills, the results were all too clear. The condition of many farmers was 'verging on absolute ruin and wholesale bankruptcy. We are very very poor.' Farmers could not tell how much they had lost. They 'just kept going from year to year'.[60] The only exceptions to this were the farmers to the north-east of Norwich. This had always been a prosperous area of good soil which had been farmed well for 200 years.

The small farmer, particularly the owner-occupier, was worst hit by the depression. Read reported, 'We have a good many yeomen in the county of Norfolk, and they have been hit hardest of all.' Tenant farmers

---

[57] Ibid., question 51924.
[58] Parliamentary Papers (1894), *Royal Commission on Agriculture*, question 16031.
[59] E. H. Hunt, 'Labour productivity in English agriculture', *Economic History Review*, second series, vol. 20 (1967), pp. 280–92.
[60] Parliamentary Papers (1894), *Royal Commission on Agriculture*, question 15956.

were also suffering, particularly the small man with little capital to fall back on. Tenants on the small estates where rents were disproportionantly high found landlords unwilling to reduce rents and so had an extra financial burden to bear.

The depression hit the clay lands badly because these were unsuitable for wheat cultivation, except when prices were very high. As early as 1874 tenants on Lord Rayleigh's Essex estate were asking for rent reductions. In 1877 the agent was advising his employer that almost any action necessary should be taken to keep tenants.[61]

In Norfolk, however, rent reductions did not come so soon, and on the Holkham estates rents remained high until the 1880s. Tenants, misunderstanding the causes of the depression, relied on the livestock side of their farms and paid rent out of capital, hoping for a good harvest next year, and with it a return to the more familiar conditions of prosperity. In 1879, Overman had entered into a new lease at the same rent as the old. He was prepared to do this because he was confident of receiving an annual reduction of about 10% to tide him over bad times.[62] By the 1890s rents had been reduced almost everywhere. Read said,

> The larger landlords have reduced their rents, some of them, I am sorry to say, hardly in time. On some estates there has been a great change in tenantry. On others timely reductions have kept the tenantry there. Now the landlords are prepared to take any rent and to keep any tenant they possibly can, and what with the landlords and the bankers, the tenants hang on somehow.[63]

In spite of these rather gloomy replies to Royal Commission questions, there were no large-scale bankruptcies in Norfolk, or wide tracts of uncultivated land.

Between 1871 and 1891, the proportion of land under the different broad categories of crops changed very little (see table 1.1). Corn slowly declined from 457,069 acres to 427,039, greens from 200,233 to 195,215 and rotation grasses from 169,247 to 164,797. The only significant change was the increase in permanent pasture from 214,479 to 288,510. By the 1890s many farmers believed that the only way to make ends meet was to lay down more permanent pasture, which would reduce labour costs. By 1879, Lord Leicester no longer practised a four-course rotation on

---

[61] J. Oxley Parker (ed.), *The Oxley Parker Papers* (Colchester, 1964).
[62] Parliamentary Papers (1881), *Royal Commission on Agriculture*, question 51987.
[63] Parliamentary Papers (1894), *Royal Commission on Agriculture*, question 15979.

TABLE 1.1 *Agricultural statistics for Norfolk 1871–91*

	1871	1881	1891
Total acreage	1,354,301	1,356,173	1,356,173
Total acreage under crop	1,048,929	1,071,728	1,090,532
Total acreage under a corn crop	457,069	444,476	427,039
Wheat	207,452	184,284	159,452
Barley	NA	203,387	205,518
Oats	NA	28,800	39,149
Rye	NA	5,252	3,785
Beans	NA	15,056	13,428
Peas	NA	7,697	7,340
Total acreage under a green crop	200,233	202,992	195,215
Potatoes	6,667	4,757	6,987
Turnips/swedes	143,818	133,719	126,392
Mangolds	37,048	47,999	48,887
Carrots	648	452	NA
Cabbage/kale	4,556	4,028	3,971
Vetch	7,496	12,037	4,237
Rotation grasses	169,247	164,472	164,797
Permanent pasture	214,479	259,788	288,510
Livestock			
Horses	55,865	43,545	45,640
Cattle	92,903	114,348	125,195
Sheep	745,037	579,691	608,081
Pigs	79,509	82,711	118,477
Number of agricultural labourers*	41,269	39,331	39,090
Number of shepherds*	1,186	1,122	987
Number of nurserymen/seedsmen and gardeners (non-domestic)*	285	2,592	3,872

Source: Agricultural returns to the Board of Trade. Discrepancies in this table are due to changing methods in collecting the statistics.
  NA indicates figures not available
* From census returns.

the lightest soils. Instead he was laying down grass for sheep for five or six years. This semi-permanent pasture required 'no expense of tillage or labour'.[64] Read thought that the only sensible way to change the system of agriculture was to keep land in grass longer and so increase stock and decrease labour. The total cultivated acreage did not begin to decline until 1881, while the number of horses kept and the size of the labour force was already going down and continued to decline faster than

[64] Parliamentary Papers (1896), (c.8021), XVII, Henry Rew, *Report on Norfolk*, pp. 596–7.

the cultivated land, which suggests a reduction in the intensity of farming methods. Contrary to common belief, machinery did not decrease labour costs, as more horses had to be kept and looked after. Machinery had to be maintained by skilled men who demanded higher wages. 'Machinery saves time, not money.'[65] It is impossible to prove or disprove the truth of this tantalising statement made to the Royal Commission, as the relevant statistics do not exist, but the decline in the number of labourers and horses kept does suggest that less machinery was being used. Machinery was of very little help in livestock farming, where few processes could as yet be mechanised.

Although the total acreage of each type of crop changed little, the balance of the crops within each type did alter. The acreage under wheat declined, while barley increased. The market for British wheat contracted under competition from America, but good Norfolk malting barley was always in demand. Oats, usually regarded as a poor-land crop, increased in acreage, presumably to feed the growing number of horses used in the towns.

The increased emphasis on livestock took several forms. The number of pigs steadily rose from 79,509 to 118,477, providing for an expanding market in a field where there was as yet little foreign competition. Cattle also increased from 92,903 to 125,195, and the production of beef involved more intensive winter feeding in the newly erected sheds, yards and loose boxes to be found on many estate farms. The more nutritious mangold was replacing the turnip as a root crop, but it did not entirely make up for the decline in turnip growing. (Turnip acreage declined by 17,000 while mangold increased by only 11,000.) No other fodder crop acreages were increasing, so there must have been a greater reliance on such feeds as cattle cake for the winter. But we have seen that more extensive systems were also being advocated. Much land was put down to semi-permanent pasture and rarely ploughed up.

The decline in wool prices from 1864 meant that sheep numbers dropped from 745,037 in 1871 to 579,691 in 1881. Mutton prices were better in the 1880s and sheep may have saved many farmers then, when numbers rose to 608,081 in 1891. But after this, there was no profit here either. An increase in the number of sheep, accompanied by a decline in the number of shepherds, suggests an increase in the size rather than in the number of flocks.

[65] Parliamentary Papers (1894), *Royal Commission on Agriculture*, question 16483.

It was possible for some farmers to make profits. The agricultural depression should not be seen as an entirely negative development. It was 'a significant link rather than a purposeless vacuum between an old and a new agricultural world'. It was 'a development era of many new practices'.[66] Unfortunately few old farmers were prepared to adapt and, although some Norfolk farmers were adjusting to the new situation, Overman and Read among them, a new group was entering farming. These were men who had made money in business and usually kept these interests alongside the farm. They had capital to invest. Overman commented that it was difficult to find men with the courage to put capital into the soil, but those there were came mainly from the business world. Read said, 'Good lands, with a certain amount of grass are still readily hired by men of means and we have about half a dozen farmers of considerable capital and a very large amount of business talent who have hired vast tracts of land and I may say have farmed them well.'[67] These farms were usually between 2,000 and 3,000 acres.

Most observant farmers agreed by the 1880s that the emphasis of farming must change. Livestock prices kept up better than grain and so farmers with animals could continue to make profits. Agriculture on the good chalks and light loams suffered least. These were the areas where sheep were kept and both Overman and Read thought that laying down land to sheep walks was the best use that could be made of it. The reduction in the number of horses kept and the increase in permanent pasture represent a decline in the intensity of farming after 1873. In 1886 the *J.R.A.S.E.* reported that it was doubtful whether Norfolk farming was in advance of that in other counties.[68]

Even the large farmers were not making profits after 1890. By this date poorer quality farms were being given up and could not be relet. 'There is a certain quality of land in Norfolk that cannot be let at any price, and this will rise if the depression continues.'[69]

The one type of agricultural employment which showed a significant increase in the late-nineteenth-century censuses was that of nurseryman and seedsman. Market gardening, particularly near the towns and railways, was a growing business, even if it was too small to affect the general agricultural pattern.

[66] P. J. Perry (ed.), *British Agriculture, 1875–1914* (Newton Abbot, 1973), p. xiii.
[67] Parliamentary Papers (1881), *Royal Commission on Agriculture*, question 51757.
[68] 'Report on the farm prize competition', *J.R.A.S.E.*, second series, vol. 22 (1886), p. 565.
[69] Parliamentary Papers (1896), *Report on Norfolk*, p. 35.

By 1900 there had been no fundamental changes in the structure of Norfolk farming although the importance of summer pasture and permanent pasture had increased. Bullock fattening was the staple industry although market gardening, dairying and horse breeding had increased.[70]

The impression given by Rider Haggard in 1902 was no more cheerful. In East Flegg there was still good competition for farms, although farmers were losing ground every day. Rents and selling values had declined by half since 1875. Profits on livestock as well as corn had declined. The number of cattle kept had increased but their value had declined from between £8 and £10 per bullock to not more than £5. Market gardening and fruit production continued to increase but the local market could easily become glutted. The farmers around Aylsham had suffered considerably. They continued to farm in the old way, buying in their stock for fattening and breeding nothing. 'In the old days, corn paid the wages and the root crop the landlord, but things were changed.' The light soil farms had not fared so badly. With care, the best soils paid their way. Lord Leicester could still let his farms. By large-scale mechanisation, farmers such as Keith at Egmere could make profits, but it was only men of capital who could afford to set themselves up this way.[71]

Norfolk farmers suffered as others in areas where grain still provided the main cash crop. The larger farmers with suitable farms and the wherewithal to change to livestock farming fared best. If they could afford to intensify production, they stood a better chance of success. New types of farming such as market gardening and dairying were beginning to develop, but they were not of great significance until after the First World War.

It is in this context of agricultural boom and depression that the history of the Holkham estates must be seen. However good a landlord he might be, the owner could not control international economic factors and, as the nineteenth century progressed, these were of increasing importance to the farming community. While the demand for home produced food was high the landed class, as owners of most of the agricultural land, were in a very powerful position, but as foreign food

---

[70] Philip Rose, 'Norfolk Agriculture in 1850', M.Phil. thesis, University of East Anglia, 1976.
[71] H. Rider Haggard, *Rural England* 2 vols. (London, 1902), vol. 2, p. 449.

supplies became available the demand for their land declined and the tenants became the stronger partners.

The landowning class in Norfolk consisted of about sixty owners of more than 3,000 acres. They were nearly all J.P.s, and Lord Leicester was for many years the lord lieutenant. The deputy lieutenants and high sherriffs were all drawn from their number, as were most of the M.P.s. They lived in varying degrees of grandeur, ranging from the Palladian magnificence of Holkham Hall to the charming country houses designed by Sir John Soane at Shotesham and Letton. Many houses were altered and enlarged by their mid-nineteenth-century owners and most were surrounded by parks and lakes.

Until the middle years of the nineteenth century, the landlords' position looked very secure. If an estate were well run, then it appeared that nothing could prevent the continuing prosperity of the landed class. With rents rising a good income seemed guaranteed. Even if there were agitation for parliamentary reform, the landed class remained the only one with independent means which allowed them the time for politics. In the county they dominated the magistrates' benches and their position as leaders of society was unchallenged. Even as late as 1881, Broderick could write,

> But all these changes (county police, highways boards, poor law unions) have by no means weakened the power of the squire who on the contrary is a greater man than ever, relative to other classes in the village community, since he is no longer jostled by independent yeomen, but surrounded by obsequious tenants and labourers. The lord lieutenant of the county, always a great landowner, seldom places any but landowners on the commission of the peace... even if he is not a magistrate, he can hardly fail to be virtually the headman of the village as lord of all the farms, cottages and allotments around his domain. He is the chief employer in the locality and the main supporter of village charity.[72]

However, by the 1880s the landlord's dominant political and economic position was being eroded by parliamentary reform and economic depression. Of the nine Norfolk M.P.'s, seven were landowners. But alongside these traditional representatives, new men were to be found. The Yarmouth brewer, Sir E. H. K. Lacon, represented North Norfolk, and the owner of the expanding Norwich mustard business, J. J. Colman, represented his home town. Agricultural depression brought with it

---

[72] G. Broderick, *English Land and English Landowners* (1881), p. 271.

disastrous falls in rent. Not all landlords fared equally badly. Rents on mainly pastoral estates did not decline as fast as in arable areas.[73] In Norfolk, Read gave evidence to the Royal Commission that the average decline in rents was about 33%. Actual figures ranged from 10% in the good soils to the north-east of Norwich, where the rents were still about 30 shillings an acre in the 1890s, to 50–75% in the very light and very heavy areas, where in the worst soils the rent was now down to 2s. 6d. to 5 shillings an acre. On medium soils the drop was about 20%.[74] The areas with the greatest decrease, which included much of Breckland as well as the very heavy clays, did not account for as much as a quarter of the county. The rents on the Holkham estates did not decline until the late 1880s, yet by 1894 they were 45.5% lower than in 1873.[75] With this type of reversal of fortunes the owning of land became an expensive luxury. Landlords who could were well advised to invest their assets in the stock exchange rather than in their estates, Although Read thought it was a very difficult question to answer he told the Royal Commission that probably the landlord had lost more capital than the tenant.[76] The value of land had gone down by half. Landlords did not really know how much they had lost until they came to sell.[77] Two thirds of the gentry could no longer afford to keep up their homes and had moved out, letting the shooting to tenants who came down for only a few months of the year and had no interest in local affairs.[78]

The collapse in rent and land values in the last quarter of the nineteenth century undermined the landowners' leading role in agricultural society. They could no longer choose from a long list of applicants for their farms, which instead were difficult to let. They wanted to keep their tenants at any price. They were prepared to take any rent and do limited farm improvements demanded by the tenant. The tenant was able to force the landlord's hand rather than the other way round. It has been said that one of the functions of the landlord was to act as a buffer between the farmer and the low prices in times of depression by lowering rents. This may well have happened in the depressions earlier

[73] F. M. L. Thompson, *English Landed Society in the Nineteenth Century* (London, 1963), p. 311.
[74] Parliamentary Papers (1894), *Royal Commission on Agriculture*, question 1600.
[75] Parliamentary Papers (1896), *Report on Norfolk*, p. 30.
[76] Parliamentary Papers (1894), *Royal Commission on Agriculture*, question 1652.
[77] *Ibid.*, question 1635.
[78] Parliamentary Papers (1896), *Report on Norfolk*, p. 107.

in the century, but this time falls in rent seem to have followed rather slowly on the slump in prices. Rather than acting as a buffer, the landlords were draining the tenants' capital and so made it more difficult for them to develop new farming techniques.

As the political and economic influence of the landowners gave way to that of the commercial classes they valued their social prestige even more, and shooting became a much prized prerogative to which they could invite their admiring city friends. In Suffolk, on Lord Iveagh's estate, game was considered far more important than agriculture. 'Instead there is a general tendency to turn many of the estates in this part of Suffolk to pleasure rather than agricultural purposes.'[79] The fact that two out of every three country seats in Suffolk were let for game shows how important shooting had become as a source of income. The number of gamekeepers in Norfolk increased from 684 in 1871 to 839 in 1891, but had declined to 492 by 1901. With the letting of shooting rights and houses to outsiders, the landowners were relinquishing their monopoly over the sport. Sometimes, as at Holkham, the rights were even let to tenants, so the one thing that socially divided the tenant of land from the owner was removed, and here again we see the decline of the influence of the landed estate.

Throughout the nineteenth century, the landed gentry and aristocracy remained numerically important in Norfolk. Of a total of 1,365,173 acres, 194,331 were owned by peers and 322,939 were in estates of over 3,000 acres.[80] However, the influence of the landowners was declining. The part they played in both national and local politics was less important by 1900. They were no longer the wealthiest group. Agricultural depression meant they were no longer involved in a prosperous business and their involvement became less as their bargaining power with a diminishing number of potential tenants became weaker. Yet despite the loss of both political and economic power, social prestige remained. Landed aristocracy and gentry commanded local respect. The social prestige of land outlived its profitability. By 1909 land was an expensive luxury, but one for which many landlords were still prepared to pay.

The fortunes of the Holkham estate followed to some extent the

[79] Haggard, *Rural England*, vol. 2, p. 382.
[80] Bateman, *The Great Landowners*, p. 507.

pattern just described, but the fact that it was so much larger than its neighbours and that its management had been outstandingly good obviously had some effect on the way in which it stood up to the onset of depression. We will now proceed to follow the fortunes of Holkham through periods of prosperity and slump and to see what influence the estate had over the activities of the tenant farmers and cottagers.

2
The landlords

The control of the estate was in the hands of its landlord. He might well delegate much of the administration to an agent, and his tenants could contribute greatly to the improvement of the land, but the final responsibility rested with the owner. A conscientious landlord could well be a very busy man, especially if, like Coke, he was an active politician as well.

Thomas William Coke, 1754–1842

Thomas William Coke was born in London in May 1754. His father, Wenman Coke of Longford, Derbyshire, was a Member of Parliament for Derbyshire and nephew of Thomas Coke, Earl of Leicester and builder of Holkham Hall. The Longford estate was a twin property with Holkham and had been purchased by one of the sons of Chief Justice Coke in the seventeenth century. In 1759, Lord Leicester died, leaving no children, and so Wenman became the heir to Holkham. He was disliked by the dowager Lady Leicester who hoped to outlive him and so prevent his coming to Holkham.

Wenman's parliamentary career meant that his time was divided between Derbyshire and London, and so Thomas' early life was spent either at Longford or at a rented house in Hanover Square. He was sent to Eton when he was ten years old and here his interest in sport and country life began. This was in sharp contrast to his more studious father. In 1771 he left Eton and completed his education in the manner traditional to the wealthy, by going on the European grand tour, and most of the next four years were spent in Italy.

In 1774, Wenman began to take more interest in Norfolk. He gave up his seat as an M.P. for Derbyshire and became a member for Norfolk instead. A year later Lady Leicester died and Wenman succeeded to Holkham. In the same year Thomas married Jane Dutton of Sherbourne, Gloucestershire, and they settled down for the hunting season at

Godwick Hall, Tittleshall. Thomas soon succeeded Lord Townshend as master of the Norfolk hounds. In April 1776, Wenman died. He had hardly spent any time at Holkham as his parliamentary duties had kept him in London. Thomas on the other hand was far more interested in country pursuits and running the extensive estates that he had inherited than in a political career. However, he was persuaded to stand for his father's seat, mainly, it seems, to keep a Tory out. 'At the mention of a Tory my blood chilled from head to foot, and I came forward.'[1] His long parliamentary career lasted until 1833.

Coke entered Parliament in the year when open war against the American colonies was finally declared, and on 4 July, Congress declared America independent. Coke soon associated himself with the Rockingham Whigs in opposition and there was plenty for them to criticise in the way Lord North's government handled the war. Many, with Fox as their vociferous spokesman, openly supported the American cause.

'When I first entered Parliament, I attached myself to Fox and I clung to him through life. I lived in the closest bond of friendship with him. He was a friend of the people, the practiser of every kindness and generosity, and advocate of civil and religious liberty.'[2]

Coke consistently voted against the North government and spoke strongly against the war in a speech on 4 December 1778, in which he moved that the House condemn the manifesto of the peace commissioner proposing unacceptable terms to the Americans.

Dissatisfaction with corruption and the unrepresentative nature of Parliament was strong during the war, and County Associations to petition Parliament for reform were set up in many parts of the country. Coke was one of the few Norfolk landowners who supported the petitioning movement, and on 23 February 1780 he presented the Norfolk petition to the House.

It was the personal obstinacy and interference of George III which kept Lord North's government in power so long, but finally in 1782 the ministry disintegrated and the Rockingham Whigs, whose first aim was to end the war, took office. It was Coke who moved that the independence of America be recognised and who presented the address to the king requesting the end of the war. Coke was always outspoken in his criticism

---

[1] *Gentleman's Magazine* (1842), part 2, p. 317, quoted by Sir Louis Namier and J. Brooke, *History of the House of Commons, 1754–1790*, 3 vols. (London, 1964), vol. 2, p. 234.

[2] *Norwich Mercury* (7 Aug. 1830), quoted by A. M. W. Stirling, *Coke of Norfolk and his Friends*, 2 vols. (London, 1908), vol. 1, p. 165.

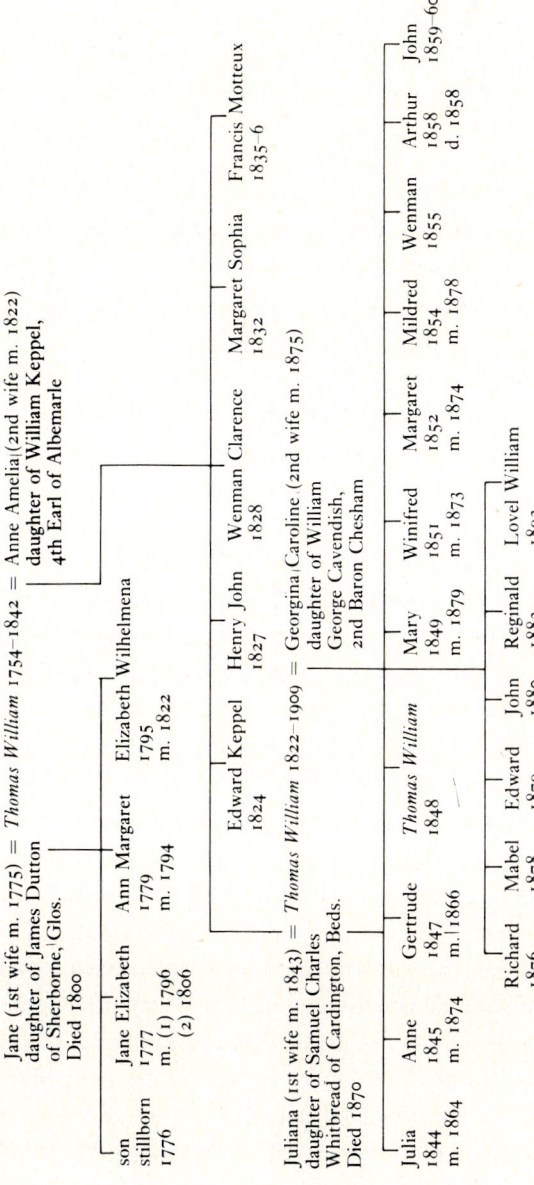

2.1 Family tree of the Cokes of Norfolk, 1776–1909.

of the king, and George III never forgot that he had played such a prominent part in the campaign to end the war. Rockingham died in July and Shelburne became Prime Minister. He was entirely occupied with the peace negotiations and lost the support of many of his own party, such as Fox, because of his lack of interest in economic and parliamentary reform. It was also felt that he could have made more favourable terms with America and Coke was one of those who voted against his peace proposals of February 1783. After Shelburne's resignation, no administration could be formed from among the many factions, and finally Coke told the House on 21 March that he would move for an address to the king if a ministerial arrangement was not come to very soon. The final solution was the very unlikely and unpopular Fox–North coalition which only lasted until December. Coke's approval of this government lost him support in Norfolk and he withdrew from the general election in 1784 to avoid an expensive and probably pointless contest. He was not reelected until 1790.

Between 1784 and 1790, Coke was able to spend more time at Holkham with his family. His marriage to Jane Dutton was a happy one. The first year was saddened by the birth of a stillborn son, but in 1777 a daughter, Jane Elizabeth, was born and another daughter, Anne Margaret, in 1779 (fig. 2.1). No sons followed and so in 1793, when a son was born to Coke's brother, Edward, he was accepted as the heir presumptive to Holkham. He was named Thomas William and, like his uncle, he was brought up at Longford, which had been lent to Edward for his lifetime.

Even Thomas Coke's biographer, Mrs Stirling, could find out little about domestic life at Holkham during this time, but it is clear that even while not an M.P. Coke did not lose contact with his Whig friends. Fox and many leading Whigs were frequent visitors to Holkham, as the entries in the game books show. One wonders what, other than shooting, was discussed on these occasions and how many parliamentary tactics were decided in the fields and woods around Holkham as well as on the race courses and in the London clubs, gambling and coffee houses.

Perhaps one of the most spectacular events at Holkham was the festivity celebrating the centenary of the Glorious Revolution in 1788. It was partly a political affair and was organised on a huge scale. The Prince of Wales, who as heir to the throne was frequently at loggerheads with his father, was seen as a champion of the Whig cause and had hoped

2.2 Thomas William Coke, owner of Holkham, 1776–1842.

to attend, but one of his father's fits of insanity prevented this. Fox was abroad, but other notable Whigs were present. Locally, invitations were sent to all those of suitable standing within the county, whatever their political affiliations, but many political opponents declined the invitation, some 'civilly' and others less so. One reply was even described as 'insolent'.[3] The evening's entertainment consisted of a ball, banquet and fireworks. Holkham Hall was filled 'from end to end'. The political flavour of the occasion was shown, by the fact that the Whig slogan 'Liberty and our cause' was illuminated over the door of the saloon where Mr and Mrs Coke were receiving their guests. The Prince of Wales' feathers in the Whig colours of blue and buff were lit up above the pediment on the front of the house, and although a toast was drunk to him none was drunk to his father. Blue and buff dominated the clothes of the many hundreds of guests.

When Coke returned to Parliament in 1790, it was the problem of the French Revolution which was dominating politics and which was to split the Whig party and Coke's circle of friends. In April 1790 Lord Windham of Felbrigg Hall, Norfolk, recorded in his diary a pleasant evening spent with Coke at his London home. 'I sat next to Burke, with Fox next to him and had a tolerable share of the conversation; the principle subjects of which were Bruce, the conduct of the judges on the impeachment [of Warren Hastings], Dunning, farming, architecture and painting.'[4] This must have been one of the last occasions when Burke and Fox met on friendly terms. In November Burke published his book, *Reflections on the Revolution in France*, in which he condemned revolutionary change. His belief in building freedom on existing conditions rather than tearing them apart appealed to the Tories and less radical Whigs, but Fox and his supporters, including Coke, were already being swept forward by the spirit of revolution and its call for freedom. As the horrors of the revolution in France became more apparent, Burke's views gained support, but by this time the opposition Whigs were split. Coke was always against interfering with the internal affairs of France as this could only prolong the horror. He could never support the French war and in a speech in Norwich in 1830 he said, 'Would to God that ministers had seen their error before they plunged so madly into a war which has nearly been the ruin of the country'.[5]

[3] Stirling, *Coke of Norfolk*, vol. 1, p. 347.
[4] *Windham Diary* (17 April 1790), p. 197.
[5] *Norwich Mercury* (23 Jan. 1830).

Whatever Coke may have thought about the desirability of the French war, he certainly made the best of the agricultural boom that accompanied it. His interest in politics declined as he devoted more time to farming and the improvement of his estates. In 1795 his third daughter, Elizabeth, was born. His two elder daughters married, but still spent much time at Holkham. In 1800, his wife, Jane, died and was mourned deeply. She seems to have been a great support to her husband in every way and fulfilled admirably her functions as hostess. Elizabeth, now five years old, became the object of Coke's care and attention. In 1809, he described her as, 'My beloved daughter, the comfort of my life', and at the age of eighteen she took on the position of mistress of Holkham and hostess for her father. Some idea of how much work this position involved is shown in a letter that Elizabeth wrote many years later to her future husband, when Coke had remarried and she was no longer responsible for the running of the house. 'She [Mrs Coke] probably finds what I have found during several years, that this house entails a perpetual sacrifice of all one's feelings and inclinations.'[6]

As the war with France dragged on, Coke was still not drawn into the atmosphere of panic or impending invasion. He did not support the setting up of local volunteer militia and refused to regard a French invasion as imminent. In fact, along with other Norfolk Whigs, he respected Napoleon for what he was doing to France. Lord Albemarle of Quiddenham, Norfolk, is said to have had a portrait of the emperor over his bed.

In 1806, Fox died and this further weakened Coke's interest in politics. He was reluctant to stand for reelection. However, at the end of the Napoleonic War Coke again found political causes to support, the most important of which was parliamentary reform. He vehemently opposed the 'six acts', designed by the Tory government to prevent subversion. At a dinner in Norwich to mark Fox's birthday, he described them as 'bills of blood'. He also championed the cause of Catholic emancipation and in 1825 he presented a petition in its favour.

In 1822, Coke married again. His second wife was his godchild, Anne Keppel, the daughter of his close friend, Lord Albemarle. She was fifty years his junior, and Coke had originally planned that she should marry his nephew, the heir to Holkham. However, neither party would agree

---

[6] A. M. W. Stirling, *The Letter Bags of Lady Elizabeth Spencer Stanhope*, 2 vols. (London, 1913), vol. 2, p. 59.

to this arrangement. Anne Keppel was upset by her own father's remarriage, not least because she would lose her position as mistress of the household to a stepmother. She was only too willing to marry her godfather of whom she was already very fond.[7] The engagement was greeted with some surprise in London society. 'Mr. Coke's absurd marriage to Lady Anne Keppel, fifty years younger than himself, is the general topic of conversation', remarked a gossip.[8] In spite of the misgivings of many of his friends, the marriage was a success and Coke took a renewed interest in family life and less in politics. The birth of a son in 1822 meant that Coke's nephew, William, was no longer heir to Holkham. 'Yet he never showed any regret at his change in fortune, and continued to treat his uncle with the same affection as formerly.' He never married, but spent the remainder of his life in a rented house in Norfolk, 'hunting energetically to the last'.[9] By 1832 Coke's new young family consisted of four sons and one daughter.

When the first step in parliamentary reform was finally achieved in 1833, Coke wrote to congratulate Lord Grey and there is a bas-relief at Holkham commemorating the signing of the Reform Bill. King William is shown as King John signing Magna Carta and portraits of Coke and the other reformers are clearly shown in the warriors grouped around.

With parliamentary reform established, Coke was ready to retire. He was seventy-nine and had been an M.P. for fifty-seven years. As early as 1823, he had expressed his dislike of Parliament to his favourite daughter, Elizabeth, who wrote to her future husband, 'To my great entertainment Majesty [Coke] expressed his disgust at being in Parliament and wished to Heaven you were in his place, forgetting, I suppose, at the moment, your obnoxious Tory principals.' Again she wrote a few days later, 'Whatever you do, keep out of Parliament! My comfort is gone and yours too whenever you engage in such turmoils – though you would speak good sense, which in these days is rather a novelty...I am too tired of the whole farce, for it is only larger children's play.'[10] Coke had valued his position as a commoner and had refused a peerage at least three times, but on his retirement he was ready to accept. Now that he had four sons, he claimed that one of his reasons for accepting the title was for the benefit of his heirs.

---

[7] Stirling, *Coke of Norfolk*, vol. 2, pp. 281–2.
[8] *Ibid.*, vol. 2, p. 283.   [9] *Ibid.*, vol. 2, p. 200.
[10] Stirling, *The Letter Bags*, vol. 2, pp. 75 and 55.

Coke was not, however, immediately honoured. He had grossly insulted George III on several occasions and so William did not think it right to enoble him. On the accession of Victoria, who had visited Holkham two years before William's death, Coke was made Earl of Leicester of Holkham in 1837. After that date he spent an increasing amount of time at Longford, which, after the death of his brother, was empty. He died there in 1842. There are many descriptions of his lavish funeral and the journey of his coffin back to Norfolk from Derbyshire. He is buried in the family vault at Tittleshall.

Life at Holkham

Although Coke was a prominent Norfolk Whig and a consistent attender of the House of Commons, he still found time for country sports and the running of his estates. Although he did not own a London house, he rented one for the parliamentary session and spent most of the session there. Late-eighteenth-century parliaments sat for between six and seven months most years, between November and May. This covered much of the hunting season and so Coke kept a pack of hounds near Mark Hall in Essex and hunted in Epping Forest three or four days a week.[11] As well as the kennels at Holkham and in Essex, he kept hounds in Suffolk and Cambridgeshire. Shoots at Holkham continued throughout the parliamentary sessions even when Coke was not there. Game books show them starting on the first Wednesday of November and continuing twice a week throughout the season. Open house was kept at Holkham and fifty or eighty guests plus their servants might well stay for several weeks. These often included royalty, such as the Duke of Sussex (son of George III), the Duke of Gloucester (nephew of George III), and the Prince of Wales, later George IV. Entertaining royalty was always an expensive business and was the financial ruin of several great families. Other than royalty, members of the shooting parties often included Coke's Whig friends, local aristocracy and a few of the gentry. Only the most eminent of Coke's tenants ever joined him, even if he were shooting across their land. On these occasions, the tenants were usually given a couple of brace of partridges, a somewhat poor reward for the amount of damage caused by the game and the shoot. Unlike some estates, there is no evidence at Holkham for tenants' shoots at the end of the season.

[11] Stirling, *Coke of Norfolk*, vol. 1, p. 243.

A splendid game larder at Holkham dates from the eighteenth century. It is two storeys high and its circular interior is lined from floor to ceiling with Derbyshire alabaster, while the shelves are of slate. The continual preoccupation with game during the shooting season was not always to the taste of all who lived at Holkham. Elizabeth wrote to John Stanhope, 'Your conversation will be more than usually delightful to me, I am so tired of mangled hares and missed woodcocks.' In a previous letter she had reported that on the first day of the battue there were nearly 800 head killed. 'George Anson killed 130 with his own gun.'[12] On another day in the same season there were '860 head and three people'!

Coke's main interests at Holkham were in sport and agriculture. He undertook very few alterations in the house. Mrs Stirling quotes him as saying, 'I shall not venture rashly to interfere with the results of years of thought and study in Italy.'[13] The park was extended considerably in the last years of the eighteenth century and most of the lodges rebuilt. The splendid Great Barn was also built in the 1790s. It served the home farm and was universally admired by all who attended sheep shearings.

Parliamentary sessions may have clashed with the shooting season, but Coke was at Holkham for the most active parts of the agricultural year and his personal interest in agriculture was most clearly shown in the attention he lavished on the sheep shearings. These began in 1776 as simple annual gatherings of local farmers to exchange ideas and inspect the Holkham home farm,[14] but from 1778 the arrangements became more formal. The meeting always took place at sheep shearing time at the beginning of July. This allowed Southdown sheep to be examined and the amount of wool obtained to be measured. The shearings began to attract farmers from further afield, and by the early nineteenth century they were large and sometimes international meetings, attended by aristocrats, landlords and farmers alike. Reports were published in the *Annals of Agriculture* and individual pamphlets. Improvements first published at the sheep shearings could easily be followed by a far wider audience.

For this sort of event to be a success, the cooperation and enthusiasm of the tenantry was necessary. Progress on the tenant farms impressed visitors as much as did the home farm. Many of the animals entered for

---

[12] Stirling, *The Letter Bags*, vol. 2, pp. 48 and 75.
[13] Stirling, *Coke of Norfolk*, vol. 1, p. 239.
[14] *Ibid.*

the competitions were from tenant farms and it was Holkham tenants who won many of the prizes.

The sheep shearings were not without their financial benefit to Coke. Sheep and cattle were sold and bulls and rams let. The income from sales and lettings in 1806 was £2,234. Usually the figure was somewhere between £1,000 and £2,000. Again, much of the business was done between Coke and his tenants.[15]

The importance of the sheep shearings was obviously very great. It brought a great deal of publicity to Holkham on a national and international scale. Bacon claimed that 'It has indeed changed in a good degree the habits and condition of agricultural society.'[16] He also pointed out the way that the sheep shearings were an example of the complete confidence that had been established between landlord and tenant. The sheep shearings are significant, not only showing Coke as a great and improving landlord and agriculturalist, but also showing the interest in experiment and development which existed among his tenants.[17]

The last sheep shearings were held in 1821 when Coke was sixty-seven. He may well have felt that there was no more to be achieved by them. With his marriage in 1822, he was again involved in domestic life and although he continued to take an active interest in his estates he may have thought that the time for the exhausting entertaining involved in having so many guests at Holkham was past.

Although contemporary descriptions show how lavishly Coke entertained and that Holkham was a great social centre of the period, the number of servants seems to have been very modest compared with other estates. In 1801, twenty-six servants were employed in the house on a yearly basis. Seven more worked in the stables and one in the kennels. Presumably more were hired for shorter periods as needed. Those paid annually included a butler, a cook, a groom de chambre, a valet, a porter, a baker and underbaker, a plateman, a footman, a housekeeper, a nurse, a kitchen maid and an under kitchen maid. Only one gardener is mentioned but he must have had assistants. There were also five gamekeepers, a carpenter and a glazier. The wages for the year amounted

[15] Holkham MSS, sheep shearing accounts.
[16] R. N. Bacon, *A Report of the Transactions at the Annual Holkham Sheep Shearings* (Norwich, 1821).
[17] For a detailed assessment of the importance of the sheep shearings, see R. A. C. Parker, *Coke of Norfolk, a Financial and Agricultural Study, 1707–1842* (Oxford, 1975), chapter 8.

to £294. The number of servants had risen by the 1840s, when there were as many as forty at Christmas time. For most of the year there were over thirty, and on top of this there were the servants of the guests. Extra people such as coal carters frequently dined in the servants' hall, as did chimney sweeps and coopers. In the winter that were also ice carters. In 1851 there were thirty-six people outside the Coke family living in the Hall: eighteen maids, two charwomen, one governess, one housekeeper, one cook and a roasting cook, one nurse, one house steward, the agents' clerk, a plate burnisher, a house porter, a footman, a postillion, three helpers in the stable, the stewards' room lad and a baker. Twenty-one of the servants were born locally. It was mostly the senior members of the household, such as the housekeeper and governess, who came from further afield.

Most of the servants were daughters of cottagers rather than of small farmers in the area. Rigby thought fears that the decline in small farmers would bring about a decline in the supply of servants were unjustified. 'How many individuals does he [Coke] benefit in this way? How many are thus trained up, not only to habits of regularity and industry, but to good manners and even to something like the polish of civilised society?'[18]

Even although Elizabeth Coke had managed Holkham for her father for several years, she still welcomed advice on the qualities necessary for a lady's maid, and was given the following list of essential requirements, which she sent to her future husband.

> She *must not* have a will of her own in *anything*, and be always good humoured and approve of everything her mistress likes. She *must not* have a good appetite or be the least of a *gourmand* or *care* when or how she dines, how often disturbed, or even if she has no dinner at all. She had better not drink anything but water.
>
> She must *run quick* the instant she is *called*, whatever she is about. Morning, noon and night she must not mind going without *sleep* if her mistress requires her attendance. She must not require high wages nor expect any profit from the *old clothes*, but be ready to *turn* and *clean* the *dirty gowns*, not for herself, but for her mistress, and then sell them for an old song as she is *bid* and be satisfied with two gowns for herself. She *must* be a *first-rate* vermin catcher.
>
> She must be *clean* and *sweet* and *very* quick. She must have ears (strong ones), eyes and hands, but as for thinking or judging for herself or being in any way independent (if especially her mistress be a Whig or of liberal *principles*) she must not think of such a thing; and let her not venture to make a complaint or difficulty of any kind. If so, she had better go at once.
>
> She may gather up as much gossip as she likes, but she must never *tell any*.

[18] E. Rigby, *Holkham and its Agriculture* (3rd ed., Norwich, 1817), p. 101.

The landlords

Implicit obedience, the first essential; extra-ordinary disinterestedness, united with a love of strict economy, the second. Honesty that will bear the closest inspection; unceasing activity; unimpeachable good health and extreme good humour *indespensible requisites*.

She must in short, do everything, gain nothing except the few pounds she gets for her wages and be alive to the fact that she has a very good place.[19]

It is not clear how seriously this advice was to be taken, but Elizabeth was very sure about the sort of housekeeper she wanted. 'Pray, don't engage a terrible looking housekeeper, if she frightens you she will frighten me much more. I want a goody sort of person who will occasionally make up a mess of broth or sago for the poor people.'[20]

The impression of Holkham life left for us by Elizabeth Stanhope (*née* Coke) and Mrs Stirling is of an establishment used to large-scale entertaining and visited by many eminent people of both local and national repute. The shooting was good and well managed and shooting parties were large. The conversation seems to have mainly been about politics, sport and agriculture. Yet the household itself was not excessive and, except for the lavish hospitality, the house was run with moderation. Towards the end of his life, Thomas Coke was spending much more time at Longford, Derbyshire, which was far smaller and perhaps more suited to a life of semi-retirement. Elizabeth Stanhope's letters from this period suggest a quieter if very happy domestic life. The Duke of Sussex was a frequent visitor and shooting continued on a grand scale, but when at Holkham Coke seems to have spent his time enjoying his second young family and the grandchildren of his first marriage who often visited him there.

Included in the list of servants for 1801 is a farm bailiff. He was the highest paid servant, receiving £157 a year. The estate's accounts at this time were kept by Crick, Coke's valet, who had little knowledge of agricultural matters. An accountant and an assistant were employed in the estate office. There was no agent with overall control and this function must have been fulfilled by Coke himself. In 1807 he mentioned to Sir Thomas Lawrence, who was painting his portrait, that 'he had no land steward, but did all the business himself, and had done it for many years'. It was unusual for a large estate not to have an agent by this date. Those that did not employ their own stewards might well use the large London firms such as Cluttons or Savilles. By the 1780s Coke employed

[19] Stirling, *The Letter Bags*, vol. 2, p. 200.   [20] *Ibid.*, vol. 2, p. 59.

outside valuers to let farms. In 1791, £241 12s. was paid to Messrs Kent, Claridge and Co. for valuing different farms.[21] The fact that different valuers were being employed helps to explain the inconsistencies in leases before an agent was appointed. Even Coke with his great interest in agricultural matters eventually found such an appointment necessary, and in 1816 Francis Blaikie took over the estate office at Holkham. It is clear from looking at the life of Thomas William Coke that it was possible to combine a successful parliamentary career with an active and time-consuming sporting life and personal estate management. As the 'richest commoner in England' Coke probably had larger estates to manage than any other member of the House of Commons, yet he seems to have combined the roles of landlord and M.P. and received wide acclaim in both fields.

Thomas William Coke died in 1842 at the age of eighty-eight. He left a wealthy and progressive tenantry. They, along with 'yeomanry, noblemen and gentlemen', subscribed generously to the erection of the monument in Holkham park. The reliefs on the monument show scenes of the sheep shearings, the granting of a lease and the digging of an irrigation scheme, all with Coke as a central figure. A corn drill, a plough, a Devon Longhorn bull and a group of Southdown sheep are also shown, thus illustrating the main elements that made up the improved husbandry of north-west Norfolk.

Thomas Coke, second earl of Leicester, 1842–1909

In 1842, Thomas Coke inherited the estate and became the second earl. He was then aged twenty and had been educated at Eton and Winchester. Since his father had moved to Longford, he must have taken an increasing interest in the running of the estates and so was well able to take them on at his fathers' death. In 1843 he married Juliana Whitbread of Cardington, Bedfordshire. She was only seventeen at the time of their marriage and we know that the trustees of the Holkham estate (the new earl still being a minor) settled £3,000 a year from the earl's private estate for her use. This marriage seems to have been a very happy one and Juliana was very much liked. Elizabeth Stanhope wrote, 'I shall be very fond of her, nothing can be more amiable or purer in mind and feeling.

[21] Parker, *Coke of Norfolk*, p. 101.

2.3 Thomas Coke, second Earl of Leicester and owner of Holkham, 1842–1909.

Yesterday she begged me to come into her room in the prettiest and warmest manner and thanked me for my kind letters.'[22]

Holkham life certainly became much gayer under its new owner. Mrs Pickering wrote of the young couple,

[22] Stirling, *The Letter Bags*, vol. 2, p. 200.

We heard they were supremely happy at Holkham, enjoying themselves like boy and girl, as indeed they were, either riding together in the park or he teaching her to drive her ponies in a pretty little pony carriage which he had bought her before they married, both rejoicing that they had turned their backs on the London season and its frivolities.

Elizabeth Stanhope describes nights of dancing in the saloon and the audit room, saying 'Leicester delights in dancing'.

The new earl also set about altering the house, and showing it off to its best. Elizabeth Stanhope found some of the pretension rather cheerless. 'Meanwhile fancy the 300 guinea grate in the gallery without an atom of fire and every door left studiously open to show the suite of rooms. So much for vanity and vexation of spirit and comfortless magnificence.' The portico and house were painted 'a sort of mud colour so different from the beautiful tone of the bricks'.[23] Inside, the hall was also altered but the major changes were made outside. Many of the lodges were rebuilt and a new range of stables was erected to harmonise with the architecture of the house. The trees around the lake were thinned out and four islands were created. A terrace was built extending 250 feet beyond the gravel of the south front, and a lawn and terrace were laid out to the north.

It is very difficult to discover much about the life of the second earl and he was very much overshadowed by the reputation of his father. He took little interest in politics, which he left to his younger brother, Edward, who was M.P. for west Norfolk from 1847 to 1852. He followed his father in the Whig tradition but broke with Gladstone over Home Rule for Ireland in 1886. At a great meeting in St Andrew's Hall, Norwich, in 1886, of 'an entirely non-political nature', he said, 'I have never been in the habit of taking part in political matters of an entirely party description.'[24] In 1845, he told his tenants at the annual audit that he was a free-trader and 'gave great satisfaction by desiring the tenants to take their own line...a politic measure to give what they were sure to take'.[25] He did have a London address at 19 Grosvenor Square, but only rarely attended the House of Lords. He was lord lieutenant of the county from 1846 to 1906 and Keeper of the Privy Seal for the Prince of Wales from 1870. He was member of the Council for the Duchy of Cornwall from 1866. Other than these rather ceremonial positions his

---

[23] *Ibid.*, vol. 2, p. 200. [24] *Norfolk Chronicle* (30 Jan. 1909).
[25] Stirling, *The Letter Bags*, vol. 2, p. 199.

main interests seem to have been in his estates which, with the help of his agents, he ran very efficiently.

He shared his father's enthusiasm for shooting parties and these continued on a large scale throughout the nineteenth century. In 1867 the Prince of Wales was shooting at Holkham and he became a regular visitor. The game books show that the amount of game shot increased steadily throughout the period. In 1805, 1,245 partridges and 315 pheasants were shot, and in 1834–5 the numbers were 2,343 and 1,443 respectively. By 1853–4 these had risen to 3,252 partridges and 3,113 pheasants and in 1900–1, they were 4,599 partridges and 4,149 pheasants. By way of comparison, 28,000 birds were being shot annually on the royal estate at Sandringham by the end of the century.

Life at Holkham continued to be maintained in style but the number of servants kept was still not lavish. Between twenty and thirty servants were employed in the 1850s and 1860s, while by the 1880s the numbers were between fourteen and twenty, with as many as thirty extra being taken on at Christmas.

The Earl of Leicester's family increased in size almost annually. His eldest child, Julia, was born in 1844. Anne was born in 1845 and Gertrude in 1847. His first son and heir, Thomas William, was born in 1848. Seven more children, one of whom died in infancy and one who died soon after his first birthday, were born between 1849 and 1860. This family was large, even by Victorian standards and it is said that when the marriage between the Earl of Leicester and his second wife, Georgina Cavendish, was being discussed, Georgina was advised not to marry Leicester as she would always be pregnant.

Lord Leicester seems to have been a gay young man who enjoyed an active social life. Lady Elizabeth Stanhope visited her stepbrother for Christmas in 1847. Christmas eve was occupied by a grand battue; 'they are to kill 500 pheasants and 500 hares, which are all to be driven to one spot – a regular massacre. How different to the old days!' The evenings were spent in energetic dancing in the audit room which went on until after two o'clock. By Christmas day most of the party were far too exhausted to get to church.

It is quite sad, the only two men at church this morning were E. Digby and his porter – not a manservant I believe. Leicester is laid up, the romping and extreme fatigue of the shooting having knocked him up. He is better today, but has not appeared. Henry fell off the table on which he mounted in the Christmas gambols last night and hurt his knee, but nothing very serious... His Highness [the Duke of Sussex] has rather fallen in my estimation by not going to church. In true royal manner he never appears until luncheon time as I believe he gets up late and has many letters to write... The billiard table is always lighted up for the gentlemen when they come in from shooting and then they sit smoking.[26]

Christmas in Holkham village that year was not as cheerful as usual.

Mr Napier says there is such a state of gloom in the village, no meat given, or jollity or anything, and he declares he must have apple tarts for the school boys and a fiddle for the girls to dance. The reason of the charities being stopped was that they most foolishly said that his lordship was obliged to give it as it was left by will, so he was right to stop it for a year, but it should not have been longer. I believe he gives coals instead... Poor Juliana's very charity which must be great, as the £500 pin-money is certainly not spent on herself, seems to go for nothing. She is very attaching to those who really know her, so true and so gentle, but probably will never be really popular.[27]

In 1870 Juliana died of bronchitis at the age of forty-four. The heavily restored Holkham church was a result of her interest and stands as her memorial. We know little of her except from the descriptions of Elizabeth Stanhope.

In 1875, the earl married again, this time Georgina Cavendish, the daughter of the second baron Chesham, and like his father, he too was soon surrounded by a second young family. Six children, five sons and one daughter, were born between 1876 and 1893. Georgina is remembered as a very refined and cultured woman with great musical talent whose abilities were stifled by her very demanding husband who became more possessive as he became older. He had an organ built for her in Holkham church, but other than this took very little interest in her music.

The upbringing and education of this large family must have been an expensive undertaking. All seven daughters of his first marriage were married between 1864 and 1879, and arranging family weddings, sometimes two in a year, would have involved some lavish entertaining. A book of household accounts from 1861 to 1878 shows that the monthly food bill varied between £100 and £200 throughout the period. The bill for November 1863 is a typical one for a month when the family was at home:

Grocer   £7 17s.
Confectioner   £6 2s. 11d.
Milk   £10 10s.

[26] *Ibid.*, vol. 2, p. 231. [27] *Ibid.*

Meat   £50
Park Farm   £45
Butter   £14
Dairy
   166½ lb butter   £11 10s.
   40 quarts of cream   £3
   38 gallons of new milk   £1 18s.
   Milk for servants   £2 5s.

In some years the family was spending as much as six months in London, and at these times the establishment at Holkham was reduced and food bills were much lower. All the earl's daughters had to be introduced to London society and Elizabeth Stanhope described the finding, renting and furnishing of a suitable London house that this involved. Then clothes had to be bought, parties given and introductions obtained.

The earl's income was such that he could well afford to entertain royalty and after 1865 the Prince of Wales was a frequent visitor. It is clear that the style of life at Holkham was not affected by the fall in rents at the end of the century, and when the earl died he left £427,000 net (£879,500 gross) 'besides immense settled estates'.

The earl was always known as a patron of agricultural causes and the estate continued to be a model of good management, while the home farm and some of the tenants pioneered new methods. All the estate correspondence was carried out by the office, but it is clear from the letter books that the earl was always consulted and sometimes voiced a very independent opinion; but by the end of his life, 'he had lived long in retirement at Holkham'.[28] This was particularly so after 1896, when he had a severe heart attack and the family were summoned. He became an obstinate old man and life at Holkham became very restricted. His wife was never allowed to leave him and he spent most of his time in a bed that he had had brought into the saloon and in which he generally wore a sombrero hat. However, he could still be very alert and Rider Haggard found him well aware of the affairs of his farms when he visited him in 1902.

He seems generally to have been respected by farmers and labourers alike. An obituary describes him as 'a compassionate friend and ever considerate to his labourers'. The fact that he was not always prepared to support farmers against their labourers is shown by the way he

[28] *Norfolk Chronicle* (30 Jan 1909).

protected cottagers from eviction by the farmers by letting cottages directly himself rather than through the farmers. Although Lord Walsingham was against agricultural unions, Lord Leicester and Lord Suffield refused to join any combination of employer against employed.[29] They asserted that men had every right to join unions. Union records are very scant indeed and there are no branch union books for the county of Norfolk. However, there is some evidence that there were agricultural unions in some Holkham parishes, although it is impossible to know how strong they were or how long they lasted. Although many great landowners were singled out for abuse from union platforms, the Earl of Leicester seems to have escaped, which again suggests that he did not oppose unions and that his views were respected by union men.

Financial affairs

The financial affairs of the first earl have been studied in detail by Dr Parker, who shows that, in common with many other estates in the early nineteenth century, Holkham was burdened with considerable debt. When Thomas William Coke inherited, this amounted to nearly £100,000, which meant a yearly interest burden of £4,000. There were also annuities and jointures to be paid which by 1803–10 amounted to £9,000. By 1822 Coke's personal expenses were estimated at £16,000, so it was not surprising that his debts were increasing and had reached £133,000. Portions of £30,000 for his three daughters and the expenses of politics could help explain this immense increase and it meant that there was certainly no spare money for investment outside the estate.[30]

Holkham was unusual in that up to the mid nineteenth century nearly all its income came from the rents collected from agricultural land. Sometimes there was a small sum from the home farm and both the brick kilns and the woods made slight profits, although the second earl claimed that his father had sold so much timber that he had to buy in any that he needed.[31] Until 1835, Coke held the lease of Dungeness lighthouse. By charging tolls from passing ships he was able to make a profit of up to £6,000 a year in the early part of the century. In 1828 a new lease was negotiated and his profits fell to about £2,000. Finally public opinion

[29] L. Marion Springall, *Labouring Life in Norfolk Villages, 1813–1914* (London, 1936), pp. 90–1.
[30] Parker, *Coke of Norfolk*, pp. 128–34.
[31] Stirling, *The Letter Bags*, vol. 2, p. 230.

forced the passing of an act in 1835, whereby lighthouses became publicly owned and their previous owners were paid compensation. Coke was given £20,954, but as the lighthouse had been part of the settled estate, he only received the interest.

For ten years from 1826 the first earl was chairman of the Wells Turnpike Trust but he does not seem to have been financially involved. He is not recorded as a shareholder, although Blaikie and many of the tenant farmers were. In 1840 Blaikie still had £4,000 invested in the trust, which paid an interest of 4%.

The size of Coke's debts was causing grave concern by 1822, and Blaikie was determined that it should be reduced. The sale of the Hillesdon (Buckinghamshire) estates in 1823 brought in £125,000 and the remaining acres at Minster Lovell (Oxfordshire) £3,500. This was used for repaying loans. The situation was helped by the lowering of interest rates from 5% to $4\frac{1}{2}$% and a return to agricultural prosperity and rising rents. This, plus a certain amount of economising at Holkham, meant that by the late 1820s there was a net surplus of income which could be used to repay debts and they were all discharged by 1842.[32]

The second earl was perhaps unusual in that he inherited an estate with no debts attached. By 1850, the sums of £15,000 bequeathed by the first earl to each of his nine children had all been paid. However, Lord Leicester did find it necessary to borrow £19,000 from his cousin, Thomas William Coke of Longford, which he repaid in 1868. No other such bonds survive amongst the family papers.

Ledgers record that about £1,000 per annum was being paid in interest on loans in the 1850s, and about £3,000 in the early 1860s, but by the end of the decade these payments had ceased entirely. Similarly, until the 1870s annuities varying from £4,000 to £7,000 a year were being paid, but after that there were no such encumbrances on the estate.

It is very unfortunate that so little remains to help us explain the second earl's financial affairs. His income from the estate was steadily rising until the 1880s and he also received up to £6,000 a year from his private estate, £3,000 of which was settled on his wife.

The figures in table 2.1 show the net estate income every ten years, after expenditure listed in the audit books has been subtracted. It can be seen that the total income reached a peak for the ten year period

---

[32] Parker, *Coke of Norfolk*, p. 192.

between 1870 and 1880 (£749,924) and fell to £356,310 between 1890 and 1900.

TABLE 2.1. *Total decennial net income of the Holkham estate 1850–99*

	£		£
1850–9	373,016	1880–9	441,521
1860–9	453,407	1890–9	356,310
1870–9	749,924		

From this the £42,000 which was spent on the mansion between 1850 and 1880 has to be found. We do not know how much was spent on household expenses and sport.

Estimates as to how much was needed to keep up a stately home and live in a style befitting the rank of the landed gentry vary, and of course much would depend on individual taste. A London house had to be kept up and country pursuits such as entertaining and sport were expensive. As we have seen, from 1867 the Prince of Wales was shooting at Holkham, and entertaining royalty was always costly.

In the 1870s the Earl of Veralum had an ordinary expenditure of £19,000, which, by 1889, he had managed to reduce to £15,000 by decreasing the number of staff in the stables, pruning game expenses, buying less wine and cutting his London season from four or five months to two. The extravagant Earl Fitzwilliam also spent £19,000.[33] In the 1850s the Duke of Devonshire thought that his income after interest payments of between £40,000 and £55,000 should be adequate for ordinary expenditure, but unlike the Earl of Leicester he had several London and country establishments to keep up.[34] The trustees of the Marquis of Aylesbury thought that the cost of keeping up the Tottenham Park establishment at Savernake need not be more than a modest £6,000 per annum.[35] It would seem therefore that, although there are wide variations in expenditure, it was possible that the Earl of Leicester could have been spending up to £20,000 a year, and there is no suggestion that he found it necessary to cut his expenditure at the end of the century.

[33] F. M. L. Thompson, *English Landed Society*, p. 106.
[34] D. Cannodine, 'The landowner as millionaire: The finances of the Duke of Devonshire, c. 1800–1926', *Agricultural History Review*, vol. 25, part 2 (1977).
[35] Thompson, *English Landed Society in the Nineteenth Century* (London, 1963), p. 106.

The landlords

The game books show that the amount of game shot was steadily increasing and there is no significant decline in the number of servants kept or in the amount of entertaining. £20,000 a year accounts for a quarter of the earl's income in 1870 and a third in 1900. There was certainly always a surplus for investment elsewhere.

A. C. Ewald lists the Earl of Leicester as one of the ten wealthiest members of the House of Lords in 1870.[36] J. Bateman names forty families with incomes of over £60,000 a year in 1883 – Lord Leicester's income was given as £59,578.[37] Although he did not quite make it into the top forty he was one of a very limited group controlling immense personal fortunes.

The ways in which the Cokes used their wealth is of great interest for many reasons. They could either use it for very lavish living, or they could invest it in concerns outside their estates. The first alternative, although it might employ much local labour, would in the long run have little effect on local or national life. The second, however, could be of great benefit to economic growth and thus landed wealth could be providing capital for others. If the earl chose to invest his wealth rather than simply to spend it on conspicuous consumption, then his influence on the economy could extend well beyond the boundaries of his estates.

It was also by means of sound investment that the aristocracy was able to increase its wealth in spite of the agricultural depression. 'They became rentiers, maintaining a style of life that was landed in its mode of expenditure but increasingly plutocratic in its sources of income.'[38]

We shall see that the earl's main interests seem to have been in the improvement of transport, firstly in road and railway schemes of purely local benefit, and then in ventures further afield, both at home and abroad, where his interests were only financial. It was his canny distribution of this surplus money that protected him from the worst effects of the agricultural depression.

Among the papers at Holkham is a list of the investments made by the first and second earls of Leicester between 1811 and 1891 (see appendix 2). It is not clear whether this is a complete list, but it does show the types of concerns that were receiving capital from the Holkham

[36] E. C. Ewald, *The Crown and its Advisers* (London, 1870), p. 129.
[37] J. Bateman, *The Great Landowners of Great Britain and Ireland* (London, 1883).
[38] Cannodine, 'The landowner as millionaire'.

estate profits and how widely the second earl was prepared to spread his resources.

There are only two entries for the lifetime of the first earl and these are both for projects in which Coke would have been interested for local and political reasons (Lynn Theatre and the Reform Club) and which were receiving his support because of this rather than for any profit he hoped to make from them. None of his wealth was helping finance the initial stages of the 'industrial revolution'.

After 1846 there are more entries in the list of investments. Five projects are listed as receiving finance from the second earl over the next twenty years and again all of them are ones in which he would have had a specific concern, such as the Royal Agricultural College in Cirencester and local businesses (the Fakenham Corn Exchange, East Dereham Corn Exchange and two railways, the West Norfolk Junction Railway and the Wells and Fakenham Railway). The two small sums to corn exchanges could not have been of great significance to their promoters but the railway investment was far more substantial, and local railway finance was the most important of the earl's investments before 1870. He was not merely concerned with the return of capital invested but also with the building of a railway link to the main area of his estates.

The Wells and Fakenham Company was formed by the Earl of Leicester and other local landowners along with some of the directors of the Norfolk Railway Company in 1853. It was incorporated in 1854 with a capital of £70,000. As well as the earl's contribution, the Borough of Wells contributed £14,000 and the North Norfolk Railway Company not more than £30,000. The line was opened in December 1857 and remained independent until 1862, when it was vested in the G.E.R.[39]

The earl was following the example of many others with money to invest by putting it into railways. But his was not yet blind investment. He was still investing where he felt he would directly benefit from the success of the scheme. After 1870, however, the earl's investments were becoming more widely distributed. As agricultural rents increased he had more surplus wealth of which to dispose, and he followed the national trend to invest in the railways of the Empire. The peak of national investment in Indian railways was in 1866, when £7,700,000 left Britain

---

[39] D. I. Gordon, *A Regional History of the Railways of Great Britain: Eastern Counties* (London, 1968), p. 207.

for India.[40] Between 1870 and 1877 the Earl of Leicester bought £40,000 worth of Indian railway stock at a time when at least £5,000,000 a year of British capital was being exported for railway building. The earl's contribution was nearly equivalent to the net profit from the estate for one year in the 1870s. Behind such entries as '1877, The Sind, Delta and Punjab Railway £11,685', we can see something of what the British Empire and the economic influence that went with it meant for the many thousands of people in Britain with money to invest. We may well be tempted to ask why so much money was going abroad when, at the time of the Great Depression, British industry was under-capitalised and in need of investment.

At home the railways continued to attract the earl's capital. The G.E.R., the N.E.R., the L.&N.W. and the G.W.R. received a total of £49,763 in the 1870s. Local projects also received some support. £1,000 worth of shares in the Norfolk County School at North Elmham were bought. £5 was put into Walsingham Coffee House Company and £500 into the Norfolk and Norwich Agricultural Hall.

Railway shares also dominated the earl's investment through the 1880s. It was mainly British shares that were bought in the first half of the decade, when £64,340 worth of British railway stock was bought. This is the equivalent of one and a half years profit from the estate. After 1886, foreign interests again dominated, but by this time attention had shifted from the Indian peninsular to Australia, Canada, South Africa and South America. Here again the earl was following national trends and between 1886 and 1890 £55,090 was invested in railways, banks and government stock in these four areas. British railways still claimed £54,915. At home the earl's interests were widening. Not only was there support for companies with whose fortunes the earl was directly concerned – such as the Farmer's Foundry Company Ltd (£20 in 1885), Lawes Manure Company (£1,000 in 1888) and Wells improvement bonds (£900 in 1887) – but from the 1880s he was buying shares in breweries. Breweries were also favoured by other members of the aristocracy, such as the Duke of Portland.

The list of investments ends in 1891. Purchases for 1890 and 1891 were very similar to those of the 1880s, except that for the first time bank shares were bought. The earl's will, proved in 1909, specified South

---

[40] L. H. Jenks, *The Migration of English Capital* (London, 1927), p. 22.

TABLE 2.2. *Total investments per decade by the second Earl of Leicester*

	Investment £	Total estate income £
1850s	11,760	373,016
1860s	2,628	453,407
1870s	88,842	749,924
1880s	190,384	441,521

African shares. These were probably bought after 1891 as they were not mentioned here.

Table 2.2 gives the total invested per decade. This shows how rapidly purchasing increased from about 12% of total estate income in the 1870s to a staggering 43% in the 1880s. This is accompanied by a decline in investment in estate improvement from about 20% to 10%, which does not cover more than one fifth of the extra money available for investment. The earl's ability to save and invest in outlets which he hoped would be more profitable than agriculture is remarkable. The large scale of investment may help explain why he felt unable to lay out more for the unremunerative if socially desirable building of cottages.

A list of income from investment for 1890 is given in the back of the book listing purchases of stock. The figure for each month is given, but there is no mention of the source of this income. The total for this year was £11,291, about a quarter of the income from rents for that year. Even as late as 1890 agricultural income was more important than that from investments.

Income from investment is included in the ledgers for 1875 and 1885. In 1875 this amounted to £3,223 and by 1885 it had risen to £6,510. Most of the shares the earl had bought were bringing in a reasonable return and it appears that very few were sold. Income came as dividends from the shares rather than as a result of buying and selling through the Stock Exchange.

No local firm was receiving much finance from the earl, whose capital can have been of little significance to any except the Wells and Fakenham Railway, which did receive considerable support. His influence on economic affairs other than agricultural would seem to have been slight. He must be classed primarily as an agriculturalist, even though, through the years of depression, he must have been relieved to be drawing income from other sources.

It seems clear that as soon as debts were paid off and the legacies laid down in the first earl's will had been dealt with, some of the surplus income from the estate was being reinvested outside the estate in stocks and shares, both the amount and proportion reinvested increasing every decade to the end of the century. As the second earl had no source of income other than his estates, the money for investment must have come from them and certainly there was a large enough surplus, at least up to 1880. The investments themselves follow very much the trends taken by investors of this period. From their inception railways were always an attractive proposition to large and small investors alike, and when the British railways were built interest followed them abroad. None of the earl's money went into British industry, which was suffering from a lack of capital for new equipment. Foreign railways, on the other hand, were being built on the past profits of both British agriculture and industry. It was not until 1887 that sums of any significance were invested in Britain, first in breweries and then in the 1890s in banks. However, foreign investment continued at a very high level and no real change of investment pattern can be detected here. The earl did not take an independent line in his investment tactics, but simply followed contemporary trends.

As yet we do not know enough about the investment patterns of the aristocracy to be able to compare the activities of the earl with those of others. We do not have enough information to say how far the aristocracy and gentry contributed to the export of capital.

His charitable activities also suggest that the earl was a man who did not get involved in too many schemes, but who remained wealthy enough throughout the period to support generously anything in which he was really interested. Although many charities received small donations his main concern was with the Norfolk and Norwich Hospital, which received a great deal of help. In 1846 the earl was made president of the hospital and took a lead in promoting new building. In 1879 he promised £13,000 as an endowment and £2,000 towards the cost of building. However, this sum is not mentioned in the list of donations at Holkham. He also gave sums to the Hunstanton, Lowestoft and Cromer convalescent homes, the Jenny Lind children's hospital, the Blind School and the West Norfolk and Lynn hospital. He set up the

Leicester Nurses' Home in Norwich and supported a nurses' home in Fakenham. His gifts to hospitals between 1840 and 1890 must have been not less than £17,112, and at least £35,000 was given in the 1890s.

Two generations of Cokes saw the estate through a period of 133 years and this remarkable degree of continuity was in itself a great asset to estate management. That both father and son were model landlords intensely interested in their estate, who did not squander the income that it brought, explains the continued fame of the Holkham estate throughout the nineteenth century.

3
The running of the estate

A nineteenth-century estate office was the centre of a complex and often diverse business. As well as controlling thousands of acres of agricultural land, it might handle mining, housing, canal and dock interests. The duties of an agent involved farming, building and managerial skills, while on some estates a knowledge of geology and minerology was also necessary. On the efficiency of the agent depended the smooth running of the estate.

The agent

Although there was no agent at Holkham until 1816 there was an estate office in which Coke employed an accountant with an assistant; but they must have been directly responsible to him and all decisions on estate matters must have been made entirely by him. It is remarkable that such a close involvement with the management of large estates could be successfully combined with an active parliamentary career.

In 1816 Coke appointed Francis Blaikie as his first agent (fig. 3.1). Blaikie remained at Holkham until 1832 and was its most able and influential steward. Previously he had worked for Lord Chesterfield at Bradley in Derbyshire. Coke had met him there, probably on one of his visits to his Longford property, and had been very impressed by his methods of management.[1] Nothing is known of Blaikie's social background or education but he was from a Scottish farming family. Many other famous agents were also Scotsmen, including Andrew Thompson, agent to Ralph Sneyd, John Yule, agent to Sir James Graham, and John Matthew, recommended by the agricultural writer, James Caird, to Sir Robert Peel. They were mainly sons of farmers and yeomen and had practical skills rather than formal education. Blaikie's derogatory opinion of book learning is often made plain in his reports. His experience had been gained in lowland Scotland, a region which was fast becoming one

---

[1] A. M. W. Stirling, *Coke of Norfolk and his Friends*, 2 vols. (London, 1908), vol. 2, p. 122.

3.1 Francis Blaikie, agent to the Holkham estates, 1816–32.

of the most progressive farming districts of Britain. This background would have provided sound practical training.

Blaikie's personal influence on the farming of the estate was probably greater than that of other Holkham agents. His interest in the characters of individual tenants is shown in his descriptions of them, usually written after no more than a single interview and included in his report of the estate made shortly after his arrival. The old-fashioned farmers were easily contented, Blaikie thought too easily so. Mr Whiteman of

Billingford and the Seyer brothers of Longham had few wants and no complaints. Some of the young men were well educated, but could not put their learning to profitable use. Mr Haegren of Quarles was well educated but more of a theorist than 'an attentive persevering and practical farmer'. Tuttell Moore at Warham, on the other hand, was 'a zealous, indefatigable and practical farmer – and no theorist'. Blaikie had little patience with men like Mr Ward of Warham whose farm could have been well cultivated. He was in high spirits when Blaikie met him. 'He talks of improving, but at present everything is wrong'.

Blaikie spent much time in discussion with tenants on his tour of inspection. He thought that the Burrell brothers at Flitcham would attend to advice given. Mr Branford at Godwick was ready to improve in any way pointed out to him. The Nelsons, father and son, were treated to a long lecture from Blaikie on the subject of the drainage needed on their Sparham farm. Blaikie thought his words were 'seemingly attended to'. Mr Kendle of Weasenham had made the mistake of trying to crop according to a four-course rotation instead of a five-course, to which the land was more suited. However, after discussion with Blaikie, 'this sensible unprejudiced man' was converted to Blaikie's reasoning and agreed to return to the five-course shift. Mr Wright of Wighton was also 'void of prejudice and may be improved'.

Blaikie was also forward looking enough to take a great interest in the sons of tenants. Mr Rix, Mr England and Mr Nelson all had promising sons. Blaikie took young England and Nelson along with him on a day's tour of inspection and was impressed by their intelligence and practical knowledge.

Blaikie prided himself in his ability to assess the characters of the tenants. Of Mr Brereton of Flitcham he said, 'He appears to be an eccentric character, but is in reality a shrewd money getting old-fashioned farmer occupying a very good and very cheap farm.'

When Blaikie arrived at Holkham immediately after the Napoleonic Wars, farming was depressed and he was worried about the future. In the 1820s there was the continuing threat that the estate would lose the revenues of the Dungeness lighthouse which it had owned since the eighteenth century. Blaikie therefore thought that economies were necessary. In his opinion the management of Thomas William Coke had been far too extravagant, especially in the amount of money spent on farm buildings. Blaikie was often critical of the building schemes put to him by tenants who were used to the liberality of Coke. 'It would be greatly to the advantage of the tenant as well as to the landlord, and much to the credit of the former if they would condescend to be guided by the sound advise that I give them in regard to the buildings on their farms.'[2] It is not surprising that while Blaikie was agent building expenses were at a lower level than previously.

An agent such as Blaikie might well have much influence on some tenants and their methods of farming. The best tenants had no need of his advice and Mr Garwood and Mr Overman come into this category.

Mr Garwood of Billingford farmed on a four-course shift, although his lease stipulated six. 'Covenants as to management are of little or no use with such a tenant. He is a complete farmer; every branch is in perfect order – the arable is beautiful and the irrigated and other grass lands much superior to that generally seen in the county of Norfolk. Mrs Garwood is a thorough housewife and good dairy manager.' Mr Overman of Burnham won Blaikie's greatest praise. His farm was 'in a superb state of cultivation. Claying or marling is here carried out with great spirit and the good effects are more perceptable upon this than on most other farms on the estate. Mr Overman is a very deserving, industrious, attentive and persevering good tenant and may be styled a "pattern farmer".' However, we have seen that there were also those who needed guidance, and Blaikie, both through his visits and his letters, was ready to give it. He was also on the lookout for promising young men who might become suitable tenants, though some farmers were beyond even Blaikie's influence.

Blaikie's concern with the affairs of the Coke family was not limited to the estate. When Elizabeth Coke was to marry John Stanhope, he took the liberty of looking into the financial position of the prospective bridegroom. Elizabeth wrote to John, 'I have just had a séance with Blaikie, who for his own satisfaction of course has written down a calculation of all your income and charges which he has solemnly given me.'[3] In spite of his concern about overspending on estate improvements, he himself had a very generous personality. Again Elizabeth wrote,

> Blaikie has returned to my great comfort. Imagine my surprise last night when he presented me with a wedding gift – a very fine topaz locket, set round with diamonds

---

[2] Holkham MSS, letter books (1827), p. 86.
[3] A. M. W. Stirling, *The Letter Bags of Lady Elizabeth Spencer Stanhope*, 2 vols. (London, 1913), vol. 2, p. 50.

and a beautifully worked gold chain three and a half yards long. When my father spoke to him on the subject, he said 'Sir, after my obligation to Lord Chesterfield's family and your own, I could do no less. You have always known that money is no object to me.' It really is a magnificent trait, but quite consistent with his extraordinary character.[4]

Blaikie retired to Scotland in 1832 and sold the land he had accumulated in Wells to Coke for £1,200. He continued to take an interest in farming matters, and corresponded with the Royal Agricultural Society. The last letter from him to survive was written to John Stanhope in 1840. He was writing from Melrose (Roxburghshire) and was very familiar with the changing level of rents and land prices in the area. He was shocked by the number of farms being let, 'not to regular bred farmers, but to others who have made money in trade and are anxious to become farmers. The fine farm of Redden near Kelso was let last week to a Railway Contractor.' He was very much against free trade and aware of the disastrous effect it might have on agriculture, but was forward looking enough to realise that it was livestock rather than corn that was basic to British agricultural prosperity.[5]

Blaikie's place in the Holkham estate office was taken by Baker, who was first employed there as a clerk in 1821. He must have been trained by Blaikie and so was probably a very competent estate manager. He continued to run the office in the ways developed by Blaikie, and used his model leases when farms were relet. He saw the estate through a change of owners when the first earl died in 1842, and when Coke had been spending more time at Longford, Baker must have had to take an increased responsibility. Although there is very little information about Baker's work and influence on the estate, the impression gained from the documents is that he was a capable if unexciting agent. He retired at the age of sixty-two, and lived in the Garden Cottage at Holkham until his death.

Although very different from Blaikie, Baker's successor was another dynamic and influential man. William Keary became agent in 1851 at the age of thirty-six. His training had not been in the office, but rather that of a practical farmer, first in Yorkshire and then on the home farm. On taking charge of the estate office he changed the system of accounting, beginning the ledgers and general payment books. He also made a thorough survey of all the estate farms and cottages and very soon acted

[4] *Ibid.*, vol. 2, p. 54.   [5] *Ibid.*, vol. 2, pp. 168-9.

on his findings. Unlike Blaikie, he favoured large and expensive building schemes and both Longlands and Egmere farm were rebuilt at great cost during the 1850s. Keary also trained agents at Holkham. An applicant for a post on a small Cheshire estate in 1859 was described as 'a pupil of H. W. Keary at Holkham'.[6] Henry Parr Jones who went to Longleat in the same year was also described as 'one of the many pupils trained by Lord Leicester's agent, Keary'.[7] Jones was said to have gained his extravagant ideas at Holkham. Two pupils are listed among the inhabitants of Longlands in the 1851 census.

Keary's interest in general farming matters continued and he remained a member of the Council of the Royal Agricultural Society. He retired from the estate in 1863 and was followed by Samuel Shellabear, who, like his uncle, Baker, had come up through the office. Little is known about his farming interests, but he conducted much of the administration involved in setting up board schools in the villages of the estate. He was chairman of the Wells school board. He was followed as agent in 1885 by Forbes and in 1888 by John Davey. There is little about these two men in the records. They were both trained in the estate office and continued to run the estate efficiently.

It is clear that, up to the 1860s, Holkham agents were more than office managers and could influence farming on the estate. Through regular farm visits they came to know the tenants well and so were able to decide which ones were worth encouraging in times of depression and might make good afterwards. They also sifted through the requests for improvements and decided which would be of real benefit to the estate as well as to the farmers. The amount of correspondence that survives in the letter books shows that all agents carried out their work conscientiously. Perhaps their most important work was something about which we can know very little. Advice could be given and opinions exchanged in conversations with tenants on their farms, at the annual audit and in casual meetings at local markets. Such discussions were seldom recorded in writing. Agents were in a better position than tenants to compare the results of different techniques tried out in the wide variety of conditions to be found on the seventy Holkham farms. The relevant experience of one farmer could be recounted by the agent for the benefit of another. A group of progressive farmers with an agent

---

[6] D. Spring, *The English Landed Estate in the Nineteenth Century* (Baltimore, 1963), p. 100.

[7] F. M. L. Thompson, *English Landed Society in the Nineteenth Century* (London, 1963), p. 152.

acting as coordinator had a unique opportunity for improving agriculture.

Shellabear was the first of the late-nineteenth-century agents at Holkham to have worked his way up through the office. His experience would therefore be that of an administrator rather than a practical farmer. Although there is plenty of evidence to show that these later agents travelled and visited farms and tenants, it is probable that their influence over farming matters declined. The letter books show Shellabear giving advice on the filling in of government forms rather than on agricultural practice.

The Holkham estate office was never large and usually consisted of the agent plus two or three clerks. In 1845 Baker was assisted by a clerk and an architect, but this was unusual. By 1895 there were three clerks as well as a groom and a horsekeeper. The salary of the agent varied between £400 and £800 a year, while that of a clerk was between £50 and £200. Except for the use of a patent copying press from the 1850s, there seem to have been very few changes in the methods used by the office. The layout of the account books altered very little throughout the century.

The Holkham lease

One of the developments in estate management which Coke was said to have pioneered well before the appointment of his first agent was the long lease containing progressive husbandry clauses, and the negotiation of leases soon become one of the main responsibilities of the estate office. One of the reliefs on the Coke monument shows Coke and Blaikie sitting at a desk signing a lease with one of the more famous Holkham tenants, John Hudson. Lord Ernle wrote, 'by offering long leases of 21 years, he [Coke] guaranteed to improving farmers a return for their energy and outlay...at the same time he guarded himself against the mischief of a long unrestricted tenancy by covenants regulating the course of high class cultivation'.[8]

R. A. C. Parker has studied in detail the development of the Holkham lease through the eighteenth century. Early-eighteenth-century leases probably included no more than traditional stipulations that the balance between permanent grasslands and arable should not be departed from, that natural manures produced on the land should not be taken off,

[8] Lord Ernle, *English Farming, Past and Present* (6th edn, London, 1961), pp. 219–20.

together with a statement of the crops that should be left for the subsequent tenant. One development appeared in a lease for a Tittleshall farm in 1721 where artificial grasses were to be planted for short leys. A more significant addition which began to appear at this date stated that not more than three or sometimes four crops of corn were to be grown successively. In a Holkham lease for 1752 the tenant was forbidden to sow more than three crops successively and one of these was to be after turnips or a summer tilling. The land should be laid down to grass for two years. Until the 1780s, leases allowed the tenant the alternative of a six- or a four-course rotation and only rarely prevented the growing of two corn crops in succession.

After the majority of Thomas William Coke in 1776 these husbandry clauses were considerably extended, tightened and improved. The leases granted in the 1790s and drafted by Nathaniel Kent show that real progress was being made. Agreements often contain positive instructions rather than negative prohibitions, but rotations, often allowing two white straw crops in succession, were frequently still used. A typical five-course rotation is given in a six year lease granted in 1797: first year turnips or vetch, second year artificial grass, third and fourth years ley, fifth year winter corn, sixth year grain.

A field book of the estate in 1789–1803 is in the muniment room at Holkham. This gives the crop rotations practised on some Holkham farms between 1789 and 1803 and in some cases 1806. On the first page the compiler states his reasons for undertaking the work.

> The benefits which result from a check of this kind upon the tenants of a large estate are very great, as it fully guards against any improper course of cropping, and by showing what has been the past system of husbandry upon any particular farm, a landlord or agent is better enabled to judge what regulation to lay it under in future.

The book shows that a great variety of four-, five- and six-course rotations was in use on Holkham farms. A barley crop nearly always followed the turnips, and one or two years of ley preceded a crop of peas, which was then followed by wheat. A typical six-course shift consisted of turnips, followed by barley, two years ley, peas and then wheat. Grain crops were, however, still frequently grown in succession. Oats often followed wheat. A seventeen year lease to Mr Brereton for a farm at Flitcham, granted in 1785, stated that there were not to be more than three successive grain crops. The existence of this field book is proof that tenant farms were receiving regular visits from the estate office and so tenants were obliged to keep to the terms of their leases.

The first lease forbidding the growing of two grain crops in succession was granted in 1801. It laid down a rotation beginning with turnips or vetch fed to sheep folded on the land. This was followed by peas or vetches preceding a crop of summer corn or grass seeds. Then came two years of ley, followed by winter corn and then peas or vetches again. After this date rotations on this model were often included in leases.

In 1816, Blaikie composed his series of leases, copies of which form a bound volume kept in the muniment room at Holkham. They contain various four-, five- and six-course rotations suitable for the many types of soil on the Holkham estate. The one point all these leases have in common is that they prohibit the growing of two successive grain crops and this remained an important element in Holkham leases until the 1860s.

Although it has often been stated that Holkham pioneered the long (twenty-one year) lease, and that most of its farms were let on a long lease by the early nineteenth century, this was not always the case, and eight and twelve year leases were still common. One of the main arguments for leases, and long leases in particular, was that they provided security of tenure. However, most tenants with only annual tenancies enjoyed this in practice and frequently passed their farms on to their sons. The importance of a long lease is probably less than Arthur Young maintained.

Only a rather random selection of leases survive from the nineteenth century, but these show that up to 1860 the rotations worked out by Blaikie were being included in new agreements. In addition, the tenants were sometimes given the responsibility of underdraining, while occasionally the landlord undertook this work and then charged the tenant 5% interest on the work done. Permanent pasture was not to be broken up, and sometimes the number of turnips grown was limited to those needed for the farm. Whatever variations there might be in detail, the fundamental principal that two grain crops should never be grown in succession was always maintained.

However, the development of fertilisers meant that by the 1860s it was possible to break this rule without exhausting the soil. Tenants who wished to depart from the terms of their lease and grow more grain wrote to the estate office and asked permission to do so. In 1864 John Hastings of Longham asked if he could sow barley instead of roots and permission was granted.[9] In 1867 he was allowed to grow oats or barley after wheat[10] and finally in 1868 he was given permission to crop the land as he thought fit.[11] Similarly, in 1855, John Hudson asked leave to grow barley instead of turnips.[12] This request was granted and reviewed annually until finally, nine years later, Hudson was given permission to 'crop the farm in any way you think fit'.[13]

As new methods of farming developed, feelings against restrictive leases grew stronger, and Holkham was one of the first Norfolk estates to abandon its traditional agreement and allow freedom of cropping. Henry Overman told the Royal Commission on Agriculture that these new leases, allowing tenants complete freedom of cropping until the last four years of the lease, when the land had to be brought back into a rotation, were first introduced in the early 1870s. If the agent ever thought the farm was in a bad state, he had the power to reimpose cropping restrictions. 'He has the power to do so and I think that is right.'[14] More intensive wheat production was not possible everywhere. Of the 700 acres that Overman rented from Lord Leicester there were only thirty or forty acres which were suited to the production of an extra crop of barley.

As agricultural depression became serious at the end of the century, tenants would not commit themselves to more than annual leases and the old cropping restrictions were reintroduced. There was no opposition from tenants, for whom intensive grain production was no longer profitable, and they could not afford the heavy capital outlay on fertilisers that was necessary.

It is difficult to say how far the types of lease imposed at Holkham influenced farming. So long as they encouraged the most progressive types of farming they were adherred to. The majority of Holkham tenants were, however, progressive farmers who would have practised this type of farming anyway. As soon as the restrictions of the rotations became outdated, the tenants put in requests to depart from the terms of their leases and these requests were granted. Finally, restrictive husbandry clauses were abandoned. Here we see the tenant leading the way and the landlord following. Leases certainly prevented bad tenants from

[9] Holkham MSS, letter books, vol. 4 (1864), p. 88.
[10] Ibid., vol. 5 (1867), p. 96. [11] Ibid., vol. 5 (1868), p. 509.
[12] Ibid., vol. 2 (1855), p. 4. [13] Ibid., vol. 4 (1864), p. 538.
[14] Parliamentary Papers (1881), (c.3096), XVII, Royal Commission on Agriculture, minutes of evidence, part 2, question 51710.

exhausting the soil and some of the smaller heavy-land farms were worked by less businesslike men who perhaps needed some form of control. This point was made by Caird, who said that leases were needed for bad farmers and not good ones,[15] and the new leases of the 1870s allowed freedom of cropping.

Although by the end of the century the annual agreements were more restrictive again, there was little the estate office could do to enforce obedience. Tenants were not easy to come by and it wanted to keep them at any price. After 1881 tenants were protected by law and we see the beginnings of the state stepping in to regulate the relationship between landlord and tenant.

The home farm

If the husbandry clauses of the lease were the one way in which the estate could enforce certain farming practices on its tenants, it was through the home farm than an example could be set and the advantages of improved techniques shown. In fact very few home farms were used in this way. They were normally run at a loss and regarded merely as suppliers of fresh produce for the house.

The Duke of Bedford was unusual in hoping to make a profit from the home farm at Woburn. He expected his bailiff to produce a 5% profit on capital invested, but there is no evidence that this was ever achieved.[16] He thought it would be a bad example to the tenantry if they saw that he lost at farming. The Duke had been told that Lord Albemarle in Norfolk and Lord Hardwick in Cambridgeshire made profits on their home farms, but it has not been possible to find out whether this was so.

There is little information about the home farm at Longlands before the 1840s. A series of accounts for the years 1817–27 survive, and Blaikie refers to experiments carried out on the home farm in his letters on agricultural matters collected in the agricultural letter books. These sources provide only very fragmentary evidence for the activities of the home farm in the first half of the nineteenth century.

The Longlands farm had a total acreage of 1,800. Most of this was very light land and therefore needed careful farming. The account books give a yearly valuation of crops, stock and implements. In 1817 crops

[15] J. Caird, *English Agriculture in 1850–51* (London, 1851), p. 171.
[16] Spring, *The English Landed Estate*, p. 46.

were valued at £4,745 worth of barley, wheat and peas, £602 worth of roots and £972 worth of hay. There were 62 horses, 160 cattle, 2,004 sheep and 134 pigs. Implements were valued at £999. Turnips were not the only root crop grown, as both swedes and mangolds are mentioned. Sainfoin and linseed were cultivated as well as the traditional clover. The large number of sheep were essential to the Norfolk rotation as it was developed on light soils. The sheep were folded on the turnip fields and by feeding there and manuring the land they greatly improved the fertility of the soil.

It is clear therefore than an intensive mixed husbandry suited to the local soil conditions was practised on the home farm. Implements worth £1,000 show that it was highly mechanised and the accounts indicate that the newer crops such as swedes, mangolds and sainfoin were being grown. The accounts do not include any figures showing the amount of labour employed.

The home farm was not run at a profit and for most of the ten years between 1817 and 1827 even Blaikie's efficient management and economy measures resulted in its making a considerable loss. It was more of a showpiece and experimental farm. The deficiency for 1821–2 was as high as £5,095, while in 1819–20 it was £3,081. The highest profits were made in 1824–5, when £971 was recorded.

Blaikie's correspondence shows that many agricultural experiments were being carried out. He wrote to Mr Shepherd in 1819 that gypsum had been tried as a manure. It had been found entirely effective, especially for sainfoin. 'How it answers for other crops remains to be proved. Experiments are in progress.'[17] Another example shows Coke's lack of interest in trying salt as a manure and Blaikie wrote to the promoter of this scheme suggesting that the Earl of Albemarle be approached, who was 'a leading patron of agriculture and an indefatigable farmer, a perfect gentleman and above all a good man'.[18]

The fame of Holkham meant that the estate was frequently sent samples of new seeds. In 1821, '8lbs of the most approved kind of yellow bullock turnip seed' arrived. Blaikie was not enthusiastic about the success of these new types. He wrote, 'There were a great many trial seeds sown upon Mr Coke's farm last year, but the produce from none of those were so much approved for as the sorts usually cultivated at this place.'[19]

[17] Holkham MSS, *Agricultural Letter Books*, 28 Aug. 1819.
[18] *Ibid.*, 20 Oct. 1812.   [19] *Ibid.*, 4 May 1821.

The results of the experiments carried out at the home farm were scientifically analysed. In a correspondence with the Duke of Bedford, Blaikie was able to state that the mangolds grown at Holkham contained 8% more sugar than the turnips.[20]

There are more records available for the period after 1842, when a complete series of cash and stock books was begun. Although they do not contain descriptions of experiments carried out, they do give much valuable information about the running of the farm in the second half of the nineteenth century. They show, for instance, that the farm was by no means self-sufficient. It was buying stock, seed, fertiliser and feed. Linseed cake, rape cake and malt dust were bought in the 1840s for animal feed, and nitrate of soda, lime, guano, spratts, mussels and 'Wells dung' were bought as fertilisers. Patent manures, such as Lawe's and Packard's manure, were bought in the 1850s. Cotton cake is mentioned in the 1880s and 1890s.

The records show the way in which the home farm could influence the standard of agriculture on estate farms. There was much business between the home farm and the tenants, who frequently bought and sold seed and stock from and to the estate. This sort of contact must have provided ample opportunities for discussion between the estate and tenant farmers, which would have been of mutual benefit. New and improved strains of stock and seed could be introduced to the estate farms and ideas and opinions exchanged.

The stock books give details of the amount of wheat and barley sold every year after 1842. Sometimes they also contain the value of these sales and, occasionally, the average yield per acre. From the 1860s, the number of livestock on the farm is also given.

The value of the cereal crop in 1843 (£2,951) was less than half that for 1817 (£4,475). The 1817 price for grain in Norwich was between 70 and 80 shillings a quarter, which was higher than it was again until 1840. In 1843 the price was only between 40 and 50 shillings a quarter, which probably accounts for the low value of the home farm crop that year. The value was less, but the actual crop may have been almost the same as in 1817.

Table 3.1 shows very clearly the changes brought about by the agricultural depression. The harvest of 1873 was poor and only half the amount of wheat as in 1863 was sold. Barley production, however, had increased from 1,902 coombs to 2,365 in the same period. By 1883 the

[20] *Ibid.*, 6 Nov. 1821.

TABLE 3.1. *Ten-yearly statistics for the home farm, 1843–1907*

			Cereals sold		Average yield per acre	
Date	No. of livestock		coombs	£		coombs
1843			Wheat 1,553	1,600		
			Barley 2,040	1,351		
1853			Wheat 3,863	4,171	Wheat	11
			Barley 863	626	Barley	10
1863	Cattle	195	Wheat 3,082			
	Sheep	1,510	Barley 1,902			
	Horses	48				
	Pigs	119				
1873	Cattle	160	Wheat 1,635	2,283		
	Sheep	2,851	Barley 2,365	2,284		
	Horses	35				
	Pigs	14				
1883	Cattle	290	Wheat 533	631	Wheat	7
	Sheep	2,259	Barley 1,005	902	Barley	8
	Horses	28				
1893	Cattle	222	Wheat 447	264	Wheat	5
	Sheep	1,389	Barley 212	105	Barley	5
	Horses	24				
1907*	Cattle	170	Wheat 320	252	Wheat	9
	Sheep	1,129	Barley 1,767	1,286	Barley	11
	Horses	25				

Source: Holkham MSS, cash and stock books, 1843–1907.
* The only accounts available for the 1900s.

quantities had dropped much further and in 1893 only 447 coombs of wheat and 212 coombs of barley were sold. Wheat continued to decline in importance in the twentieth century, although the quantity of barley rose again. By 1907 the yields had also improved to the levels of 1853 (nine coombs of wheat and eleven coombs of barley per acre). This figure is slightly above the county average of thirty bushels per acre calculated by Sir John Walsham. Yields had dropped considerably in the 1880s and 1890s when as the result of the drought of 1893 they were down to five coombs per acre of both wheat and barley.[21]

[21] 1 coomb = 4 bushels
1 coomb wheat = 18 stone
1 coomb barley = 16 stone
1 coomb oats = 12 stone

As cereal production declined the role of livestock changed. With the converting of arable land into semi-permanent pasture in the 1890s, fewer horses were needed. The number of horses declined steadily from 1857.

A large number of sheep had always been kept at Holkham and played an essential part in the system of farming. Over 2,000 were grazed until the 1890s. However, as the price of both wool and mutton declined, fewer were kept and in 1907 the number was down to 1,129.

The general pattern seems to show intense cereal cultivation in the middle of the century, with an increase in cattle and sheep in the 1870s and 1880s when grain production slumped. In 1907 both wheat and livestock production were low but barley had increased again. With the importing of both cheap meat and cereals from the New World, it was only good-quality Norfolk malting barley which could find a profitable market.

James Caird visited the home farm at Holkham in 1850. He was impressed by the large barns which allowed a considerable proportion of the crop to be stored under cover. Large sheds and yards accommodated the cattle. The herd of pure Devon cattle were very fine specimens of the breed. About 250 cattle were kept, including twenty working bullocks. There were forty cows and 2,500 sheep, 700 of which were pure Southdown ewes. Thirty-two horses were kept as well as 150 pigs. These figures seem high when compared with those in the stock books, but they probably include many animals that were normally sold off by Michaelmas. The farm was cultivated on the four-course system. Guano and superphosphates were the manures most frequently used. 'In the operation of the course, the usual details of good farming are practised.'[22]

Perhaps as a result of the management of the businesslike William Keary, the home farm made a profit after 1842, although the profit was never more than a few hundred pounds. Keary was an agriculturalist of some renown and in 1848 he wrote a prize essay for the *Journal of the Royal Agricultural Society* on the management of cattle at Longlands.[23] He was one of those who inspected the twenty-one farms competing for the farm prize competition in 1870.[24] In 1851 he was

---

[22] Caird, *English Agriculture*, pp. 166–7.
[23] H. W. Keary, 'Management of cattle at Longlands', *J.R.A.S.E.*, vol. 9 (1848), pp. 424–51.
[24] H. W. Keary, 'Report on the farm prize competition, 1870', *J.R.A.S.E.*, second series, vol. 6 (1870).

3.2   The home farm at Longlands.

promoted from the position of farm manager at a salary of £170 a year to that of agent for the estate at £500 a year.

One of the first improvements that Keary undertook as agent was to rebuild the home farm. The cattle yards and sheds erected in the 1790s were left, but more cattle-yards, implement sheds and waggon lodges with granaries above were built. A large range of estate workshops, including a steam engine house, was also added. Architectural embellishments meant that the farm buildings were quite in character with their park-like setting about two miles from the house (fig. 3.2).

Throughout the nineteenth century the home farm was run on a progressive basis. Its influence was probably at its height during the years of the sheep shearings, when it was visited by aristocrats, gentry and farmers, but under Keary's management it remained influential and Caird was impressed by what he found in 1850. Four- and five-course rotations were practised. New crops were grown and large numbers of stock kept. Small areas of experimental crops were also tried. There were many business contacts between tenants and the home farm, which they often visited.

By the end of the century the home farm had lost much of its influence.

It was running at a loss and Lord Leicester was putting much of his land down to semi-permanent sheep walks. He was disappointed that his tenants were not following his example.[25] Agricultural depression discouraged experiment and Longlands was no longer a focus of attention for those interested in agricultural improvement. Instead they were looking to the huge farms, often resulting from amalgamations, run by newcomers with capital made outside farming, such as Keith at Egmere.

Other estate activities

Other than the home farm, the only other enterprises directly managed by the estate were the woodlands and the brick kilns.

The planting of trees was not only valuable for the timber, but the afforestation of the dunes along the coast was essential for their stabilisation and the protection of the farmland behind. The dunes were first planted in the 1870s with Corsican pines; Austrian pines were used as windbreaks in exposed places and Scotch pines in sheltered areas to provide variety. In 1832 Coke had the satisfaction of seeing a ship built at Wells from oaks which he had planted. As well as the woods at Holkham, there was an area of woodland at Fulmodestone and another at Tittleshall. There were also smaller woods in Warham, Waterden, South Creake, Weasenham, Kempstone, Longham, Billingford, Bintry, Sparham and Egmere. The wood accounts begin in 1816, when the net income from them was £1,315. The figure was always over £1,000 until 1831. In 1832, it dropped considerably to £491. The lowest figure for the period was £55 in 1844. By 1845 the sum had risen to £1,670. After 1849, only the large woods in Holkham, Fulmodestone and Tittleshall were exploited and the figures for these three are given separately. Holkham was by far the most important. In 1853, the income from Holkham was £1,130, from Fulmodestone, £138 and from Tittleshall, £996.

The highest income recorded was for 1855–6, when Holkham produced £3026, Fulmodestone £276 and Tittleshall £413. The total for the three woods remained over £1,000 until the 1880s, after which the figure varied between £500 and £800. The income from woods reached its highest in the 1850s, when the rents were also high, and then

---

[25] Parliamentary Papers (1895), (c. 7400–111), XVI, *Royal Commission on Agriculture*, part 3, p. 597.

dropped at the end of the century, when rents could well have done with a boost from an alternative source. Therefore, although in some years the woods were providing a sizeable return, more for instance than the home farm in the middle of the century, they did not help to provide an alternative source of income in the agricultural depression.

All the sums quoted above are for sales of timber. The woods also provided most of the requirements of the estate for repairs and improvements. Much of the wood kept in the large timber yards at Longlands must have come off the estate.

As well as providing its own timber, the nineteenth-century estate also fired its own bricks. Until the 1870s there were brick kilns at both Holkham and Tittleshall, but at that time the Tittleshall brick kiln was closed. Holkham brick kilns occupied a large site opposite Peterstone farm and were worked until the 1930s. Most recently they consisted of four large drying sheds, one kiln and a steam engine house. Machines for making field drains and cutting bricks survive on the site as well as two pug mills for mixing clay. There are many broken roofing tiles, which show that they also must have been made here. Clay pits extend over a large area and the concern was obviously a big one. Nothing remains of the brick kiln at Tittleshall, which was much smaller and served the mid-Norfolk estate.

Although the main function of the brick kilns was to serve the needs of the estate, some bricks were sold. It is likely that Samuel Wyatt, who worked as an architect at Holkham at the end of the eighteenth century, negotiated through his brother, who was agent to the Earl of Penrhyn, the sale of Holkham bricks to the earl in exchange for slates from his quarries. The audit books only give details of the sales of bricks after 1850. Only very few were ever sold from the Tittleshall kiln; for instance in 1855 sales amounted to £12. Bricks used on the estate were valued at £303, while the outgoings involved in running the kiln were £420. The figures for the later years of the Tittleshall kiln also show it running at a loss.

The Holkham kiln was more profitable. In 1855 sales were worth £260, bricks used on the estate were valued at £1,596, and the outgoings were £951. The net profit for 1865 was £716; for 1875, £779; for 1885, £422; and for 1895, only £97. As was the case with the woods, the brick kiln was not in a position to buoy up the estate income in the years of depression. Rather it was declining along with rents. The only other source of income available to counterbalance the fall in rents was the earl's increasing investment in stocks and shares, but throughout the nineteenth century most capital was put into agriculture and it was in this that most interest was taken.

Income from rents and investment in farm improvement

The landlord's concern with the productivity of his estate was shown most clearly in the interest he took in making permanent improvements, and much of Thomas William Coke's fame was the result of his high investment in his estate. At his death it was claimed that he had laid out half a million pounds in improvements, and it made good financial sense for the landlord to establish conditions in which improved agriculture could flourish. This meant the provision of compact and convenient farms with the necessary basic facilities like farm buildings. Such a system was mutually beneficial. Good farms attracted good tenants and high rents, while good tenants were worth helping through hard times. However, it is questionable whether heavy investments in farm improvements could produce increases in rents which justified this outlay.

The level of rents on the estate is a clear indication of the level of prosperity enjoyed by the landlord and the amounts of money he had available for investment in his land. It is possible to extract from the audit books a series of figures for buildings and repairs as well as the total sum collected in rents (appendix 3), and so levels of rents and expenditure on improvements can be ascertained and the proportion of income ploughed back in improvements calculated (figs. 3.3 and 3.4).

Rents were rising from the end of the eighteenth century and this increase was particularly marked in the later years of the Napoleonic Wars from 1810 to 1815. The amount in arrears fluctuated dramatically from year to year, but was usually at a relatively high level until 1800. The arrears for 1797, when grain prices were at their lowest since the beginning of the war, were as high as £6,105. This figure was only surpassed once before 1878. After 1800 grain prices were generally at a high level and arrears very much lower.

At the end of the war the steady increase in rents came to an end. Arrears at Holkham were up to £3,168 and grain prices dropped to a pre-1800 level. Between 1816 and 1820, arrears were lower and rents

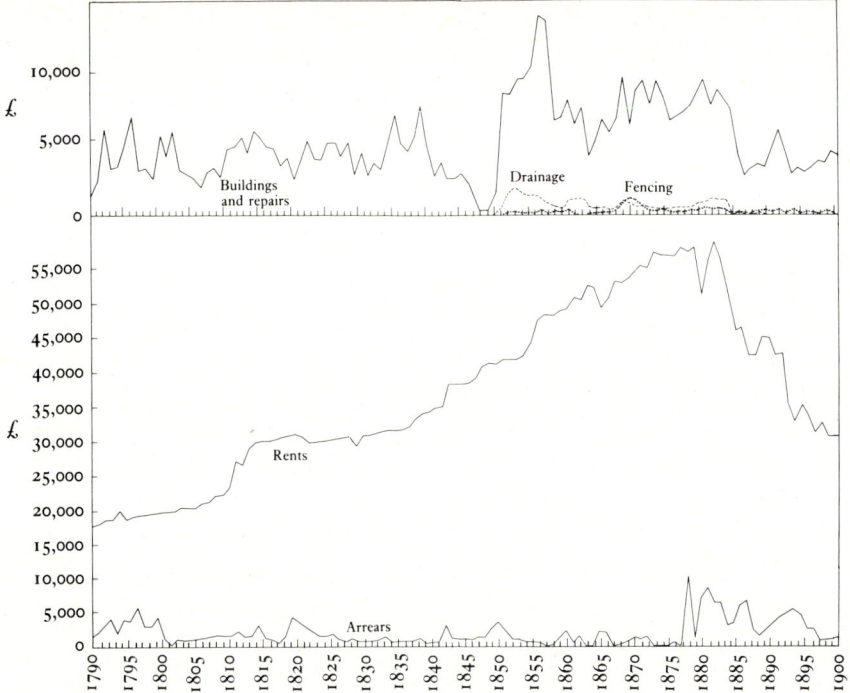

3.3 Arrears in rents, rents collected and the amount spent on improvements, 1790–1900.

slowly rose from £30,000 to £31,000. In 1823, the rents again slipped back and did not regain the 1822 level until 1830. The price of grain fell to its lowest in 1830 but was generally very low from 1825. The remarkable thing about the Holkham rents through this period is not so much the increase to 1815, but the fact that there was so little decrease in the period 1815–30.

From 1830 rents were rising at a steadily increasing rate. Between 1843 and 1844 there was a large increase from £35,953 to £39,265. They remained stable until 1848, when they began to rise again. When Keary became agent in 1851 he introduced the corn rent principle in new leases. This meant that part of the rent varied with the price of wheat and barley. This was not very popular with tenants and did not last long. However, while it was in force, the estate rental fluctuated annually with the price of grain. Except for a sharp drop in rents received in both 1865 and 1880, the general rent level continued to rise until 1882, when it reached a peak of £59,709. From that date rents fell steeply and continuously so that by 1900 they had fallen to the 1828 level.

Arrears were generally at a low level, except from 1850–2, when they were over £2,000. Between 1852 and 1878, arrears were usually below £2,000 and often below £1,000. As farmers' capital became depleted and the post-1873 depression dragged on, arrears rose steeply. They remained high until rents were adjusted downwards, and not until the last years of the nineteenth century were they again at a low level of under £1,000.

The figures for rent increases at Holkham mean little unless we know how much the acreage of the estate increased during this period. It is very difficult to sort out the dates, size, and cost of purchases of new land. Some, but not all, are recorded in the audit books, cash books and ledgers. The catalogue of title deeds shows when deeds first came into the estate's possession. Between 1793 and 1853, £44,559 is recorded as having been spent on new purchases. Most of the purchases were of very small pieces of land, often less than ten acres. Also of importance were exchanges of land which, along with the purchase of small estates intermingled with Holkham property, meant that farms could be reorganised into compact and workable units. Between 1776 and 1851 the estate had increased from 30,000 acres to its maximum size of 42,000. No new purchases are recorded after 1853, so the rents after that time were not affected by a change in acreage.

With two important exceptions, rent movements at Holkham are what we would expect in the context of national farming prosperity. The wartime conditions of 1796–1815 meant a boom in agriculture with rents rising. The enquiry of the Board of Agriculture, held in 1804, showed an average increase in rents over the whole country since 1790 of nearly 40%. On many estates rents doubled. Landlords who had the good fortune to own large areas of enclosable land made the most of the boom conditions of war. In 1797 Sir John Sinclair estimated that the rent of newly enclosed land increased by 9 shillings an acre.[26] It was particularly the enclosure of lands that could then be added to existing farms and so did not involve the expense of building new farmsteads that was profitable. Most of the open fields on the Holkham estate had been enclosed by this date, and it was the enclosure of wastes and commons, which were then added to existing farms, that was carried out. During the Napoleonic Wars over £6,750 was spent by the estate on enclosure, mostly in the later part of the period. The rent increases following an

---

[26] R. J. Thompson, 'An enquiry into the rent of agricultural land in England and Wales during the nineteenth century', *Journal of the Royal Statistical Society*, vol. 70 (1907), p. 589.

enclosure can be seen at Hall Farm, Longham. The two commons in the parish were enclosed and the small irregular fields rearranged between 1814 and 1816. Although the farm gained land from the common it lost some fields to the east of the parish and the acreage changed very little while the rent rose from £225 to £577.

Over the war period total rents on the Holkham estates rose from £19,039 to £30,833. R. A. C. Parker calculated that, allowing for new purchases, the rent on a constant acreage rose from £12,332 in 1776 to £25,789 in 1815.[27] This growth is far greater than the average for the selection of Norfolk and Suffolk estates studied by B. A. Holderness.[28] This, however, included many small ill-managed estates, where little improvement had been undertaken. This suggests that, if rents were to rise considerably, some investment in improvements was needed and did pay off.

There is much evidence to show that Norfolk did not escape depression. Richard Preston wrote in 1816, 'In Norfolk alone, landed property to the value of one and a half million pounds is on sale without buyers for want of money'.[29] Witnesses to the Select Committee on the State of Agriculture, which reported in 1833, gave a pessimistic picture. Mr Wright, a land agent in Norwich, said, 'If there were a farm now let in bad condition, it would not let so readily as it used to, as tenants are more cautious in expanding and do not like to lay out capital on an uncertain speculation.' He estimated that rent decreases of between 10% and 15% were usual on farms let on an eight year lease in 1824 and then relet in 1832.[30] The problems of letting a farm that was out of condition were experienced on the Holkham estate as elsewhere. Lodge Farm and Manor House Farm, Castle Acre, were both in a poor state in 1822. 'The two farms had been refused by three persons before Mr Hudson took them.'[31]

Bacon wrote in 1844,

At the beginning of the Napoleonic Wars, the rental in Norfolk had risen considerably and from 1805 to 1816 a further rise took place of from 25% to 30% on the light lands

[27] R. A. C. Parker, 'Coke of Norfolk and the Agricultural Revolution', *Economic History Review*, second series, vol. 8 (1955–6), pp. 156–66.
[28] B. A. Holderness, 'Landlords and capital formation in East Anglia, 1750–1870', *Economic History Review*, second series, vol. 13 (1972), pp. 434–47.
[29] Richard Preston, 'Review of the present ruined state of agriculture and the landed interest', *Pamphleteer*, vol. 7 (1816), pp. 149–67.
[30] Parliamentary Papers (1833), (612v), *Select Committee on agriculture*, p. 97.
[31] H. M. Jenkins, 'Lodge Farm, Castle Acre', *J.R.A.S.E.*, second series, vol. 5 (1869), p. 461.

and in the district of marshland from 40% to 80% and upon the good soils from 40% to 50%. The ruinous fall in prices, with a reduction in expenses which followed, did not however depress it in the same rates, the variations being from 10% to 15% and 20% and the reason for this is obvious. No sooner was a farm vacant, or likely to become so, than, notwithstanding the distress, such was the number of applicants, that in accepting a tenant the enquiry was rather not who among the competitors possessed sufficient means or skill to carry on the farm in the most advantageous manner both for the proprietor and tenant, but who could afford the highest rent. The value of farms will be regulated like every other marketable commodity, by the number of applicants.'[32]

It is this last sentence which explains why Holkham did not suffer as much as some other estates. Poor land would be the first to go out of cultivation and much marginal land remained uncultivated for more than a hundred years. Holkham farms, on the other hand, were among the best in the country and competition for tenancies could be fierce. The estate was able to select competent men who could afford to pay high rents. Those who chose to hang on through the depression knew that it was no use asking for rent reductions because there were plenty of others willing and ready to pay the higher rent. John Blyth of Burnham told the Board of Agriculture in 1816 that Holkham farmers were men of substance who had enough capital to survive a series of depression years.

The farms in the neighbourhood of Burnham are mostly let on lease for 14 or 21 years, and are in general larger than in any other district in this country; as such, greater capitalists are engaged in them and when rent has been paid, it has been from other resources: in many farms, that of not having purchased the full number of cattle and sheep for feeding, or from not having bought the necessary quantity of oil cake for manure, from which omissions great deficiencies must arise in the product of the farms, which will in the end be truly calamitous to the community at large.[33]

One of the main reasons why Holkham rents did not drop as much as those on many estates in this period must have been that the Holkham farmers were men of capital and could pay rent in the way that Blyth described. The Duke of Bedford thought that Coke was reponsible for the fact that his tenants were such wealthy farmers. He wrote to Coke in 1816,

Since I left Holkham I have witnessed nothing but disheartening prospects...Norfolk is at this moment a splendid exception to the rest of the kingdom, and you must derive infinite satisfaction in the reflection that 38 years of persevering and unwearied efforts

---

[32] R. N. Bacon, *Agriculture of Norfolk* (London, 1844), p. 39.
[33] Board of Agriculture, *Agricultural State of the Kingdom in February, March and April, 1816* (1816), p. 196.

in promoting a beneficial system of husbandry, should have created such a mass of capital among the tenantry of Norfolk as to enable them to bear up against the evils which are overwhelming every part of the empire'.[34]

A second reason was that, as we have seen, the post Napoleonic War depression was selective in the type of farm it hit hardest. Marginal land and small farms let at high rents were affected first – in this group was the landed property valued at one and a half million pounds that was for sale in 1816 – but there was still a demand for good farms. As Blyth said, the Holkham tenants were men of substance who had made large profits during the war. This meant that these farms were less likely to become vacant as their tenants could withstand a few bad years, even if this was sometimes at the expense of good husbandry. The fact that the Holkham farms practised a system of mixed agriculture would also have made them more resilient.

In Norfolk, Holkham stands out as the largest and best organised estate and so there are no local ones with which it is comparable. It is necessary to look beyond Norfolk to find another as well documented and administered. The Bedford estates, administered from Woburn Abbey, were just over 48,000 acres and the house of Russell maintained an interest in the improvement of its agricultural assets throughout the nineteenth century. The work of the various members of the family has been studied by David Spring, and in 1897 the Duke of Bedford published a book in defence of the landowner–tenant system.[35] There are two main areas of Bedford property, one in Bedfordshire and Buckinghamshire and one in the rich Lincolnshire fens, and the figures for each area are given separately. In Bedfordshire and Buckinghamshire the rents reached a peak of £33,530 in 1817 and then declined to between £28,000 and £30,000 and, except for 1834, they did not rise above £30,000 again until 1837. The acreage of the estate was increasing slightly through this period. Income from Lincolnshire remained steady until 1821, when rents were reduced. They were increased again in 1828 and reached the 1817 level again in 1831. The Duke of Bedford, however, was not disheartened and wrote to Thomas William Coke in 1830, 'The times are bad, but I, like you, have not had a single defaultation of rent or reduction applied for.' The Duke thought the reason that their estates

---

[34] Stirling, *Coke of Norfolk*, vol. 2, p. 121.
[35] Spring, *The English Landed Estate* and the Duke of Bedford, *The Story of a Great Estate* (London, 1897).

were suffering less from this depression than some others was that other landlords had over-let land and 'screwed up rents to the highest pitch the tenant could stand'.[36] However, as the figures show, the Holkham estate fared even better than the Duke of Bedford's as the total rent collected hardly declined at all. Visitors to Holkham in 1830 were surprised at the state of agriculture there compared with the adversity of other areas, 'even of Norfolk estates in the immediate neighbourhood'.[37]

Chambers and Mingay described the depression between 1821 and 1823 as one affecting both grain and livestock,[38] and it certainly hit the Holkham estate harder than any other event in the first half of the nineteenth century. The amount of rent collected dropped from £31,680 in 1822 to £30,990 in 1823 and £30,950 in 1824, while arrears reached a peak of £7,584 in 1821. This fall in rents may not seem very significant when compared with that on other estates, but it was in fact the only fall experienced by the Holkham estate. The depression of 1833-6 is described by Chambers and Mingay as affecting only arable farming[39] and, although grain prices were particularly low in 1833 and 1834, rents and arrears on the Holkham estates were not affected. This again shows the important part livestock was already playing in the estate's farming.

The depression was over by the late 1830s. Grain prices were rising but were still well below the wartime levels. However, farmers at Holkham were still paying rents at the Napoleonic War levels. Holkham fits into the general pattern as described by Chambers and Mingay: 'There is no widespread rise again until the later 1830s but it seems that farmers in general were then paying rents which were still not far from double the pre-war level, while their prices had fallen to a level only 18%-20% higher than pre-war.'[40] Thompson says that, to keep rents at this level through the depression, much of the landlord's money had to be put into farm improvements.[41]

As grain prices rose in the late 1830s, so did rents. Farming remained a profitable business through the 1840s, being hardly affected by the repeal of the Corn Laws (1846), until the early 1870s. Grain prices fell

---

[36] Stirling, *Coke of Norfolk*, vol. 2, p. 121.
[37] Ibid.
[38] J. D. Chambers and G. E. Mingay, *The Agricultural Revolution, 1750-1880* (London, 1966), p. 127.
[39] Ibid.   [40] Ibid., p. 129.
[41] Thompson, *English Landed Society*, p. 235.

to their lowest for the period in 1850, but this was still well above the level of the early 1830s. The price never again reached the wartime levels, but this was compensated for by the rising trend of livestock prices which encouraged a more intensive mixed farming to which the Holkham estate was well suited.[42]

Mid-century rent increases at Holkham were very similar to those at Woburn. At Holkham the rise in rents between 1835 and 1870 was £22,000 on an estate of 42,000 acres. Over the same period, the rise on the Bedford estates was £27,596 on an estate of 50,000 acres. The main increases on the duke's Lincolnshire estates were post-1855 and were directly associated with drainage improvements and the erecting of new farm buildings. Rents then remained very steady until the post-1873 collapse. On the Bedfordshire and Buckinghamshire estates there was an erratic pattern of rent increases accompanied by an equally erratic expenditure. The increases were mainly post-1842 and rents fell after 1875.

Norfolk is traditionally a grain-growing area, but the many cattle kept on the Holkham estates must be one reason why rents did not fall with the slump in grain prices after 1873 but continued to rise until 1882. Secondly, although debts might be waived in particularly bad years, and temporary reductions made, rents would not be permanently lowered until a lease ran out and, as many of the Holkham farms were let on twenty-one year leases, reductions would be delayed. Thirdly, Holkham farmers were prosperous and, as in the late 1820s, could withstand a few bad years and pay rent from savings. However, this did not cushion them against the continual down-swing of prices in the 1880s and 1890s and eventually depression caught up with both tenant and landlord. Arrears were high in 1878, in 1881, and again in the bad years of 1894 and 1895. By 1900 rents had evened out at a low level and arrears were again under £1,000. Here we see the way in which a well organised and highly capitalised estate was better able to face a depression than less progressive ones. When Rider Haggard visited the Earl of Leicester in 1902 the old man told him that the demand for his farms was greater than at any other time during his period as earl. He thought large farmers were doing well, but inevitably stressed the problems of the landlord who still had to keep

---

[42] E. L. Jones, *The Development of English Agriculture, 1815–1873*, Studies in Economic History (London, 1968), p. 19.

up the buildings on half the rent.[43] Rents certainly had been considerably reduced by then. According to the Royal Commission on Agriculture, by 1895 Holkham rents had been reduced by 45.5% since 1878. On some farms the reduction was 50% or more.[44]

The delay in rent reductions cannot be paralleled on other estates. The reductions on the Duke of Bedford's estates began in 1875. On the Marquis of Bath's estates rents reached their peak in 1878,[45] although in 1894-5 rents were only 6% lower than in 1878 and still 6% above 1869-73. The total fall of 11% is less than half the general level of reductions in this period. The Wilton estates were past their peak by 1874 and by 1890-4 they were 42% below their peak. The picture for the Savernake estate was very similar. On the estates studied by R. J. Thompson, rents continued to rise until 1878, but between then and 1892 there was a 25% fall.[46]

The Holkham pattern of rents in the nineteenth century gives us two surprises: one is for the post-1815 period and the other for the period after 1875. On both occasions the estate showed a remarkable ability to weather depressions. Even the well managed Bedford estates could not survive so well. Holkham is unique among the large estates in that it had no major urban or industrial interests. It relied entirely on agricultural profits and so the incentive to keep the land profitable was very great.

Expenditure on improvements on the Holkham estates

The careful choice of tenants and the drawing up of detailed husbandry clauses in leases by good agents who made frequent inspections of their employer's farms were some of the ways in which the continued good condition of the estate could be ensured. But the most important contribution the landlord could make towards better agriculture, which in turn benefited his estate, was the provision of the capital for the rebuilding of farmsteads and the improved layout of farms. Thus one of the most significant duties of the estate office would be the sifting

---

[43] H. Rider Haggard, *Rural England*, 2 vols. (London, 1902), vol. 2, p. 467.
[44] Parliamentary Papers (1896), (c.8021), XVII, Henry Rew, *Report on Norfolk*, pp. 31 and 35.
[45] F. M. L. Thompson, 'Agriculture since 1870', *V.C.H. Wiltshire*, vol. 4 (London, 1959), pp. 95-6.
[46] R. J. Thompson, 'An enquiry into rents', p. 589.

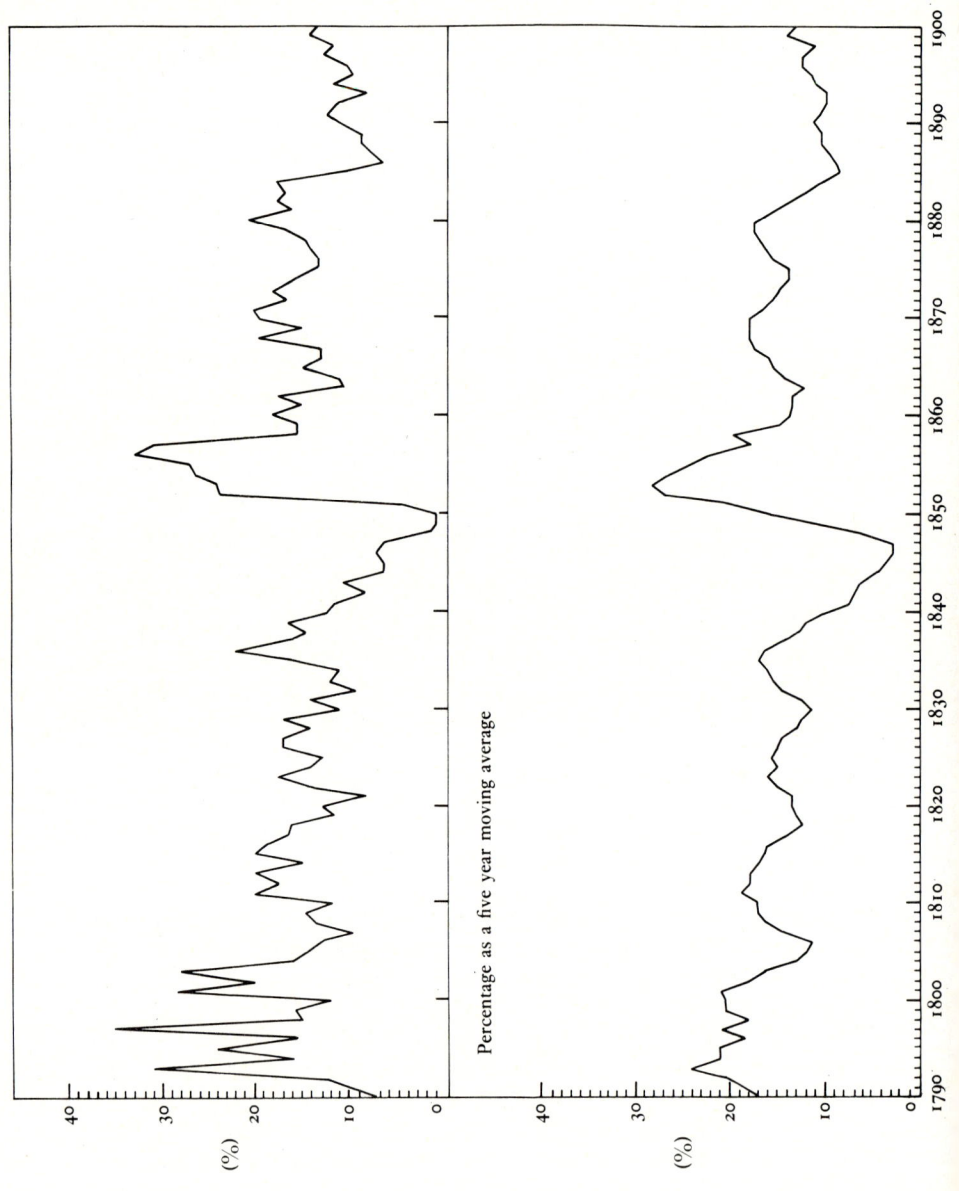

of tenants' requests for improvements and the supervising of the projects that were undertaken.

The only figures for expenditure are those in the 'Buildings and repairs' column of the audit books (appendices 3 and 4). As well as considering the actual figures, it is also worth while calculating the percentage of income from rents spent on repairs (fig. 3.4). The actual yearly percentage is shown in the upper graph, while the lower one is drawn from five year moving averages, as it is easier to isolate long term trends where some of the yearly irregularities have been smoothed out.

Expenditure during the prosperous years of the Napoleonic Wars varied. It was generally high during the 1790s, reaching a peak in 1797 when at least 35% (£7,084) of income was reinvested in farm improvement. This is the highest percentage for the period up to 1909. After 1800 the percentage figure was down, although increasing rents meant that the actual figure spent did not vary much.

The post Napoleonic War depression coincided with the arrival of Blaikie in the estate office. He made it very clear that he felt tenants' requests for improvements had been far too extravagant and that Coke had been spending too much. In 1827 he wrote,

Mr Coke's tenantry generally are much in the habit of erecting unnecessary buildings, and frequently do so without due consideration; such buildings are not only attended with uncalled for expense to the landlord in the first instance, but entail a lasting encumbrance on the estate. For every particle of building not absolutely wanted is an encumbrance to the estate and a deterioration to the property. These remarks apply more immediately to Mr Coke's estate than to any other in the kingdom.[47]

Blaikie's views on farm building, coupled with the fact that farming was depressed and there was a crisis in Coke's financial affairs, means that it comes as no surprise to find that estate expenditure on farm buildings was down. Although after 1822 the rates of investment are generally higher there is no marked change in the pattern of expenditure when agriculture became generally more prosperous in the 1830s.

The first real change came between 1843 and 1852 when expenditure went down dramatically and was at its lowest (less than £600) in 1849 and 1850. There is no break in the rent pattern at this date and the decline must have been due to the death of the first earl and the fact that the second earl began by carrying out expensive schemes in the house and park before turning his attention to farm buildings with the

[47] Holkham MSS, letter books (1827), p. 86.

appointment of W. Keary in 1851. It is very noticeable that the greatest irregularities in the expenditure curve are caused, not by the national or international economy, but by family affairs.

Lost ground was quickly made up. In his tour of the farms when he took up his appointment as agent, Keary noticed much that needed improvement. He had been a very capable farmer and so had a practical knowledge of what was required. Expenditure rapidly rose to nearly one third (£4,343) of the income in 1856. Over £9,000 was spent in the 1850s at Longlands, building estate workshops, so that more of the materials for improvements could be produced and processed on the premises. Keary had gained a reputation for extravagant building by 1859 when Henry Parr Jones went from the estate office at Holkham to work at Longleat. His work at Longleat soon came under criticism for its 'quite unwarranted magnificence'. This, however, was excused when it was found that Lord Leicester put up most extravagant buildings. 'His [the earl's] pride has been to make them as fine as possible. He now begins to see the mistake, and said the other day of some workshops he had erected, that the pulling of them down would be a better deed than the building of them.'[48] It is obviously personalities rather than economic considerations that were responsible for the very great expenditure of the early 1850s. Expenditure remained at a high level, between 11% and 20% until 1885, and rarely fell below 15%.

We noticed that the fall in wheat prices in the 1870s did not result in an immediate fall in rents, and similarly expenditure did not fall until after 1880. As rents fell, so did expenditure. After 1890 the percentage remained fairly steady, between 8% (£2,620) and 14% (£4,475).

Expenditure on draining was not listed separately until after 1851. From the figures available, it is clear that the period of highest expenditure on drainage was 1850–60, being as high as £1,707 in 1852–3 (fig. 3.3). After 1865 drainage was only occasionally significant. Blaikie's letters and a few scattered comments show that before the 1850s drainage was the tenant's responsibility. In 1851 Keary commented that much of the heavy clay lands, especially on the central Norfolk estates, still needed draining. Perhaps as a result of his report, more was spent on drainage during the following years. An interest in drainage schemes at this date can be seen on many other estates, especially on the very heavy

---

[48] Quoted by Thompson, *English Landed Society*, from Longleat MS, Whitwell Eluin to Lord Bath, 6 Feb. 1961.

clay lands of the midland counties. The mass production of clay pipe drains had just become a commercial proposition and after 1846 government loans were available for drainage schemes. Between 1847 and 1872 the government paid out £5,381,000 in loans. There is no evidence in the Holkham records to show whether any of this money found its way to the Holkham lands. There is some controversy as to how effective all this drainage was. Some of it was badly constructed and James Caird concluded that only 20% or less of the land which could have benefited had been drained by 1873.[49]

Little new hedging was done at the estate's expense between 1851 and the early 1880s. Presumably, the early-nineteenth-century enclosure hedge lines or the pre-enclosure fields were considered adequate. The terms of leases show that tenants were responsible for the maintenance but not the re-laying of hedges.

From the estates he studied, F. M. L. Thompson concluded that landlords made more improvements in times of depression, both to attract new tenants and to avoid having to reduce rents. This, however, does not seem to have been the case at Holkham. High levels of investment coincide with times of farming prosperity, and investment is in fact lower after the Napoleonic Wars and in the early 1830s. In Staffordshire, J. E. C. Peters found a pattern of expenditure similar to that at Holkham and he concludes, 'The survey area may be exceptional as it conflicts with Thompson's statement that little or no building was undertaken between 1792 and 1815.'[50] The explanation may be that ill-managed estates found that they needed to improve their farms and increase expenditure in depression years, while well run estates which were steadily improving and kept their farms in good repair all the time did not have the same problem in getting tenants in less prosperous years.

When discussing the depression of the 1870s, Thompson said, 'For the first time an agricultural depression did not produce an expansion of owners' investment in an effort to maintain levels of rent, for any such endeavour was seen to be futile.'[51] Expenditure on the Holkham estate did not decline until after 1885. Unlike that on the estates studied by

---

[49] In Jones, *The Development of English Agriculture*, p. 23.
[50] J. E. C. Peters, *The Development of Farm Buildings in East Lowland Staffordshire* (Manchester, 1969), p. 215.
[51] F. M. L. Thompson, 'The English Great Estate in the nineteenth century', *Contributions and Communications to the First International Conference of Economic History, Stockholm* (Paris, 1960), p. 395.

Thompson, investment seems to follow the pattern of boom and slump rather than to be a foil to it. This can be seen when local corn prices are compared with improvements. They both follow very roughly the same course. When prices were high, so were investments. When farmers were optimistic, they put in more requests for new buildings, and if high rents were coming in the estate was more inclined to comply with them than when there were large amounts in arrears. The great number of articles on the improvement of farm buildings which appeared in the *Journal of the Royal Agricultural Society* in the 1850s suggest this was a period when there was great interest in the subject, and so new building was in no way limited to periods of slump.

Unlike the improvement of land by the initial enclosure of either open fields or wastes, which could sometimes result in the doubling of rent, further investment, often in an attempt to counteract depression, might not produce an economic return. F. M. L. Thompson wrote, 'Essentially, landowners thought of the whole complex of improvements [post 1815] as a rescue operation, and for them its results were in sharp contrast to those of the age of enclosure.'[52] There are many examples to show that returns of well under 5% and, in some cases where the capital was borrowed, even losses were being experienced. However, benefits from land improvement were divided between the tenant and the landlord, so high returns to the investor could not always be expected. Without expenditure, the rent on some estates might have declined further.

Landlords were frequently disappointed by the way rents did not rise in proportion to the money invested. Between 1859 and 1867 the Marquis of Bath spent over £48,000 on his estate. In the same period rents increased by £4,000 per annum, but the marquis did not think that the improvements had affected the rent increases. He wrote, 'This is to be accounted for by the increase in property rented and re-let, in lands purchased, in life leases that have expired and partly, no doubt, to the improved value of some farms by the outlay on them by draining and buildings, but the latter, I fear, is a small item.' The marquis then commissioned an enquiry to see exactly what had happened. The report said that there had been no great extravagance in outlay, and that farm buildings had been erected at a reasonable cost. The net increase in rents was equivalent to a yield of 5% on the outlay. The main effect was to

---

[52] Thompson, *English Landed Society*, p. 237.

maintain the rent-producing power of the estate and not to increase it. In conclusion, Thompson said of Wiltshire, 'The great improving landlords had their estates neatly farmed by the most capable tenantry available. They had however been investing their money uneconomically, and in so doing were largely responsible for creating an over-capitalised agriculture, for the new buildings and drainage they provided led to an uneconomically precarious system of farming.'[53] If we look simply at the figures for expenditure and income, then it appears that Thompson is right. However, it is necessary to be sure what exactly money was being spent on. If the buildings were for the methods of farming that were to remain profitable after the 1870s, then there is no reason to assume that farming was over-capitalised. It was the cattle sheds necessary for intensive livestock farming rather than increased grain storage that were being built at Holkham, and it was livestock rather than cereal farming that was profitable in the last quarter of the nineteenth century. Rather than creating an 'uneconomically precarious system of farming', the improvements to the Holkham estate were helping to diversify farming so that it was better able to cope with the depression that was inevitable when the great wheatlands of America were opened up. It must also be remembered that improvements to an estate increased its value if it were sold, irrespective of the effect they had on rents.

The audit books record a sum of about £485,259 as being spent on 'buildings and repairs' between 1790 and 1882, the year when rents reached their peak. A further £44,559 was spent on the purchase of land and £7,000 on enclosure (between 1776 and 1851, the acreage of the estate increased from 30,000 to 42,000 acres). Thus the total invested in the estate as recorded in the audit books was £536,818. Over the same period rents rose from £18,461 to £59,709, an increase of £41,248; £536,818 was therefore invested to produce an increased income of £41,248. This represents an annual return of about 7.6% by 1882. However, this takes no account of the building material and workmanship provided by the estate. If we follow the example of the mid-nineteenth-century estate office and add two thirds of the sum spent on improvements to allow for this, the resulting percentage is about 4.6%. Neither calculation allows for an increase in the value of land.

There are many problems with these figures. We do not know how

[53] Thompson, 'Agriculture since 1870', p. 95.

much the value of the estate would have risen without improvements. We do not know how accurate is our figure for the amount spent on improvements. By using the peak figure for rents we have calculated the highest percentage return for the period, which only applies for a single year. Calculations spanning different periods would give different results. However, many of these drawbacks must apply to other estates, and it is unlikely that the return in the years immediately before rents began to decline was less than 5%. In spite of investment, the rents had decreased by 1900 so that they had reached the level of 1828. Keary introduced a new clause into his leases whereby the estate was ensured of a return on improvements made to farms. After 1850, 5% was charged for drainage work and $7\frac{1}{2}$% on the cost of building work carried out. This clause was often maintained until the 1870s.

In his report to the Royal Commission on Agriculture in 1895, the commissioner calculated that the return on investment on the Holkham estate was $2\frac{1}{2}$%. He arrived at this figure by adding up the total spent on improvements and purchases between 1776 and 1895 and working out the percentage return of this from the rent received in 1895, when the rents were far lower than fifteen years previously.

F. M. L. Thompson suspects that investment in improvements had little effect on rent movements, compared with that of land values. 'Two of the most striking features about investments in farm improvements in the nineteenth century were the low returns which it yielded and the uniformity of rent movements on estates with different levels of owners' outlay.'[54]

The point is borne out if we calculate the amount spent on improvement and the percentage return in the form of increased rents for the ten year periods between 1790 and 1900 (see table 3.2). Periods of high rent increases are not necessarily ones of high investment, but times when farming was prosperous and land values high. An apparent 26% return on investment between 1840 and 1850 reflects the good years of 'high farming' mid-century, coupled with the low investment of the first years of the second earl at Holkham, rather than any particular lucrative investment project.

When rents and investments on individual farms are considered, it is very rare for any connection between rent increases and periods of

---

[54] Thompson, 'The English Great Estate', p. 393.

TABLE 3.2. *Amounts spent on repairs and percentage return in rent increases, 1790–1899*

	Rent increase or decrease £	Amount spent on repairs £	Percentage increase or decrease (approx.)
1790–9	+1,912	35,853	+5.0
1800–9	+2,759	35,929	+7.5
1810–19	+8,384	48,386	+17.0
1820–9	−292	45,432	−0.6
1830–9	+2,389	46,580	+5.0
1840–9	+6,982	26,997	+26.0
1850–9	+7,292	81,148	+9.0
1860–9	+3,691	67,818	+5.5
1870–9	+4,537	81,921	+5.5
1880–9	−5,918	59,657	−10.0
1890–9	−14,173	39,060	−36.0

Source: appendix 3.

expenditure to be obvious (table 3.3). Again it is land values which are reflected. The rent pattern from farm to farm is very similar, while investments are not. At Castle Acre there was considerable expenditure at Lodge Farm and Wicken Farm to bring them up to the standard required by the new tenants in 1823, but there was no immediate increase in rent. £927 was spent in 1824 at Lodge Farm and this was followed by a rent rise of £122 between 1833 and 1834, thus providing a 15% return on capital. Improvements at Wicken farm between 1868 and 1870 were followed by a decline in rent, but by 1883 the rent had increased by £253, giving a return of 15% for a few years.

The figures for Longham Hall Farm show, in contrast, the immediate affect that enclosure had on rents. The enclosure map for Longham is dated 1816. Some common land was added to Longham Hall Farm and the fields were newly laid out. £992 was spent on new premises. The rent increased by £225 to £567, although it was not maintained at this level for long. The building work carried out after 1880 was accompanied by a fall in rents and was undertaken in an effort to keep the tenant, who had threatened to quit several times.

Wicken Farm, Tittleshall, was one of the poorest farms on the estate and in 1851 the rent was the lowest per acre (17s. 2d.). The land was

TABLE 3.3. *Rent and expenditure on five Holkham farms, 1790–1900*

	Rent £		Expenditure £
Wicken Farm, Castle Acre			
		1797	2,249
		1802	73
1823	538		
1833	574		
1843	601		
1853	782		
1863	1,294	1865	484
1873	1,283	1868–70	1,850
1883	1,547		
1893	974		
Lodge Farm, Castle Acre			
		1797–1800	2,600
1823	700	1824	927
1833	700		
		1840	194
1843	822	1843	80
		1847	117
1853	867		
1863	1,363	1863	513
		1866	183
1873	1,370	1876–9	1,439
Longham Hall Farm			
1790	243	1790s	492
1800	337		
1810	342	1816–20	992 and enclosure
1820	567	1820s	1,400
1830	400	1830s	647
1840	435		
1850	435	1850s	544
1860	596	1861	174
1870	968	1877	406
1880	1,013	1889	258
1890	621	1893	183
1900	479		
Wicken Farm, Tittleshall			
1790	50		
1800	50		
1810	86		
1820	120		
1830	100	1839–40	362

TABLE 3.3. (*cont.*)

	Rent £		Expenditure £
1840	100		
1850	100	1851	13 underdraining pipes
1860	123	1868	429
1870	183		
1880	251		
1890	150		
1900	65		
North Hall Farm, Warham			
1790	550		
1800	550	1808	148
1810	584		
1820	639		
1830	684	1831	333
		1836–9	445
1840	934		
1850	937		
1860	1,176		
1870	1,198	1879	802
1880	1,305		
1890	1,017	1890–1	406
1900	812		

Source: Holkham MSS, audit books.

heavy and more was spent on underdraining here than anywhere else. Very little was spent on improvements, yet the rent rose along with the land values and a total expenditure between 1790 and 1880 of £804 was accompanied by a rent increase of £200, or a 25% return on the investment.

A high percentage return can be calculated for the large, well run and well equipped light-land farm, North Hall Farm, Warham. £1,728 was spent and the rent increased by £755 between 1790 and 1880. However, in 1890, £406 had to be spent to equip the farm for a new tenant, while at the same time the rent was reduced by £200. It is always economic trends in agriculture generally rather than expenditure levels that are reflected in rents.

All these calculations have been made from the audit book figures and no attempt has been made to add anything to take account of materials and labour provided by the estate and not accounted for. This would reduce the percentages considerably and bring them down to a more realistic level.

It is worth drawing attention to the fact that on the Holkham estate high investment was accompanied by higher rent rises than on many other estates. Once the windfall rent rises that resulted from enclosure were over, and there was no other new land to be brought into cultivation, an increase in the intensity of farming was the only way to increase returns. The terms of leases could encourage the maintaining of soil fertility, but fixed capital investment was also needed. Both these methods were used at Holkham. Its leases served as models for other estates and over half a million pounds was spent on improvements in the nineteenth century. Not only did rents rise, but the more prosperous class of tenants who were attracted to these well equipped farms were able to hold their own better in periods of depression. Thus we have seen that not only did rents rise more steeply during periods of prosperity but Holkham was also better able to withstand depression than many other estates.

It is perhaps unfair to judge the value of high investment purely in terms of profit to the landowner. He certainly hoped to gain financially from improvements, and without them he would have found it difficult to keep his rents up or to find new tenants. However, there are other considerations to be taken into account. Agricultural advance relied to a large extent on landlord's capital. The landlord–tenant system, as it existed in England, meant that additions to the fixed capital of the agricultural industry had to come from the landlord. Tenants would find it far easier to run a well equipped farm progressively and intensively, and their profits would increase with landlord investment. The wealth of many mid-nineteenth-century Holkham tenants is proof of this. There were also less tangible rewards. The admiration of his fellow landowners at the Holkham sheep shearings would have been something that Coke would have felt was well worth paying for. There was a genuine feeling of commitment to improvement among the greater and many of the lesser landowners. All were spurred on by the standards set by men such as Coke of Norfolk and the Duke of Bedford.

4
The tenant farmer and his farm

E. L. Jones, writing in 1968, said, 'Of the three main agricultural classes, landowners, farmers and labourers, it is surprising that we know least about the economic condition of the middle group...the business history of the farm is unwritten.'[1] The main reason for this must be the lack of available information. Farmers, unlike progressive estate offices, did not keep detailed accounts. Henry Overman, an intensive and intelligent farmer on the Holkham estates, told the Royal Commission on Agriculture in 1881 that he could not calculate how much profit he made on a cow.[2] In 1894, the Norfolk farmer and agricultural writer, Clare Sewell Read, said that it was impossible for farmers to know how much money they had lost: 'They just keep going from year to year.'[3] This lack of records for the nineteenth-century period of agricultural development, boom and depression is particularly regrettable as most modern historians accept that many of the improvements of the 'agricultural revolution' were the result of the work and experiment of the tenants rather than the landlords, and contemporaries also recognised their importance. Marshall found that they travelled widely and sent their sons to learn from more distant farmers.[4] Adam Smith wrote that great proprietors were seldom great improvers, and although Arthur Young reported in glowing terms on the activities of certain landowners, it is the work of the tenant farmers that features regularly in his reports.[5]

Thomas William Coke recognised the value of good tenants and is said to have maintained that the interests of landlord and tenants were identical. 'A good understanding between landlord and tenant' was

---
[1] E. L. Jones, *The Development of English Agriculture, 1815–1873*, Studies in Economic History (London, 1968), p. 25.
[2] Parliamentary Papers (1881), (c. 2778–1), XVI, *Royal Commission on Agriculture*, minutes of evidence, part 2, p. 735, question 51731.
[3] Parliamentary Papers (1894), (c.7400–1), XVI, *Royal Commission on Agriculture*, minutes of evidence, part 2, p. 69, question 15978.
[4] W. Marshall, *Rural Economy of the Midland Counties*, 2 vols. (London, 1796), vol. 1, pp. 182–5.
[5] G. E. Mingay, *English Landed Society in the Eighteenth Century* (London, 1963), p. 164.

quoted as the root of Holkham prosperity.⁶ Many contemporaries reported on the care with which Coke chose his tenants and the fierce competition there was for his farms. This means that those who were lucky enough to be chosen as tenants much have been men of unusual calibre, and from the scattered evidence available it is possible to discover something about the type of person who became a successful tenant on this model Norfolk estate.

The sources available for studying the activities of the tenants are limited. Very few farm accounts survive and it is difficult to trace descendants of the nineteenth-century farmers. The estate records include descriptions of the tenants and their farms at several dates, and the letter books include correspondence with them. Contemporary accounts of the agriculture of the county also often include descriptions of visits to individual farms and opinions expressed by tenants.

Holkham tenants

About 150 families held farms on the Holkham estate during the 110 years from 1790 to 1900. About twenty-five of these held more than one farm and remained tenants for most of the 110 years. Six of these families were sometimes occupying more than three farms. It is not always clear whether they were farmed as one or whether they were worked separately by different branches of the family. If the farms were some distance from each other they would probably be separate concerns, but we do know that the farms of the Hudsons at Castle Acre were farmed as one by the son with his father, a tenant farmer in no more than name. That there was a certain amount of intermarriage within the group is shown by the half-dozen double-barrelled names where both parts are Holkham names. Even where the name changes, tenancies sometimes went on through the female line. At Sparham the Winters were tenants from the 1820s. A daughter married a member of the Forby family and they took over the tenancy in 1850. Again a Forby married a Sayer and the Sayers took over the farm in 1898.

Many tenants stayed on their farms for a very long time. Thirty-one farms were held by the same family for over fifty years, two of these for the entire 110 years being studied. Fifteen were worked by the same family for forty to fifty years and twenty-three for thirty to forty years.

⁶ A. M. W. Stirling, *Coke of Norfolk and his Friends*, 2 vols. (London 1908), vol. 1, p. 257.

Assuming that a man might not have the experience and capital, or at least the credit facilities, needed to work a medium-sized or large Holkham farm until his thirties or forties, the normal working life of a tenant farmer may have been between twenty and thirty years, and perhaps the forty-one farms which were held for this length of time include this sort of one-generation farm. Fifty were held for ten to twenty years and fifty-six for under ten. The last two categories include farms held before 1790 and after 1900, and twenty-seven of the fifty-six held for under ten years changed hands in the last the years of the nineteenth century.

We know very little about the individual characteristics of most of these tenants, although there is some evidence for the farming practice of the more famous and progressive. A little is known about some who became tenants at the end of the nineteenth century and in some cases their families are still farming. However, there are certain characteristics they must have had in common. Most were local men with long associations with farming in their area. Of the seven Holkham tenant farmers living in Tittleshall in 1851, all were born in Norfolk. John Forby, aged sixty, had taken on the leases of his father's farm and was born there. Elizabeth Forby, aged sixty-nine and a widow, was born in Mileham, perhaps the daughter of a Holkham tenant there. George Belcham came from Wells and Mary Bell from Burnham Market, where again their families may have been connected with the estate. George Brandford, aged sixty, was born in Norfolk just before his father came to Godwick, and his heirs remained there until 1894. Thomas Rix, aged sixty-four, was born in Great Dunham, bordering on the Holkham estate, and his family came to Tittleshall in 1807 and remained until 1874. Isaac Riches was born in Castle Acre and his family were also long term tenants at Tittleshall. The same very local origins of tenants is shown in other parishes at this date.

One of the most important differences between the Holkham tenant and many of his contemporaries was in the size of farm occupied. Of the seventy farms of the estate in 1850, six of those on light land were over 1,000 acres, while twenty-eight were more than 500. Mingay calculates that £2 an acre was a minimum figure for a tenant's working capital[7] and therefore £1,200 would be needed for a 600 acre farm.

---

[7] G. E. Mingay, *Enclosure and the small farmer in the age of the Industrial Revolution*, Studies in Economic History (London, 1968), p. 22.

Obviously there can only have been a very limited number of eligible applicants with enough capital to farm intensively. James Caird wrote in 1850,

> Mr Coke determined to get men if he could, to take into their hands that improvement of farms which he could not accomplish himself; for it is through an enlightened tenantry that a large estate can be permanently and profitably improved...as farms became vacant, therefore, they were let to men of capital and intelligence. Fine sets of buildings and houses suitable for a superior class of tenantry were erected...It was not enough that he should bring his tenantry to the standard of the day – they must be prepared to advance with the general progress.

For this reason Coke organised the annual sheep shearings as occasions when his model farm and those of nearby tenants could be viewed, ideas exchanged and livestock judged. The result was a highly capitalised agriculture, in which

> The half a million pounds claimed to have been spent by the landowner on permanent improvements was matched by the amount spent by the tenants on artificial foods and manures...The wisdom of the course taken by Mr Coke is shown...in the continued progress of improvement; for there is no standing still, no belief that perfection in farming has been attained, though probably no farmers in England have more right to rest content with the point they have reached than the best of Lord Leicester's tenants.[8]

This rather eulogistic description, referring back from the 1850s to the early nineteenth century, needs verifying from earlier sources, but it does show the reputation that Coke and his tenants had gained.

From Blaikie's report of 1816 it is clear that not all farms had a progressive occupier. Two small farms on heavy land in the parish of Tittleshall were in a very bad state. One was 'poor land in a wretched bad state, but capable of improvement.' However, there was 'no hope of the present occupier, and his son seems to have a weak intellect'. The other was 'in a miserable state; the land much out of cultivation'. Drainage was needed, but again there was no hope of improvement by the present occupier. At Croxton Farm in the parish of Fulmodestone, much drainage and marling was needed, but the tenant was not likely to improve.

Most of the Holkham tenants were described by Blaikie as 'zealous' and 'industrious', although he did not always approve of their methods. The temptation of high profits had led many of them to abandon the five- or six-course shifts which were often laid down in their leases and

---

[8] J. Caird, *English Agriculture in 1850–51* (London, 1851), pp. 164–5.

instead to try a four-course rotation which allowed more land to be under the highly profitable grain crops. However, Blaikie thought that some of the land on the estate was not good enough for this intensity of cropping. Mr Plowright of Wighton had changed 'injudiciously' from a five- to a four-course shift. 'The present state of this land shows the impropriety of attempting by means of stimulating manure [oil cake] to force crops in a four course shift upon land not equal to the task.' Blaikie often found fault with the practices of tenants who were otherwise described as 'good', 'deserving' and 'industrious'. Those who were most highly praised by Blaikie were men whose names frequently appeared in the agricultural literature of the period. Blaikie found much to praise in the farming of Mr Garwood of Billingford, Mr Overman of Burnham and Mr Bloomfield of Flitcham. Bloomfield was a well travelled man and in 1819 visited many of Coke's agricultural associates in America. Mr Overman of Weasenham was highly praised and 'may be considered worthy of being held out as a model for all young agriculturalists to imitate'.[9]

So the Holkham tenantry was headed by about a dozen very progressive farmers who had enough capital to improve their large farms and bring them up to a high standard of cultivation. Below this were the majority of 'industrious', 'persevering' and 'deserving' tenants whose farming practice was not always perfect. They were often responsible for over-cropping, but Blaikie thought he had persuaded many of them to return to five- or six-course rotations and the depression which followed the peace with France in 1815 made intensive wheat growing less worthwhile. A few farms were still occupied by old-fashioned and backward farmers. These were mostly small farms on heavy land where improvements were difficult.

The only other agent who recorded his opinion of the tenantry was William Keary. His brief remarks are included in his description of the estate, written in 1851. Fourteen farms were 'badly managed', six were 'fairly farmed' and nineteen were 'well looked after'. There is no comment on the management of the others.[10] It would seem therefore that the best tenants hardly made up a third of the total farmers on the estate.

[9] Holkham MSS, F. Blaikie, 'Report on the estates of Thomas William Coke, Esq. in the county of Norfolk' (1816).
[10] Holkham MSS, H. W. Keary, 'Report on the Holkham estates' (1851).

The most detailed report on Norfolk agriculture in the nineteenth century was written by R. N. Bacon as a *Journal of the Royal Agricultural Society of England* prize essay in 1843. He obtained much of his information by sending questionnaires to over eighty of the most famous Norfolk farmers. He received replies from thirteen Holkham tenants, and it is very fortunate that manuscript answers to these questionnaires are now in the Norfolk Record Offffice, so it is possible to discover the systems of husbandry practised by progressive Holkham tenants.[11] Bacon's list of famous Norfolk agriculturalists included several Holkham farmers. Bloomfield of Warham, Kendle of Weasenham, Wrightup of Ashill and Tutell Moore of Warham were all included among the 'first generation' (pre-1840), while the 'second generation' were still farming. These included J. Overman of Burnham and H. Overman of Weasenham, Hill of Waterden, Beck of Mileham, Everitt of South Creake and Hudson of Castle Acre.[12]

All the Holkham tenants who answered Bacon's questionnaire farmed on the four-course system, although some used a five-course shift on the poor land. All used large quantities of both farmyard and artificial manures. Farm machinery was generally used. Corn was drilled, although one farmer occasionally dibbled. Threshing machines were generally used, although Mr Gayford threshed his barley by flail.

Very few farmers bred their own cattle, and not all had breeding ewes. Instead, stock tended to be bought in and fattened up. Few dairy cattle were kept, and pigs were normally only fattened for domestic use, although Mr Hart bought and kept forty to fifty pigs for market.

There was no sign of complacency among Holkham tenants, who thought there was still room for improvement in farming methods. Production had not yet reached its highest level: 'This will develop as knowledge increases.'

Bacon was very impressed by the class of tenant he found at Holkham. They were farming with a great deal of capital. 'They are generous, independent, hospitable, free, intelligent and very many have carried on intellectual pursuits and acquirements far beyond the race of farmers in former times.'[13]

If we compare the farming methods of the 1840s and 1850s with those

[11] Bacon MS 4363, N.R.O.
[12] R. N. Bacon, *Agriculture of Norfolk* (London, 1844), p. 110.
[13] R. N. Bacon, quoted by C. S. Read, 'Agriculture of Norfolk', in W. White, *Norfolk Directory* (London, 1883), p. 74.

reported by Blaikie in 1816, it is clear how much more intensive the practice of Holkham tenants had become. More artificial feeds and fertilisers meant that very little land was too weak to support a four-course shift, and in many cases two successive grain crops were possible. Both tenant and landlord continued to invest heavily in improvements and intensive farming, and so were able to carry the progressive methods of north-west Norfolk a stage further.

The optimism about the future which is so obvious among Holkham tenants who answered Bacon's questionnaire was finally broken by the agricultural depression. However, even the decline in wheat prices in the 1870s does not seem to have resulted in an immediate loss of confidence. The livestock side of many farms had been developed considerably since the 1850s and this helped counteract the effects of the depression. It was not until the 1880s that rent arrears began to mount up and rents had to be reduced. In 1881 four Holkham farms had been vacated: 'one man had gone out because of declining health, one is dead, another thinks he had better go out before he has lost all he has got and I am afraid the fourth has lost all he had got'.[14] Many tenants were broken by the depression and by the 1890s farms were difficult to let. Ten farms were vacated between 1880 and 1890 and a further eighteen between 1890 and 1900. Six changed hands between 1895 and 1896. For the first time they had to be advertised. Good tenants with capital had done much for the estate in the mid nineteenth century, but these were difficult to find by the end of the period. The Royal Commission on Agriculture reported, 'Perhaps Lord Leicester is an exceptional landlord, and no doubt it is a tradition on his estate that no good tenant is allowed to leave it, but even large reductions of between 42 and 56% have not always been able to keep tenants.'[15] Farmers were not bringing up their sons to the land, 'as for £1,000 a man could be put into a profession whereas to farm he needed £3,000 which he stood a good chance of losing. Nearly all the people who hold small official positions in the district are farmers' sons or broken down farmers.'[16]

Table 4.1 shows the periods over which the same family held a Holkham farm. For instance, in 1810 twenty-five of the farms were held by the same family as in 1790. It can be seen that the most stable twenty

---

[14] Parliamentary Papers (1882), (c.3096), XVII, *Royal Commission on Agriculture*, minutes of evidence, part 2, question 51768.
[15] Parliamentary Papers (1894), *Royal Commission on Agriculture*, p. 31.
[16] H. Rider Haggard, *Rural England*, 2 vols. (London, 1902), vol. 2, p. 453.

TABLE 4.1. *Periods over which the same family tenanted a Holkham farm*

						20 yr period
1870					31	40 yr period
1850				26	17	60 yr period
1830			37	21	12	80 yr period
1810		21	14	9	9	100 yr period
1790	25	9	5	2	2	
	1810	1830	1850	1870	1890	

year period was between 1830 and 1850 when thirty-seven (over half) of the farms were held by the same family. Twenty-one of these families remained for the succeeding twenty years, making 1830–70 the most stable forty year period. Twelve of these managed to stay for a further twenty years, but this number was halved in the next ten years.

The evidence given to the Royal Commissions has shown that the greatest periods of change were the years of depression. Between 1822 and 1826 there were seventeen new tenants, and the period 1810–30 is the twenty year period with the greatest number of changes, with only twenty-one farms remaining in the same hands. The changes between 1870 and 1890 are far fewer, although we know that by 1900 twelve more long-standing tenants had left and that in all, twenty-eight farms changed hands between 1880 and 1900. The effects of the post-1870 depression were considerably delayed as far as tenants giving up is concerned.

We know very little about the new tenants. Some of them, as had always been the case, were local. The Sayers at Sparham were an old local family who married into a Holkham tenant family there. When some farms were given up, they were taken over by established tenants. At Weasenham, the Overmans, who had held Weasenham Hall Farm since 1820, took over two other farms in 1888 and 1890, and the family still farmed here until the 1950s.

Some of the long established families kept going after 1900, although often it was one branch of the family holding only one farm. This was true of the Leeds, who remained in Castle Acre, although they had left West Lexham and Burghwood Hall, Mileham, in 1870. The Betts family, who had farmed four farms, remained at Panworth Hall, Ashill, until 1900. The large Middleton family had held seven farms, but by

1900 they only remained at one. The Hudsons at Castle Acre had farmed in several places, but by 1900 they were only at Beck Hall, Billingford.

Other well known names did disappear, although families may have carried on down the female line. About ten of the families who had held more than one farm for a considerable time during the nineteenth century had gone by 1900.

From the list of about twenty new names it is possible to know something about only a few. Mr Everington, who took on John Hudson's old farm in Castle Acre in 1870, was the son of a London merchant and a farm student of Clare Sewell Read before he took his own farm, firstly near Dereham and then moving to the Holkham estate. The family held Lodge Farm until the early 1970s.

Holkham farms were being advertised in Scottish newspapers by 1880 and the best known of the Holkham tenants by the turn of the century was an Aberdeenshire man, Mr Keith, who took the Egmere farm in the 1880s. Although he may have been the only Scot on this estate, he was one of the many who came south for cheap farms and he brought capital with him. He ran a highly mechanised farm that was making profits in the 1890s. 'Even the hedges were clipped by machine.'[17]

It is a pity that it is impossible to find out how much the life style of Holkham farmers had changed during the nineteenth century. There are many requests in the letter books for additions to farm houses to suit them to a more fashionable way of life. The popular bay windows were often added to plain Georgian façades totally unsuited to them. Blaikie's report contained descriptions of farmers' wives who were skilled in cheese and butter making, but working wives are not mentioned in later records. The 1851 census returns show that from two to four servants were kept by most farmers, with sometimes a groom or a housekeeper. Farm sales catalogues at the end of the century show that farmers had chaise houses in which there was a brougham and a luggage cart, plus a dog cart and usually a couple of gigs, but these catalogues give no indication of the condition of these vehicles.[18] However, this would suggest that the large tenant farmers were living in some style.

The size of the Holkham estate, and the unusual calibre and wealth of many of its tenants, had one significant result for the village

---

[17] *Ibid.*, vol. 2, p. 471.
[18] Sales catalogues for the auctions of live and dead stock at Lodge Farm, Castle Acre in 1877 and 1907, kindly lent to the author by Mr R. D. Everington of Blakeney, Norfolk.

community. In many villages, dominated by a great house and squire, the squire would provide most of the employment and initiate philanthropic activities. In a Holkham village this role was often taken over by one or two large farmers. They would initiate schemes for church restoration, road and bridge improvement and the setting up of schools. They would then request the estate for financial help, or the right to dig brick earth or gravel on their farms, or to use timber. Mrs Forby at Tittleshall was responsible for a fund to 'help the poor' to which Lord Leicester subscribed regularly. The position of some memorial plaques, near the alter of their local church, in the place reserved for the gentry in other villages, shows the respect that a tenant might command to the end.

Although the style of many Holkham farm houses certainly puts their tenants a cut above the ordinary farmer, there was one preserve of the landed classes that even they did not manage to infiltrate. No Holkham tenant farmer, however influential, appears in the list of magistrates for the nineteenth century. J.P.s were almost exclusively drawn from the local gentry.

This rather general survey of the activities of Holkham tenants can be backed up with more detailed information about several farming families. These include two, the Hudsons and the Overmans, who rose to national fame as a result of their farming achievements, and one, the Hastings, who were probably more typical of the competent but less well known farmers.

The Hudsons were the most famous farming family on the estate, although they did not lease a farm from Holkham until 1822. John Hudson was a founder council member of the Royal Agricultural Society in 1843 and his portrait hangs in the society's London headquarters (fig. 4.1). He was a frequent contributor to the *Journal* and helped both Bacon and Caird when they wrote their reports on Norfolk. Born in Grimston near Kings Lynn, he came to Castle Acre in 1822 when he leased Lodge Farm, and his father took the neighbouring Manor Farm. Between them they farmed 1,497 acres at a rent of £1,238. The early 1820s were years of depression and the two farms had already been turned down by three people when Hudson took them. Both farms were 'poor' and 'foul'. Yields were as low as twenty bushels of wheat and twenty-four bushels of barley per acre. The roots grown had not enabled the outgoing tenant to winter more than ten bullocks.[19]

[19] H. M. Jenkins, 'Lodge Farm, Castle Acre', *J.R.A.S.E.*, second series, vol. 5 (1869).

4.1 John Hudson, tenant of Lodge Farm, Castle Acre, 1822–69.

John Hudson immediately set himself the task of improving the farms and, by 1869

after being cleaned and fertilised by the liberal use of rape cake, the land gradually improved; and now after the expenditure of between £2,000 and £3,000 per annum on oil cakes and other feeding stuffs, as well as from £800 to £1,000 a year on artificial manures, according to their price, the 1,000 acres will winter 100 to 140 steers according to the root crop.[20]

John Hudson managed both farms until his father's death in 1840. Manor Farm was then run by executors until 1857, when John's son, Thomas Hudson, took over. John Hudson was not slow to publicise his success. In 1845 Barugh Almack described his four-course system. He was famous for the degree of capitalisation in his livestock farming and he gave details to Bacon of his intensive system which allowed him to double the amount of stock kept. Two hundred acres of the farm were pasture. A four-course rotation was followed throughout the rest, 'there being annually 300 acres of wheat, 300 of barley and 300 of clover and trefoil'. All the crops were well manured. Twenty-five shillings an acre was spent on guano and superphosphates for the turnip crop. The land was marled once every twenty-one years.[21] Thirty-six horses (one for just over every twenty acres) and sixteen bullocks were required to work the farm.

As a result of feeding sliced turnips and cake to sheep in the fields, Mr Hudson claimed to have increased the output of the land by a third.[22] This, along with the very high consumption of cake by both sheep and cattle, accounted for an increase, between 1823 and 1850, of from four hundred sheep and thirty bullocks to 2,500 sheep and 150 bullocks. The barley crop, which in 1823 did not exceed twenty-two and a half bushels per acre, had nearly doubled by 1850.[23]

John Hudson died in 1869, while farming prosperity was at its height, and the farm was run by executors until 1878 when a new family of tenants took over. The farm sale when the executors gave up was a large one. The livestock consisted of twenty-four cart horses, five riding and carriage horses, seventy-four cattle including dairy cows, and 1,017 sheep. The farm had a good selection of farm implements, including about thirty ploughs and the same number of harrows, as well as scarifiers, cultivators and rollers to prepare the soil. The harvest machinery consisted of a reaping machine, a threshing drum and two elevators with horse gearing. Several Gardeners' turnip cutters prepared the root crops for animal feed. There was harness for five teams of horses as well as fifteen waggons and eleven tumbrils. A nine horse power portable steam engine provided power in the field. The prices that the

[20] Ibid. [21] Bacon MS 4363, N.R.O.
[22] Caird, *English Agriculture*, pp. 165 and 168.
[23] Ibid.

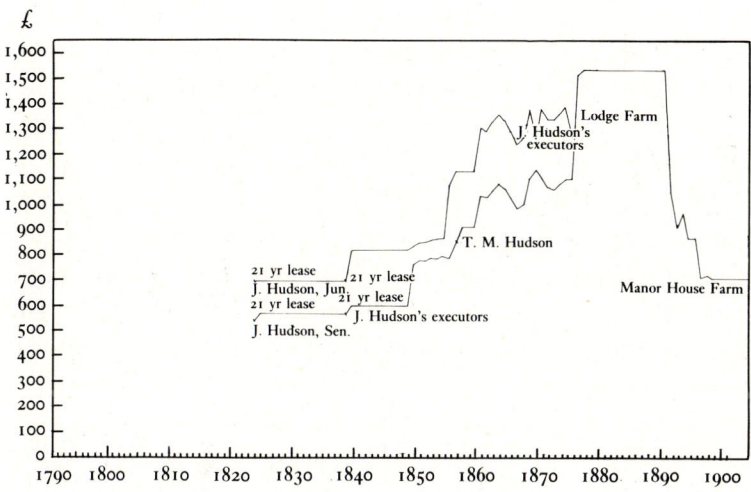

4.2 Rents on the farms tenanted by the Hudson family.

stock and implements made is not recorded so we do not know the value of the Hudsons' capital investment. The sale that followed the death of John Hudson's successor at Lodge Farm in 1907, and which appears to have contained a similar quantity of implements and stock, raised £4,556.[24] This suggests that John Hudson probably had between £4,000 and £5,000 tied up in stock and implements. Seed, manure and cattle feed were additional expenses and so it is clear that a progressive tenant farmer of the mid nineteenth century had to be prepared to invest heavily in his enterprise.

Lodge Farm was given up in 1878, but John Hudson's son, Thomas Moore Hudson, continued to farm at Manor Farm throughout the depression. He was a respected member of the local community, and was a manager of Castle Acre school until his death in 1903. The depression affected Hudson in spite of his tradition of progressive farming, and from 1881 his rent was frequently in arrears (fig. 4.2). The rent was reduced in 1890, but was still difficult to pay. In 1893 and 1894, it was paid in two parts, one in January and one after harvest. In February 1894, the agent wrote acknowledging a cheque for £250 and saying, 'Lord Leicester will be glad to receive the balance at your convenience, and does not wish you to realise at a sacrifice.'[25] Even the best farmers could

[24] Farm sales catalogues as in note 17.   [25] Holkham MSS, letter books.

not make profits and slowly the payment of rent had eaten into the resources so that many were forced to give up farming. This made it difficult for landlords to find tenants and Lord Leicester was prepared to overlook the non-payment of rents to keep his farms occupied.

The Overmans had farmed at Holkham for longer than the Hudsons and locally it is said that in the mid eighteenth century Mr Overman was agent to a north-country estate, where he was murdered by miners. Thomas William Coke was an executor of his will and so set up each of Overman's sons in a farm. If this is true it was a very shrewd move on the part of Coke as they subsequently proved to be very able farmers. One was said to be 'the first to further the new agricultural schemes, and as an experiment was allowed to draw up the covenants of his lease himself'.[26] His farm at Burnham was frequently visited and admired by those attending sheep shearings and the farm was still intensively run by John Overman in the middle of the century. The answers to Bacon's questionnaire give few details, but Caird was impressed by the high standard of cultivation there when he visited in 1850.

Caird also visited Henry Overman at Weasenham who had embarked on a scheme unusual for Norfolk. He kept a herd of dairy cows. Most of the milk was made into butter and in the 1850s it was sent to London.[27] By the 1880s, Overman's interest in stock had provided him with the expertise to judge at the Royal Agricultural Society and the Smithfield show. He was a witness of the enquiry of the Royal Commission into Agriculture (1881) and at this time he was still a dairy producer, although he was not sending butter to London, but twice a week by train to Norwich.[28]

Henry Overman's father, Robert, farmed at Weasenham until his death in 1850, when the apparent success of his farming is shown in the fact that he is said to have left £10,000 to each of his ten children! Mr R. Overman was the tenant of Egmere from 1852 to 1872. This was one of the best laid-out farms on the estate and a new set of model farm buildings was erected when Overman took it on. It was a large farm of 1,300 acres. An 'estate book' kept throughout his tenancy shows the crop rotation practised. In nearly all the fields the classical four-course rotation was followed, although sainfoin, cowgrass and lucerne were

[26] Stirling, *Coke of Norfolk*, vol. 1, p. 267.
[27] Caird, *English Agriculture*, p. 170.
[28] Parliamentary Papers (1881), *Royal Commission on Agriculture*, p. 735, question 51705.

frequently sown instead of clover. Occasionally from 1854 onwards, a crop of wheat was followed by a crop of oats before the roots were planted. Between 1852 and 1858 more intensive wheat cultivation was carried out in one field. The rotation was wheat, trefoil and red clover and then wheat again. This pattern was acceptable to the estate. Overman left Egmere in 1872, although the family continued to farm at Weasenham until very recently.

In contrast to the Hudsons and Overmans, the Hastings family at Longham did not achieve national fame and it is particularly interesting to follow the fortunes of what may have been a more typical family of Holkham tenants. Their farm at Longham was in one of the outlying estate parishes and was not visited at sheep shearing time. Unlike the Hudson and Overman families, who were new to the estate in the nineteenth century, we know that the Hastings were renting land in Longham from the Holkham estate in the early eighteenth century. The family leased Hall Farm in 1757 and remained there for 150 years, which must make it one of the longest-standing tenant families at Holkham.

The most prominant member of the family was John Sutton Hastings, who took on the tenancy of Hall Farm in 1816 when he was twenty-six. After surviving the post Napoleonic War depression, he farmed there through the prosperous mid-century and died while farming was still enjoying boom conditions in 1869. The beginning of his tenancy coincided with the work of enclosure which followed the parish enclosure act of 1813. Not only were the commons enclosed, but the irregular Tudor fields were swept away and a new compact farm with good-sized rectangular fields was laid out (fig. 4.5). A new house was built and new farm buildings provided. The house still stands, but the buildings have been altered considerably to suit modern needs. When Blaikie visited the farm in 1816, improvements to the buildings were still in progress. 'Much money has been expended on the improvement of this farm, with a very far distant prospect of return and a very large sum is still needed to complete the projected improvements.' Much of the land was poor, especially that recently enclosed from common. Some of the heavy land had been drained, but more work was needed. Seventy acres had been marled and this had improved it greatly. Many marl pits can still be seen near the present farm buildings. Blaikie's description shows how much work was needed on the part of the tenant to bring a farm up to the improved standards of the early nineteenth century, and if the land was poor or, like the newly enclosed common, had never been cultivated before, the process could be a long and wearying one. Blaikie reported that Hastings was very depressed by the work involved. 'Mr Hastings is a zealous and industrious tenant, but heart-broken by his present undertaking.' The fact that the price of wheat was falling at the end of the Napoleonic war must have made Hastings wonder whether it was all worth while. Blaikie added a footnote to his report. 'Mr Coke has promised to take him by the hand', although it is not clear what the landlord did to encourage this tenant.[29] The building work continued and by 1829 a total of £2,338 had been spent on building the new house and premises for the entirely remodelled farm. This is typical of the sort of sums spent on other farms on the estate. The farm covered 584 acres and, by 1850, the rent had risen to £606.

We have a detailed description of the farming of Longham Hall Farm written by John Hastings in answer to Bacon's questionnaire. Hastings described the soil as light, which meant that it was suitable for turnips and barley, but not wheat. The land was farmed on a four-course rotation. It had to be well farmed if it were to produce good yields and many of the newly introduced artificial fertilisers were used as well as the traditional ones. Seeds were not sown broadcast, but seed drills were used. Again crops were reaped and threshed mechanically.

Hastings were prepared to experiment with new seeds and techniques, but generally he returned to the old. 'I have grown experimentally almost every sort of wheat that I have seen.' He also carried out many experiments 'to ascertain the comparative value of artificial manures, but the results were not satisfactory enough to ascertain any'. He had also grown new grasses, but had gone back to the old. One modern development of which Hastings did approve was the growing of mangolds. He had grown twenty acres and thought they were 'more valuable than was generally supposed'. They were used as cattle and sheep feed and roots were often consumed on the fields by the animals so that the land was well manured. Hastings kept a flock of Southdown sheep, which he bought in the spring and sold when they were fat, breeding only a few himself. He kept no dairy cows but fattened about forty cattle in yards through the winter. As well as sixteen working horses there were two teams of Devon oxen for ploughing. The use of oxen for ploughing was fairly common in Norfolk throughout the nineteenth

[29] Holkham MSS, F. Blaikie, 'Report on the estates of T. W. Coke' (1816).

century. John Hastings thought there were still many improvements to be made in farming, and that production had not yet reached its highest level. 'This will develop as knowledge itself increases.'[30]

We see here a farm that, in spite of the poorness of much of its soil, was being run on progressive lines by a farmer flexible enough to try new methods and optimistic enough to believe that there was still much to be discovered and many improvements to be made. Gone is the depression found by Blaikie in 1816.

During the prosperous years for British farming in the middle of the nineteenth century, John Hastings, by now in his seventies, continued to farm progressively and try new methods. In common with many other Holkham tenants he was intensifying his livestock side as this was becoming the most profitable branch of farming with meat prices rising faster than cereals. In 1858, the estate spent £574 on new livestock sheds and in 1861 new loose boxes cost £174, but Hastings still felt he needed more. In 1863 the agent wrote, 'with the largely increased accommodation afforded by the new buildings and alterations upon your farm, I cannot think that you will find much difficulty in finding room for your stock'.

The use of fertilisers was reducing the necessity for following a four-course rotation, and in 1864 John Hastings asked if he could depart from the terms of his lease and grow barley after a wheat crop. As on other estate farms, permission was granted.

John Sutton Hastings died in 1869 at the age of seventy-nine. The fifty-three years of his tenancy had seen many changes. The low grain prices of the post Napoleonic War period had been followed by years of high prices and agricultural prosperity from the late 1830s. By the middle of the nineteenth century, the rise in the value of meat was outstripping that of grain and the evidence shows that John Hastings was astute enough to see these changes and to alter the balance between cereal and livestock production accordingly.

He was also following the contemporary trend towards growing more cereals with the aid of fertilisers at the expense of the root crop. This reduced the quantity of home produced cattle feed so he had to buy in cattle cake, which was a more effective way of fattening cattle. Both cereal and livestock production were therefore becoming more intensive. At the same time farms were becoming less self-sufficient. They relied on purchased fertilisers and animal feed to keep up this increased production,

[30] Bacon MS 4363, N.R.O.

and in time of high prices for both meat and grain this was very profitable. By 1869, agriculture had been prosperous for thirty years and John Hastings cannot have realised how soon depression would hit farming and what difficulties lay ahead for his heirs.

The situation at Longham was typical of that in many villages where almost the entire parish was owned by the Holkham estate and the land let to tenant farmers. There was no resident squire and the tenant had to take the initiative in many matters which would normally be the squire's responsibility. In 1859 John Hastings was instrumental in the building of Longham school. Much of the finance was provided by the Holkham estate and Hastings was allowed to dig brick earth from his farm for the bricks to build it. The school was to be run on the voluntary system and Lord Leicester was prepared to contribute a share based on the rateable value of his property.

In 1867 John Hastings persuaded Lord Leicester to rebuild Longham church, and he supervised the work while it was in process. Hastings himself built 'a double cottage for two married couples or four widows not under the age of 60 years'. He endowed them with six acres of land which he hoped would provide coal for the poor as well as for the upkeep of the cottages. His interest in parish affairs is recorded on his monument in Holkham church, which states that 'during more than half a century he was a steady friend and benefactor of this parish'.

After the death of John Sutton Hastings, his son, John Hastings, took over the farm (fig. 4.3). He continued to run it much as his father had done and was just as anxious that it should be improved. The large barns of the early nineteenth century in which wheat could be hand threshed with flails were obsolete by the 1870s and in 1875 the barn was converted into a dressing house where the wheat dressing machine could stand, a cutting house where the straw was cut and a cake house where feed could be kept. These alterations cost the estate £406, but it refused to build additions to the farm house which would have brought it up to the standards admired by farmers made wealthy by thirty years of high grain prices. The porch, bay windows and extra servants' quarters requested were not built, but a spacious dining room was.

John Hastings, junior, took over the farm just as grain prices began to fall. Livestock production at Longham had been intensified in the 1860s and so the farm was kept going, with the livestock subsidising the grain in the hope that things would improve; but the good days did not

4.3 John Hastings, tenant of Longham Hall Farm, 1869–84.

return and, as he continued to pay high rents from accumulated capital, his reserves dwindled. Cheap grain continued to come into England and in 1882, when John Hastings became ill, his son, another John, first gave notice to the estate that he intended to quit at Michaelmas and asked for a loan to keep him going until then. Lord Leicester, who was faced with demands for rent reductions from many tenants, said he could not afford such a loan, but neither did he want any more farms in hand and so Hastings was persuaded to stay on at the farm. In December 1883, Lord Leicester allowed the rent to stand over until the following February. In 1884 John Hastings died and his son was left with the

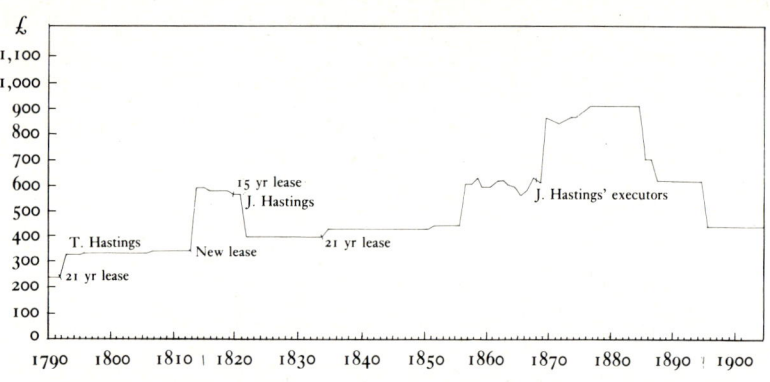

4.4 Rents on Longham Farm.

difficult task of trying to make the farm pay. The estate agreed to lend £500 for two years at 5% as well as providing a mortgage on some family property in the neighbouring village of Gressenhall. In 1885 the rent at Longham was finally drastically reduced from £1013 to £700 (fig. 4.4). The tenancy became a yearly one and the large reduction was only granted because 'the family had been tenants so long'. In fact similar reductions were being made on most of the estate farms.

John Hastings could not even pay this rent and in 1887 he was £877 in arrears and again handed in notice. The agent wrote in reply, 'His lordship is extremely sorry to lose such an old and good tenant, but he feels it would be unfair to the rest of the tenantry were he to give further special remission in your case. He wishes me to say that he must accept your notice to give up your occupation next Michaelmas.' However, new tenants were not easy to find in these years of depression and eventually John Hastings was asked to stay on after a further rent reduction to £600, plus £21 for the shooting. In March 1888, the agent was relieved to hear that 'after mature consideration you see your way to continue in the above occupation'.[31]

John Hastings no longer possessed the capital to make the farm pay, even in the slightly improved conditions of the late 1880s. Capital had drained away in the 1870s, when the family had optimistically thought that the depression would not last. In 1891 notice was handed in for the third time. The estate was again sorry at the prospect of his leaving, but this time they thought someone was interested in taking on the farm,

[31] Holkham MSS, letter books.

and John Hastings was warned that the prospective tenant might come and view it. Nothing came of this and in August 1891 negotiations with Hastings resulted in his staying at Longham. The rent was to stay the same, but the estate was to carry out certain repairs and would build a new field yard for cattle and a turnip house in the southern corner of the farm. This work was carried out at a cost of £184.

The 1890s were as bad for the farmers as the 1870s. In 1892, 1893, 1895 and 1896 there were droughts which affected livestock even more seriously than cereals. In 1895, Hastings again threatened to quit, but agreed to stay until 1897 when his rent was reduced to £477. In 1896 and 1897 he was allowed a rebate of £42 on this amount. After this the rent of £479 was regularly paid until John Hastings' death in 1907, when his widow finally left Longham. It seems that with the rent lowered by about 60% from its 1885 peak it was possible to keep the farm going. The sale catalogue for the farm sale of 1907 shows that a recent venture on the farm had been the breeding of Hackney carriage horses and there was some good breeding stock for sale.[32] It is quite possible that this type of concern was more profitable than the more traditional farming enterprises.

The story of John Hastings shows the tragedy of the agricultural depression as it affected one man, and it can be repeated all over the Holkham estate as well as all over eastern England. The new farm built at the time of the enclosure act was continually modified to suit new agricultural practice, but the depression at the end of the period could only be weathered by those with capital from outside farming. New men from trade and industry were taking farms and by introducing a great deal of mechanisation and often farming more than one farm they were able to get a reasonable return on their investment. Farming had to become more commercial if it were to survive in the twentieth century, and a new type of man was replacing those who, like the Hastings, had farmed successfully for at least the previous two hundred years.

This survey of the Holkham tenantry in general, with a more detailed description of some farmers, shows that, particularly in the early and middle years of the nineteenth century, the tenantry contained many outstanding men. It has been much easier to find information about their work than about that of the less progressive farmers. They expected the estate to provide adequate farms and buildings, but other than this they

[32] Farm sales catalogues as in note 17.

needed little encouragement or advice from the estate on farming practice.

These are the men quoted by contemporary commentators such as Arthur Young and Noverre Bacon, and also the ones that modern agricultural historians see as being the backbone of the 'agricultural revolution'. However, the majority of farmers did not fall into this unusual class. Instead they were intelligent people willing to learn and experiment and it is here that the influence of a progressive estate could be most valuable. The example of the home farm and the advice of the agent as well as the statutory husbandry clauses in leases were all important tools in the hands of the landlord. Long established families of practical farmers probably had little contact with agricultural theory except through the annual sheep shearings at Holkham; yet Bacon's report shows that they experimented with new crops and had great faith in the value of science to agriculture. They did not show the conservatism and opposition to new techniques that contemporaries often associated with long established farming families.

Nineteenth-century agriculture in the progressive and much publicised area of north-west Norfolk was therefore headed by a small group of highly intensive and progressive tenant farmers backed up by a well run estate and a generous landlord. This situation must have been an ideal one for the development of 'high farming'. But even this could only delay and not prevent the bankruptcies and distress caused by the late-nineteenth-century agricultural depression, which is shown so vividly in the affairs of John Hastings.

The farms

Thomas William Coke relied heavily on the intelligence and adaptability of his tenants to create the improved agriculture for which he became famous. They in their turn needed his capital to enclose their fields and to build the premises needed for their intensive methods. Although open field bye-laws were not inflexible, experimentation was far more difficult in open than in enclosed fields and so enclosure was almost an essential prerequisite of intensive farming. The progressive farmer would want to pasture his livestock either on improved permanent grass or leys sown with good artificial grasses as part of a rotation, rather than on poor, often over-stocked commons. Enclosed farms commanded a higher rent, often double that for open field strips, and so the rearrangement of the open fields and commons in a parish into compact individual holdings was one of the simplest ways for the landlord to increase his income from the estate. Chambers and Mingay calculated that the average cost of enclosure in the late eighteenth century was about 28 shillings an acre. The gross return on landlords' investment was, on average, between 15% and 20%, but much higher where waste land was enclosed. 'Enclosure was thus by far the most profitable use of capital in connection with the land'.[33]

This lucrative form of investment was only open to Thomas William Coke to a very limited extent. Surveys show that most of the open fields on the Holkham estate had been enclosed by 1780. Strips did still exist at Kempstone and Billingford, but as they were held in blocks by individual tenants, they were not farmed as such. More open areas of heath, common and sheep walks, where grazing rights were shared by tenants, did survive. Between 1806 and 1816 the estate spent over £7,000 on its share of the cost of enclosures and most of this was in parishes where common land rather than strip fields was being fenced. Coke's share in the cost of the enclosure of commons at Sparham and Billingford was £1,294. Between 1811 and 1814, £2,184 was spent at Wells and Warham. Enclosure of commons also took place at Fulmodeston, Longham, Kempstone and Mileham. Enclosure awards for Ashill (1786), Billingford (1806 and 1864), Bintry (1795), the Burnhams (1821), South Creake (1856), Elmham (1830), Fulmodeston (1808), Lexham (1795), Longham (1814), Sparham (1809), and Wells and Warham (1811) are held at County Hall in Norwich. The existence of an enclosure act does not necessarily mean that there had been little enclosure in a parish before. It may well simply represent an attempt to rationalise and legalise an already existing situation. Once approval for enclosure had been given, farms could be laid out afresh. A new farm was created at Dunton as a result of enclosure, but usually the land was rearranged among existing farms.

Figure 4.5 shows the parish of Longham before and after enclosure. The work which took place in 1816 involved not only the enclosure of two commons and the reduction of the area of waste land in the north of the parish but also the rationalisation of the entire field layout. The

---

[33] J. D. Chambers and G. E Mingay, *The Agricultural Revolution, 1750–1880* (London, 1966), p. 84.

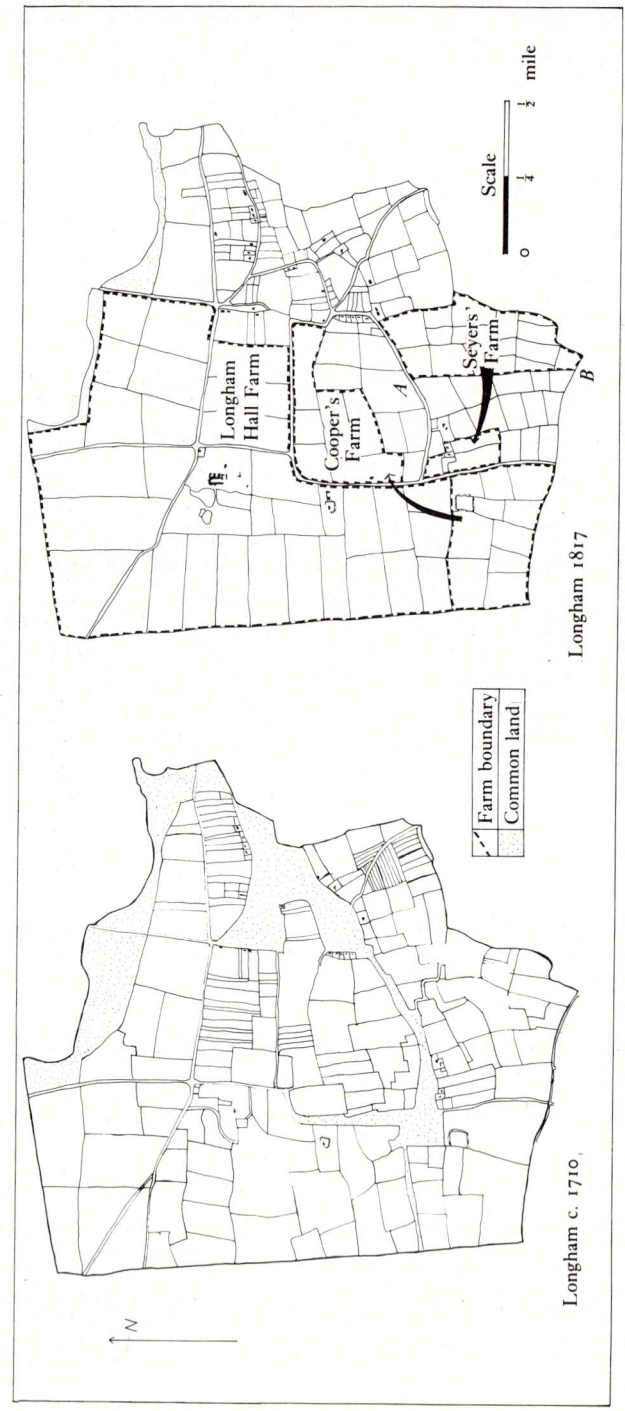

4.5 Longham before and after enclosure.

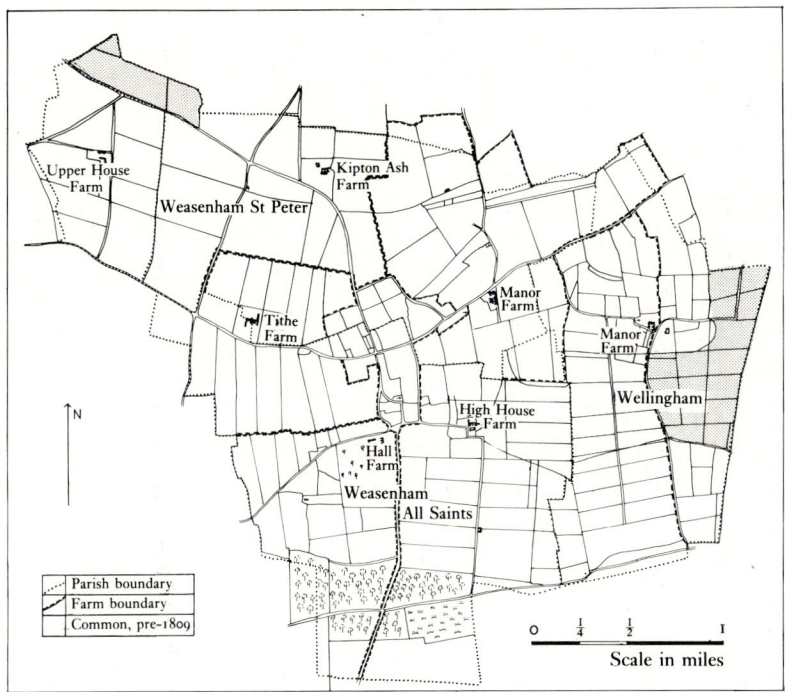

4.6 Weasenham farms, c. 1850.

strips that existed in 1710 were all removed. The fields of Longham Hall Farm to the west of the house were completely relaid. The straight boundary A–B in 1817 represents the boundary between Coke's and the Hargreaves' estate.

The commons in Wellingham and the two Weasenhams were enclosed in 1809 at a cost of £1,444 (fig. 4.6). As at Longham, this was accompanied by a reorganisation of fields. Manor Farm, Wellingham, became the most regular farm in the three parishes with a straight road through the centre of its fields, so that there was access to nearly all of them from a good hard road. The audit books show that, in 1796, 1,272 acres of intermingled holdings were bought at Weasenham by the estate. This helped towards the creation of consolidated farms and ended the strip system of cultivation there. As a result of these purchases and enclosure, it was possible to create well planned farms with large regular fields with good access from a road, as at Tithe Farm and High House Farm.

Although there was common land at Tittleshall in the sixteenth

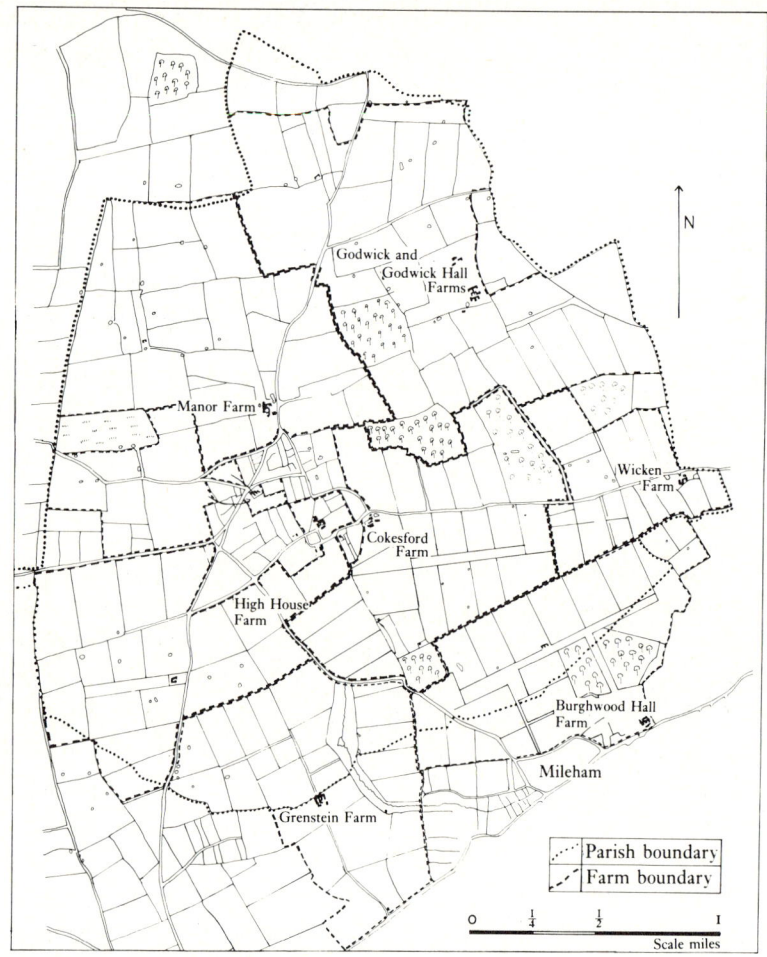

4.7 Tittleshall farms, c. 1850.

century, this had all gone by the nineteenth century and no parliamentary enclosure took place. There was an act for Mileham in 1814 and it was at this date that Grenstein Farm and Burghwood Hall Farm, both partly in Mileham, were reorganised (fig. 4.7). Again all the large rectangular fields can be reached from good roads. The area of marshy land on Grenstein Farm was reduced by drainage to a small strip beside the stream. Cokesford Farm was also newly planned sometime before 1850, but the layout of the other Tittleshall farms is more confused. The fields are large, but not always regular, which suggests the amalgamation of existing fields rather than a completely new system.

Although there was not a heavy expenditure on enclosure at Holkham in the Napoleonic War period, the work that was done was thorough and efficient. The farms that were remodelled were convenient to work and attracted a far higher rent than before.

All types of land were represented on the estate and often marling of light soils and draining of heavy ones was carried out on the same farm. While the improvement of buildings was the responsibility of the landlord, the improvement of the soils seems to have been carried out at the tenant's expense. Where the estate did undertake drainage they charged a 5% interest on the cost of work done as a surcharge on the annual rent. Similarly, little was spent by the estate on fencing after enclosure, although Dr Parker has found many references for the earlier period to payments by the estate to tenants for fencing.[34]

The drainage of the coastal marshes was undertaken by the Cokes during two specific periods, first in the 1720s and secondly in the 1850s. As a result of embanking and ditching between 1720 and 1722, the coastline to the west of Lady Ann's Drive was pushed seawards to roughly the present high-tide line, while to the east further work remained to be done and a large area of marsh between Holkham and Wells was not reclaimed until 1857–9. Once the necessary ditches and banks had been built and a new coastline created, a belt of conifers was planted to help stabilise the sands and by 1860 the coastline was much as it is today.

The produce of the enclosed, drained and marled land was processed, from wheat sheaf to grain, straw and chaff, or, in the case of root crops, fed through the cattle to make meat and manure, in the farm buildings, and the condition of his farm buildings was of prime importance to the farmer. 'To farm successfully with defective and ill-arranged buildings is no more practical than to manufacture profitably in scattered ill-arranged workshops in place of one harmoniously contrived, completely fitted mill.'[35] So wrote John Bailey Denton in 1863 and, although the development of industrial buildings has been increasingly studied in recent years, farm buildings have received little attention. However, there are several ways in which the study of farms can help in understanding changes of agricultural practice and the part played by

[34] R. A. C. Parker, *Coke of Norfolk, a Financial and Agricultural Study, 1707–1842* (Oxford, 1975), pp. 40–2, 84–8 and 86–100.
[35] J. B. Denton, *The Farm Homesteads of England* (London, 1863).

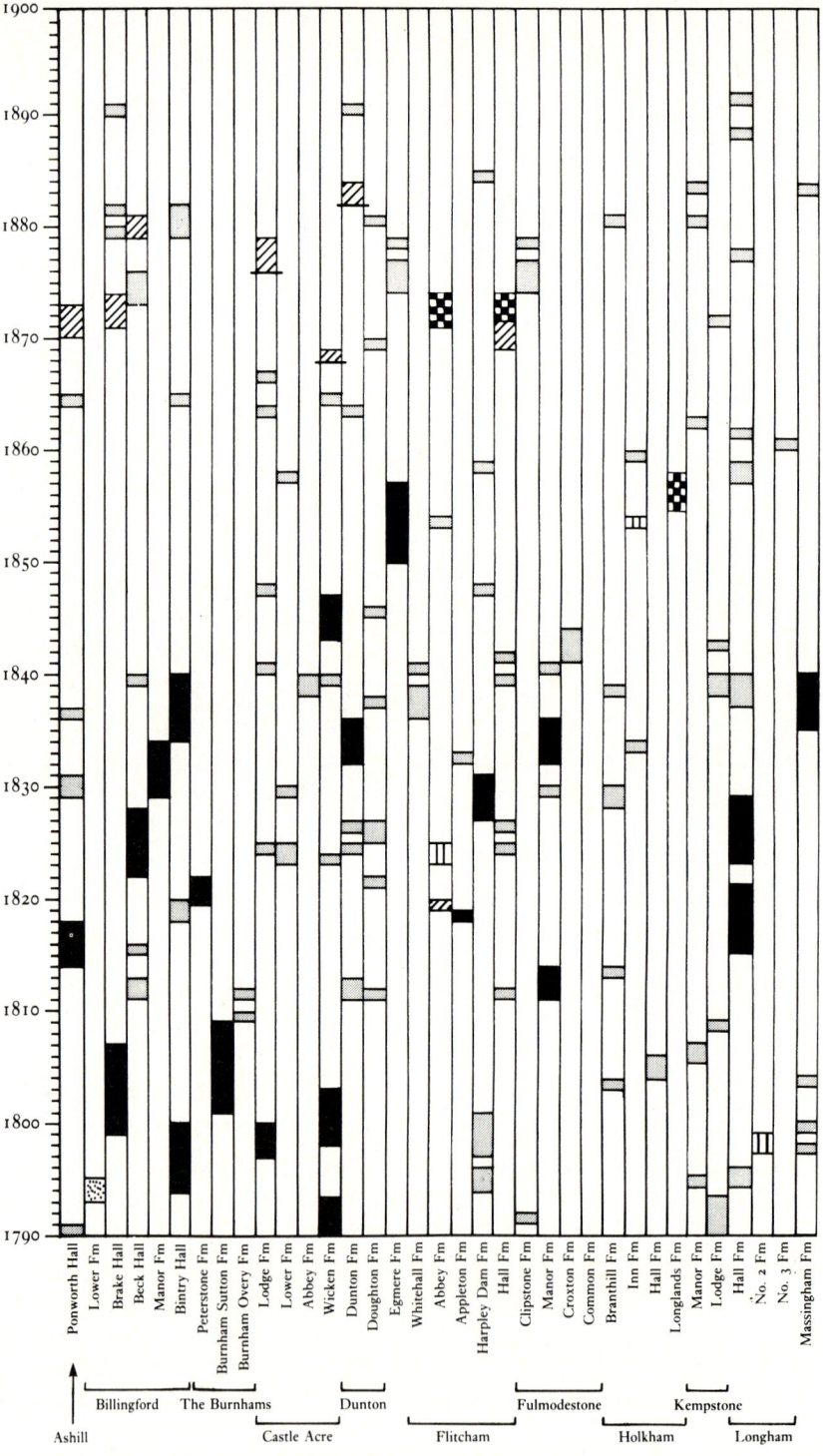

4.8 Types of improvement work undertaken on the Holkham estates, 1790–1900.
■ New houses and premises; ▩ new implement sheds; ▨ new cattle sheds;
▥ new house; ▢ new barn and granary; ⊢⊣ year of new lease.

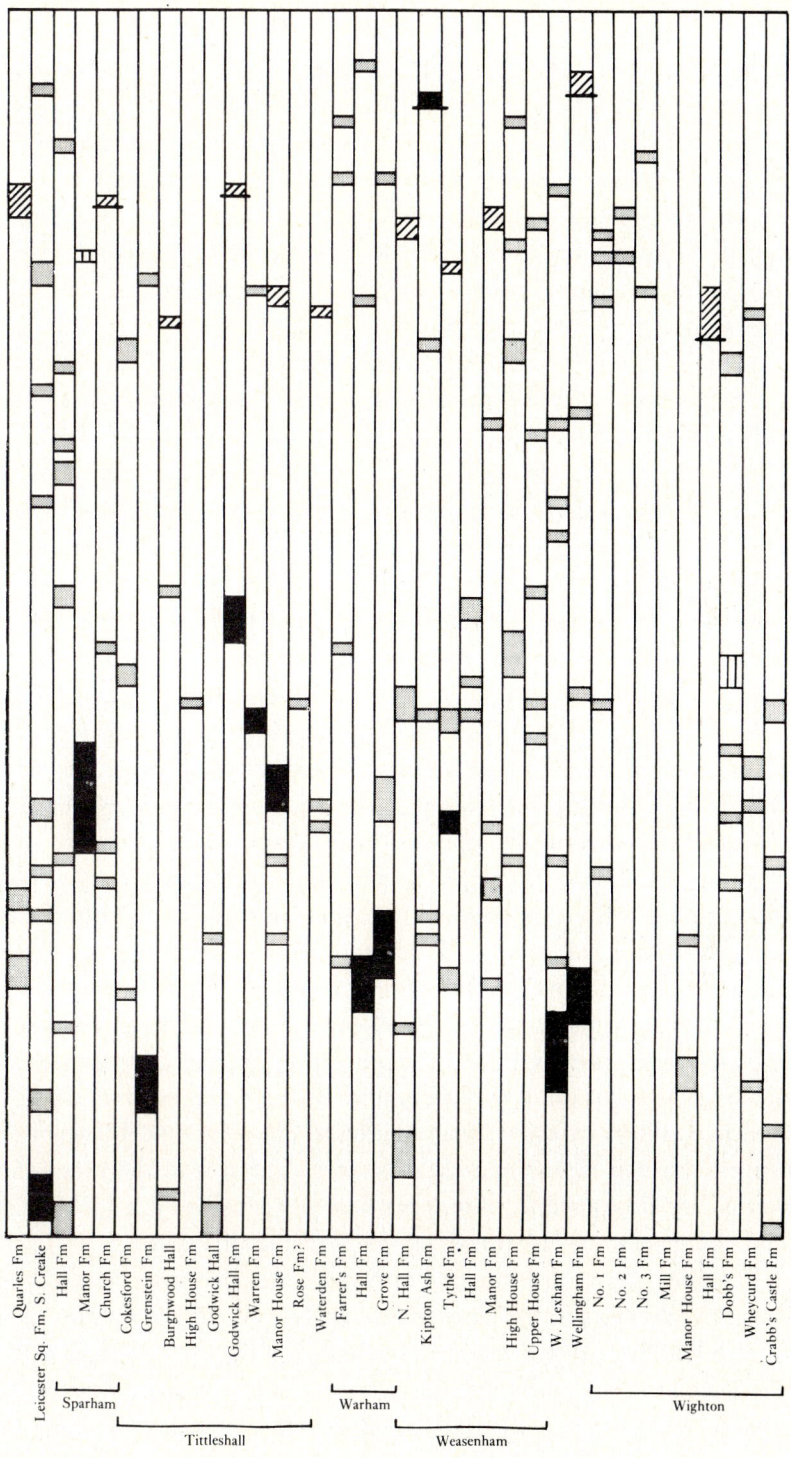

the landlord in improving farming techniques. In his book on the history of farm buildings, Nigel Harvey takes up Bailey Denton's theme when he says that the study of farm buildings is important because 'they are the central storage depots and processing shops of the farm they serve and on their efficiency depends much of the efficiency of the farming system. They are interesting because they record with peculiar clarity many of the technical and economic changes which have come to the farming industry in recent centuries.'[36]

However, the type of farm building erected is not only an indicator of the state of technical progress reached at a particular date; the optimism or doubts and fears of the farmer are also reflected. We have already seen that in the 1840s Holkham farmers felt that production could only increase as more intensive methods were introduced. They were full of optimism and ideas for improvement to their premises. However, by the 1880s, this had all gone. Changes were the result of depression. New types of enterprise were being tackled and so a limited amount of new building was required simply to enable the tenant to stay on. Through studying the farm buildings themselves it is possible to determine exactly on what the money was spent. If it was providing for the methods of farming that were to remain profitable after the 1870s then there is no reason to assume that farming was over-capitalised.

Much of the fame of the Holkham estate came from its high investment in farm building and during the nineteenth century at least £700,000 was spent on improving the seventy or so farms. For this reason Holkham is an ideal estate on which to study the development of farm building design and its effectiveness as an aid to improved agriculture. Plans of many of the farms survive. Nearly all the farms can be located and substantial parts of the nineteenth-century farm buildings are still standing. Most of the farms are unusually large and so were likely to need particularly extensive farm buildings. Plans for model farms were being published throughout the first three quarters of the nineteenth century and it is possible to compare what was actually built at Holkham with the theoretical farmsteads of the agricultural journals.

The audit books at Holkham give much detailed information from which to start the study of farm buildings. Not only is the amount spent on each building project recorded, but details of the work done are given. Fig. 4.8 shows in a simplified form the types of work undertaken. No

[36] N. Harvey, *A History of Farm Buildings in England and Wales* (Newton Abbot, 1970).

4.9 The Great Barn at Holkham.

expenditure of under £100 has been shown as these smaller sums could not have constituted a major improvement. However, the audit books do not include all expenditure. In some cases the sum recorded seems a realistic one, while in others it appears far too low. Some improvements which we know of from other sources, such as date stones, are not recorded at all. For instance, the building of the Great Barn at Holkham (fig. 4.9) is not mentioned in the estate records. Despite these problems, the figures do indicate the types of improvement being undertaken at Holkham. They give the minimum figure for expenditure and, even if they cannot be used in absolute comparison with those of other estates, they can be considered relative to each other. For instance, periods of high and low expenditure at Holkham can be isolated. The result is a fairly accurate picture of the types of improvement carried out on the Holkham farms over 110 years covering both periods of agricultural boom and depression.

It is very difficult to find out what estate farms looked like at the end of the eighteenth century. Many were considerably altered in the hundred years that followed and it was usually these improvements rather than the original buildings that interested commentators. It is very fortunate that the earliest description of the Holkham farms was written in 1790. This means that it is possible to assess the state of the farm buildings at the date this study commences. Among the estate records

4.10 A farm at Great Massingham, c. 1800.

is a book entitled 'Holkham estate valuation of sundry farms, estimated progressively as leases expire and are renewed from Michaelmas, 1789'. This describes nineteen of the farms sometime between 1789 and 1793. Although there is not always much detail, there is enough information to reconstruct the type of farm buildings that were usual. There is also a similar survey and valuation of the Warham farms, written probably between 1780 and 1790 soon after they were purchased from the Turner estate. The authorship of the survey of 'Sundry farms' is uncertain, although it includes a description of Great Massingham Farm signed by Nathaniel Kent. The Warham survey is definitely by Kent and, as the style is similar throughout both, it is probable that they are both his work. Altogether twenty-four farms are described. Only one had fewer than two barns. Seventeen had two barns on the home premises, three had three and two had four. All the farms had one stable and many had more than one. Only two did not have a cart house. However, livestock accommodation was less common. There is no mention of cattle sheds, although many of the farms had cow and calf houses and most had pig cots. One farm had a smith's and a carpenter's shop.

The only other evidence for individual farm buildings in Norfolk in this early part of the period is contained in a survey of the Cholmondesley estates made by Samuel Hill in about 1800 and now at Houghton Hall.

This survey gives the name of the tenant, the rent and the acreage of his farm. More important for the purposes of this study are the small watercolours of each farm which illustrate the survey. William Bank's farm in Great Massingham (fig. 4.10) is a typical picture from this survey. It shows an unplanned farm. A barn and a waggon lodge with a granary above and possibly a stable abutting on to it have been built along one side of a yard, while two other outbuildings, one possibly a piggery, have been built in front of them. The whole layout seems very cramped, but this is similar on the other farms illustrated. As in the Holkham descriptions, all eleven of the Houghton farms have barns near the house. Only three have waggon lodges and three have stables. There is very little livestock accommodation. A few small huts must have been either dog kennels, pigsties or poultry houses, but no cattle sheds can be seen. This rather haphazard arrangement of buildings was criticised by many early writers on farmstead design. In 1779 Lord Kaimes wrote that barns and offices were set down straggling and confused, as if by accident; 'here a barn and there a stable'. Pitt and Waistell also noted these shortcomings.[37] In his Staffordshire survey Peters found the more muddled layouts were not generally replaced by a more economical grouping until after 1815.[38]

Nathaniel Kent's survey of Norfolk for the Board of Agriculture was published in 1796. He wrote, 'Farm buildings in this county are upon a very respectable footing, but in my opinion they are upon too large a scale.'[39] Kent must here be referring to the large west Norfolk farms and probably especially to those with which he was familiar on the Holkham estates. The small freeholders of east Norfolk could not afford large buildings. He was very concerned about cottage conditions and thought that, rather than squandering money on grand houses and buildings, there should be more improvements in labourers' housing. A general rule which he thought should be observed when new buildings were put up was that nothing should be built that was not really useful. Buildings should be on a 'small compact scale, and as much as possible upon squares or parallelograms not in angles or notches'.[40] In his book,

---

[37] C. Waistell, *Designs for Agricultural Buildings* (London, 1827).
[38] J. E. C. Peters, *The Development of Farm Buildings in East Lowland Staffordshire* (Manchester, 1969), p. 51.
[39] N. Kent, *General Survey of the Agriculture of the County of Norfolk* (London, 1796), p. 110.
[40] *Ibid.*, p. 113.

Hints to Gentlemen of Landed Property, Kent explains in more detail what buildings he thought were necessary.[41] These should include,

> besides a comfortable and convenient house, good accommodation for livestock, such as stables, cow sheds, calves' pens and pig cots. These may be frequently supplied by lean-to's, or otherwise built at moderate expense; but barns, which are very expensive, may often be contracted, and much unnecessary charge saved. What should be most recommended is stacking, which ought to be done much more than it is.

We see here that as early as 1776 the pre-eminence of the barn was already being challenged, and the importance of livestock accommodation, which was to be increasingly recognised throughout the nineteenth century, was being stressed. In Norfolk, however, the barn remained a very large building, as Norfolk farmers could not be persuaded to give up their traditional practice of keeping most of their unthreshed grain in a barn rather than stacking it in a yard. The size of a barn can never be taken as an indication of the quantity of grain cropped. Instead it is governed by agricultural traditions.

The great flood of agricultural literature which was published from the last quarter of the eighteenth century contained much advice on the planning and construction of farm buildings. According to Nigel Harvey the first imaginary model farmstead was published by Arthur Young in 1770, and the first plan of a named farmstead which could be used by others as a model appeared in 1783.[42] As agricultural practice improved, so the farmer demanded more of his farmstead. As more British farmland came under the control of large landowners who let to tenant farmers, the reponsibility for providing the buildings fell more and more on the gentry and aristocracy, many of whom were not practising farmers. Some, such as the Cokes and the Dukes of Bedford, became famous for their interest in improved buildings, while others, such as the Dukes of Marlborough, were better known for their neglect.[43]

The progressive farmer expected his farmstead to perform two main functions. Firstly, it must help conserve good quality manure that was produced by his livestock and which could then be spread on the land to promote a heavy grain crop. This was especially important during the years of high grain prices in the Napoleonic Wars. Secondly, as better strains of cattle were reared and a growing population demanded more

---

[41] N. Kent, *Hints to Gentlemen of Landed Property* (London, 1775), p. 152.
[42] Harvey, *History of Farm Buildings*, p. 111.
[43] Caird, *English Agriculture*, pp. 27–8.

meat, good housing for more livestock was also required. Arthur Young complained in the 1770s that this aspect was not yet as fully appreciated as it should be. He said that there was no other country in Europe where there was so little housing for cows. 'We are told that in France not a quadruped is abroad.'[44] However, by the end of the century, the value of sheltering cattle was becoming appreciated. A third consideration which was not so important in this period of cheap labour was the arrangement of the buildings to allow for efficient movement of foodstuffs, animals and products for market. The three main components of the farmstead were the barn, the livestock sheds and the manure-collecting yards. In the better planned farms, much consideration was given to the arrangement of these buildings to reduce the amount of cartage involved. The needs of progressive agriculture were the same throughout the country and, although differences might occur in detail according to soil variations and accessibility to urban markets, the fundamental principles of design were the same everywhere. This meant that model plans published in the *Annals of Agriculture* and elsewhere could provide useful guidance to landlowners throughout Britain. In agriculture as in industry, building design was becoming standardised and regional differences were disappearing.

Many of the early commentators, especially the authors of the various county surveys, noted many farmers whose buildings seemed to have been built 'at random, without order or method, whose buildings had accumulated over the generations'.[45] This is the type shown in the illustrations in the Cholmondeley estate survey. However, for those who wished to improve their buildings, there were plenty of model plans to help them, and Marshall summarised the generally accepted principles of farm design in his book, *The Landed Property of England*, published in 1804.[46] Firstly, the barns, stables and granary should be readily seen from the farm house. Secondly, the farm buildings should be in the form of a rectangle, enclosing a yard which could either be used as fold for cattle or, where cattle were usually stalled, simply as a receptacle for dung. Marshall thought that the angles in the corners of a square yard were too sharp and so could not be easily mucked out. He suggested that it would be better if the building formed a polygon, 'although a complete

---

[44] A. Young, 'Tour of Norfolk', *Annals of Agriculture*, vol. 3 (1782), p. 58.
[45] W. Pitt, 'Buildings of a farm', *Annals of Agriculture*, vol. 9 (1788), p. 400.
[46] W. Marshall, *The Landed Property of England* (1804), p. 160.

set of buildings has not yet been erected on such a plan'. Certainly none were erected on the Holkham estate.

Marshall described some sheds of 'a very advanced design' which he said were in general use in the progressive area around Blofield.

> Some of their bullock sheds are large expensive buildings. Mr Batchelor has a very good one. It consists of a central building 36 feet long, 19 feet wide and about 11 feet high to the eaves, with a pair of wide folding doors at each end, and with a lean-to on each side extending the whole length of the building and about 11 feet wide. The centre building is the turnip house, the lean-tos are the sheds for the bullocks, which stand with their heads in the turnip house, from which they are parted by a range of mangers only...This shed holds 20 bullocks, 10 on each side, fastened by the neck with chains, swivels and rings, playing freely upon posts seven feet high. At each corner of the turnip house is a triangular shaped bin for the topped and tailed turnips. In autumn the entire building is sometimes used as a temporary barn and in the summer, the central part is an excellent waggon shed.[47]

Plans published in the *Annals of Agriculture* in 1796 showed buildings built in a semicircle behind a farm house. Sometimes they were joined together, while in other plans they were entirely separate.[48] Circular ox-stalls were built at Saxham in Suffolk, and in 1798 the *Annals of Agriculture* commented, 'The idea is a very useful one and merits preserving',[49] but these sentiments were not shared by the Holkham estate and they were never built there. The plans published by Loudan in 1812 were mostly more ornamental than practical.[50] His suggestions include a plan of a round house surrounded by a moat which was to provide water power for working threshing machinery.

By the post Napoleonic War period the rectangular plan was generally accepted but many variations of layout within it were possible. An unusual adaptation was used on the Stafford estates in Sutherland, Shropshire and Staffordshire, where many new farms were built between 1813 and 1820. Most of these new farm plans incorporated a paved way for waggons inside the rectangle enclosed by the buildings.[51] The fold yards were walled off from the paved way and occupied the central part of the enclosure. This made it much easier to move both animal feed

---

[47] W. Marshall, *Rural Economy of Norfolk*, 2 vols. (London, 1787), vol. 2, pp. 274–5.
[48] A. Crooker, 'An essay on farm houses and their appendant offices', *Communications to the Board of Agriculture on Farm Buildings* (London, 1796), pp. 66–71.
[49] 'Circular ox stalls built by the late Hutcheson Mure Esq., at Saxhum, Suffolk', *Annals of Agriculture*, vol. 20 (1798), p. 502.
[50] J. C. Loudan, *Observations on Laying Out Farms in the Scotch Style adapted for England* (London, 1812).
[51] James Loch, *Improvements on the Stafford Estates* (London, 1820), p. 98.

The tenant farmer and his farm

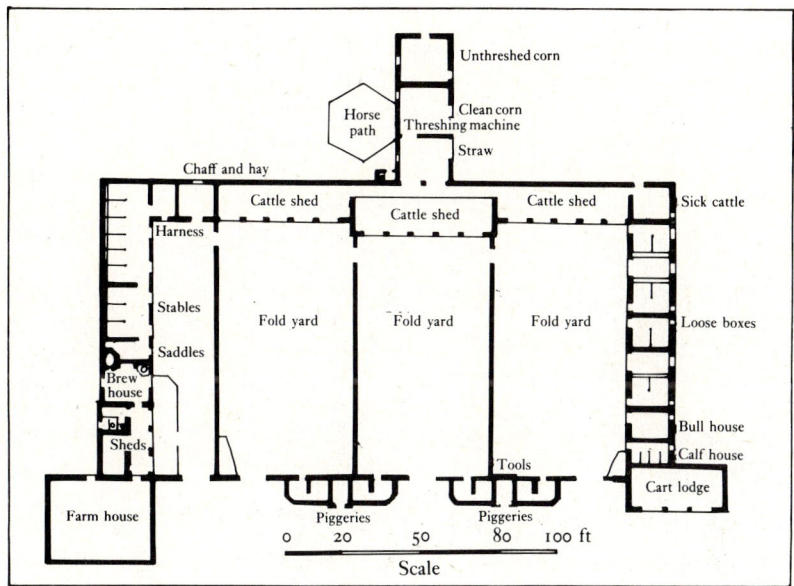

4.11 Model farm plan by Waistell (1827).

and goods for the market within the enclosed area. Where the more conventional layout is used, as at Holkham, movement of feed and goods was around the outside of the buildings rather than through the interior yard area. The more usual types of farm improvements at Holkham are similar to those published by Waistell.[52] Perhaps two of the most interesting plans in his book are those of Caterham Farm, Surrey, before and after improvement. The earlier plan shows scattered buildings partly enclosing a 'field' yard. These include four large barns, stables, cart sheds and a small cattle shed. This is probably very similar to some of the Holkham farms visited by Kent in the 1790s, and also those on the Cholmondeley estates at that date. The improvements at Caterham involved the demolition of one barn and the building of new stables and cattle sheds. The gaps around the old 'field yard' were filled in and the now completely enclosed area divided into two fold yards, a stable court and a kitchen court adjacent to the house. The resulting irregular quadrilateral plan is similar to that of some of the Holkham farms, which suggests that on those farms improvements incorporated old premises.

One of Waistell's model plans is produced here (fig. 4.11) as an

[52] Waistell, *Designs for Agricultural Buildings*, plates 11 and 12.

4.12 Round house at Wheycurd Farm, Wighton.

example of the type of farmstead aimed at by the 1820s. The yards were now subdivided to allow for the different feeding of various types and ages of stock. The barn was no longer in such a dominating position and the provision of a horse path within a round house attached to a barn for working barn machinery was often allowed for in the later plans. Very few horse paths seem to have been built at Holkham. None are mentioned in the audit or letter books. One is shown in Bacon's plan of the Great Barns, drawn in the 1840s (fig. 4.21). One survives at Wheycurd Farm, Wighton (fig. 4.12) and until a few years ago there was one at West Lexham. These could date from the early nineteenth century. Young mentions a threshing machine at Kempstone.[53] As labour was cheaper in Norfolk than elsewhere, the incentive to mechanise was not so great.

Between 1790 and 1900 nearly all the farms on the estate went through one major phase of improvement and many through two. These phases were mainly concentrated between the years 1790–1840, and 1868–90, and the type of work carried out in each phase is different.

Between 1790 and 1820 about thirty major rebuilding projects were undertaken by the Holkham estate, many taking several years to complete (fig. 4.8). Fifteen of these involved the complete rebuilding of farm houses and premises at costs varying from £1,500 to £3,500. We must now look at some of these developments in detail to see exactly what improvements were taking place and how far they met the needs of a progressive tenantry. These rebuildings had much in common and the premises at Waterden, Grenstein and Panworth Hall are typical and remain almost unaltered.

Those at Waterden are the earliest set of 'model' buildings to survive as a whole (fig. 4.13 and fig. 4.14). The first description of them was written by Arthur Young in the *Annals of Agriculture* for 1784. Having praised Thomas William Coke for his new farm buildings, Arthur Young wrote, 'Nothing in this style can exceed the buildings that Mr Coke has raised at Waterden. Every convenience to be imagined is thought of, and the offices so perfectly well arranged as to answer the great object to prevent waste and save labour.'[54] Blaikie was equally impressed in 1816 and described Waterden as 'perhaps the finest set of farm premises in

---

[53] A. Young, *A General view of the Agriculture of the County of Norfolk* (London, 1804), p. 20.
[54] A. Young, 'A tour of Norfolk', *Annals of Agriculture* (1784).

144 A great estate at work

4.13 Waterden farm premises from the north-east.

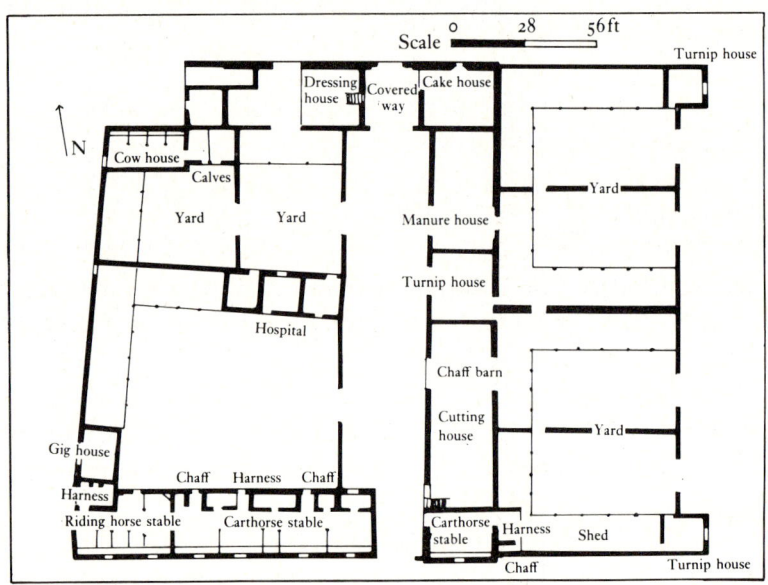

4.14 Plan of Waterden Farm.

Great Britain'.[55] Today it is still one of the most imposing groups of Holkham estate buildings, dominated by two large barns linked by a covered way. The buildings described by Keary in 1851 were similar in layout and capacity to those that survive, but date stones indicate that the flint and brick cattle yards in the foreground of fig. 4.13 and a smithy, not shown, were rebuilt in 1871, when £721 was spent by the estate at Waterden.

[55] Holkham MSS, F. Blaikie, 'Report on the estates of T. W. Coke' (1816).

The tenant farmer and his farm

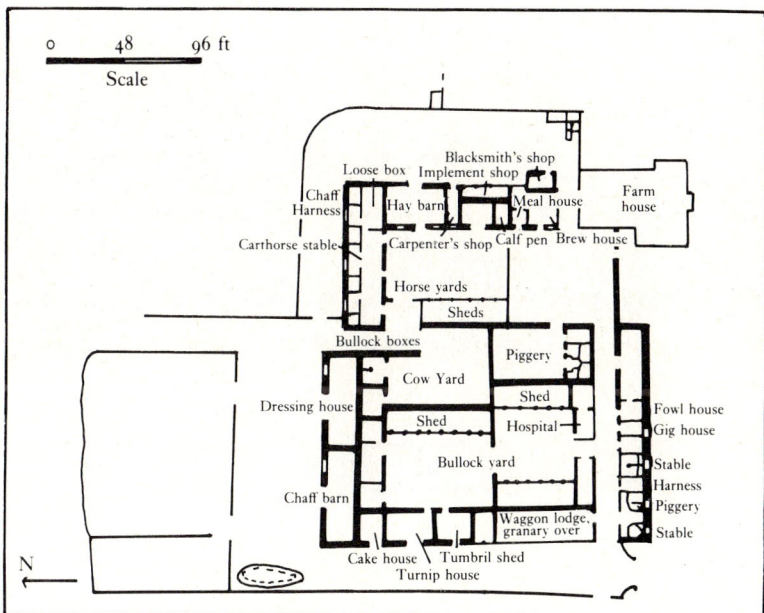

4.15 Plan of Grenstein farm. Tittleshall.

Grenstein Farm was rebuilt about 1810 and Blaikie describes the farm as having extensive buildings: 'The general arrangement is good, better than many on the estate. The farm is new modelled at great expense. How great a pleasure there is in looking over this beautiful and well arranged farm.' Very little money was spent on the farm during the next fifty years, although some new brick and flint sheds were built in 1875. A plan of the farm was drawn in 1880, when a few minor alterations were carried out, but basically the 1880 plan, shown in fig. 4.15, is that of the 1810 farm, and is also the same as the farm which stands today. Except for the yards and sheds within the main rectangular layout, which are the 1875 flint and brick additions, the farm is built of brick. The plan is similar to those produced by improvers such as Waistell and it consists of a thoughtfully laid-out, symmetrical set of buildings, with accommodation for both grain and cattle. The fact that it is so symmetrical suggests that no attempt was made to incorporate the old buildings, but that a completely new start was made. Keary described these premises in 1851: 'The premises are extremely well situated for the occupation of the farm. There are two very large barns, a cart-horse stable for 16 horses, a hay house, cow house, piggeries, three yards and

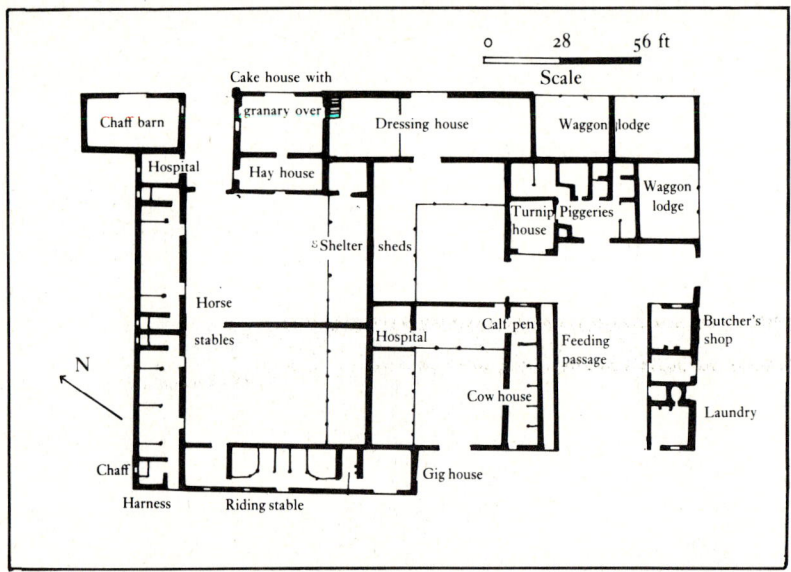

4.16 Plan of Panworth Hall Farm. Ashill.

open sheds for grazing cattle, a waggon lodge with granary over, and a cake house.' It is interesting that a well equipped farm in the early nineteenth century still required two large barns. At the date of the building of these premises, barn space was still very important to the Norfolk farmer. As Arthur Young said, 'The farmers are however generally advocates, not only of barns, but of great barns.'[56]

The premises at Panworth Hall, Ashill, were rebuilt about ten years later than those at Grenstein, but the principles behind the arrangement of the building was very similar. Between 1813 and 1818, £2,006 was spent at Ashill. The description given by Keary is that of the farm shown in the plan prior to alterations in the early 1870s (fig. 4.16).

> The farm contains a high percentage of inferior land and the lands most difficult to work are those furthest from home. Much has been drained by the present tenant, but much remains to be done. It is well farmed on the four course system with beans rather than turnips sometimes planted on the heavy land. The house is brick faced with flint and covered with blue pantiles. It was entirely reroofed recently. It is a pity that slates were only used on the lean-to. The house has two good sitting rooms, kitchens, dairies, five bedrooms and servants' rooms. There is a good thatched barn, a cart horse stable for 16 horses and two yards and sheds adjoining for the same animals, a bullock yard and sheds for 20 cattle, and an enclosed house for tying up 10 or 12, a cow house for six

[56] Young, *The Agriculture of Norfolk*, p. 20.

to eight cows, and piggeries. Also two waggon lodges with granaries over one of them, a riding horse stable and a gig house. Many of the roofs are bad. Detached and at a short distance is a barn built of mud, bricks, wood and thatch. It is an old building and in tolerable repair. Also a bullock yard and shed with a pantile roof, which is in want of repair. Also a field barn with a pantile roof and bullock yard and sheds which will graze 30 cattle.

These three farms are of a type that continued to be built into the 1840s. They were all built in the boom years leading up to the Napoleonic Wars and in the war years themselves. Shortly after Grenstein Farm was modernised it was taken over by Mr Beck, whose family stayed until 1890. The improvements at Panworth coincide with the arrival there of a member of another long-standing tenant family, Mr Wrightup, who stayed until the 1870s. The Hills at Waterden, who were there in 1780, remained until the 1840s. At this time all these men were optimistic progressive farmers enjoying the advantages of high grain prices, needing large barns to house their crops and wanting cattle to create the manure in yards to spread on the fields and produce even greater crops of grain. The large barns, often with two or more threshing floors, were the most striking feature of these early farms. One development, however, is worth noticing. Keary mentioned an enclosed shed for tying up cattle at Ashill and this building with its feeding passage behind is shown on the plan. We do not know whether this was part of the original plan, but it was certainly there by 1850, and is a pointer towards the more intensive methods of farming livestock which were to become important in the second part of the nineteenth century.

Although we have the visual evidence for the results of the estate's work, and we know roughly how much building schemes cost, we know very little about how the work was undertaken. On only very few occasions is the name of an architect mentioned. Only between 1818 and 1836 was there a person described as an 'architect' permanently employed by the estate office. It is difficult to know what is meant by this term. The two men mentioned, Emerson and Savage, received salaries of £100–£120 a year, compared with £300–£600 for the agent and £155 for a clerk. They were not architects of any note and may well have been little more than draughtsmen who drew up plans from specifications laid down by the agent in consultation with both landlord and tenant. The simple, straightforward designs of the farms so far described supports this view. This lack of professional architects is also

4.17 Farm houses on the Holkham estate designed by Samuel Wyatt. (a) Kempstone Lodge, (b) Lodge Farm, Castle Acre, (c) *(facing page)* Wicken Farm, Castle Acre.

found by Dr Peters in Staffordshire. He concluded that the design and layout of the buildings might be produced by the farmer, the owner or the agent cum architect. The use of professionally trained men was a late development, usually post-1850.

c

Holkham is unusual in that during the last years of the eighteenth and the first few of the nineteenth centuries Samuel Wyatt, a professional architect of some renown, was employed by the estate, not only to work on the mansion, but also to build farm houses and premises. He was not primarily an agricultural architect. He was the clerk of the works at Chelsea Hospital from 1792 to 1807, and most of his work was for wealthy clients, designing both town and country houses. However, Holkham was not the only estate where he built outbuildings as well as houses, although here he designed his most elaborate farm premises. He was probably responsible for building about eight farm houses and at least three sets of premises for Coke. This is more than he designed for any other client. Three of his farm houses are illustrated in fig. 4.17 and represent some of the finest domestic building on the estate. Arthur Young, writing shortly after Samuel Wyatt finished working at Holkham, said of the farm houses on the estate, 'Very many of them are erected in a style much superior to the houses usually assigned for the residences of tenants; and it gave me much pleasure to find all that I viewed furnished by his farmers in a manner somewhat proportioned to the costliness of their edifices.'[57]

Kempstone Lodge farm house contains many architectural features typical of Wyatt's style in his design of country houses. These include

[57] Ibid.

the tripartite downstairs front windows with an arch above, and the matching wings on either side of the house. In 1851, the house was described as 'combining every requisite of a gentleman's residence'. It contained a drawing room, dining room and ante-room, breakfast room and study as well as a kitchen, housekeeper's room and servants' hall. Upstairs were five or six bedrooms, dressing room and servants' apartments.

At Lodge Farm, Castle Acre, an addition to a much earlier house was built between 1797 and 1800, and was designed by Wyatt. It consisted of the four bays on the right-hand side of fig. 4.17b. It is similar to a house built at Wighton Hall Farm. The bay windows on the front and on the side are later additions. The house probably contained two sitting rooms, kitchens and five or six bedrooms, which is more typical of the sort of accommodation provided for a tenant farmer. It has fewer architectural features which can be attributed to Wyatt, but a blocked in semicircular window on the gable wall at attic level can be seen in the photograph and is typical of his work.

This type of window can be seen better in fig. 4.17c, Wicken Farm, Castle Acre, but this house has been much altered. The porch, the shutters, the bay window and the oval window in the pediment are all recent embellishments. Basically, we have a house not very different from the other Castle Acre one, but on a larger scale. This farm was completely redesigned by Wyatt between 1787 and 1797, when over £3,000 was spent on improvements.

The barn at Wicken Farm, Castle Acre, is one of a group of three built by Wyatt at South Creake and Holkham as well as at Wicken. All three are very similar and show many of the features obvious in the houses. Wyatt was not an agricultural engineer, but an architect, and his aim was to build farm premises which were also fine pieces of architecture. It is likely that the barn at Wicken Farm (fig. 4.18) was originally surrounded by lean-tos similar to those at the Great Barn (figs. 4.9 and 4.21), as the audit books specifically mention the building of a barn with lean-tos. When Kent wrote his survey in 1796, both the Great Barn and South Creake barn had probably been built and they may have provoked his comment about extravagantly large buildings. Arthur Young mentioned both of these barns in his county report of 1804.

One of Mr Coke's barns at Holkham is built in a superior style; 120 feet long, 30 feet broad and 30 feet high, and surrounded with sheds for 60 head of cattle; it is capitally

4.18 Barn, Wicken Farm, Castle Acre.

4.19 Barn, Leicester Square Farm, South Creake.

executed in white brick and covered with fine blue slate. At Syderstone [fig. 4.19, in fact Leicester Square Farm, South Creake] he has built another enormous barn with stables, cattle sheds, hog sties, shepherd's and bailiff's houses surrounding a large quadrangular yard, likewise in a style of expense rarely met with.[58]

Both the barns at Wicken and South Creake were part of new sets of farm premises. The rest of the premises at Wicken have since been replaced, but those at South Creake remain and they are shown in fig. 4.20. The buildings within the yard are later additions, but the rest are

[58] *Ibid.*

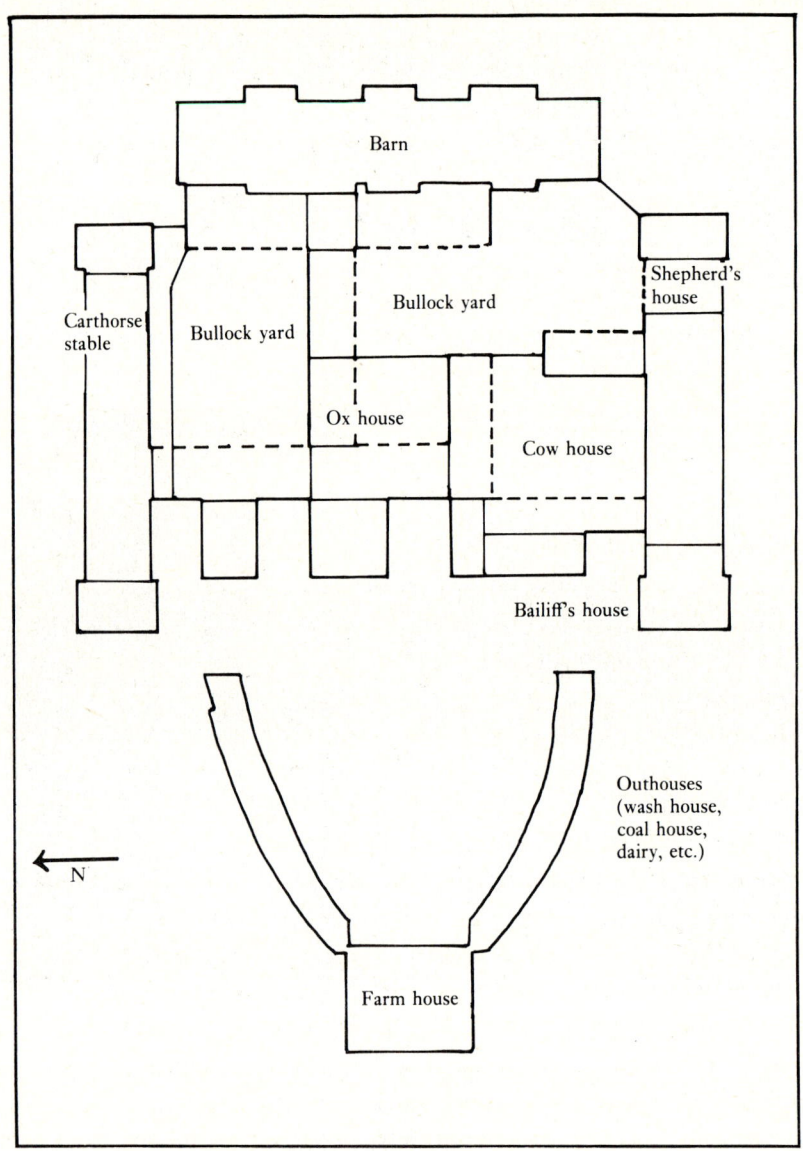

4.20 Plan of Leicester Square Farm, South Creake.

original. This ambitious scheme was built to serve a farm of 865 acres, where, according to Keary, the land was not good enough to grow wheat except when prices were high. It is now farmed by a company who are only too well aware of the poorness of the soil. In 1793, £1,363 was paid by the estate office for the 'erecting of a new barn, stables, cow houses, fences walls, pig cotes, etc.', and in 1801 a further £2,134 was paid towards 'a new farm house and offices adjoining'. A date stone of 1791 on the stables shows that work had commenced by then. South Creake is an early example of the rebuilding of a farm and it is fortunate that it should remain with so few alterations. The original layout around a yard would have been very acceptable to progressive farmers, while the features which give it architectural merit show the status which farm buildings could be given. The barn is the dominating feature and there are fine views of it when the farm is approached from the east (fig. 4.19). The sets of domestic outhouses which curve away from the charming house towards the farm buildings give the whole plan a pleasing symmetry. The back windows of the house look directly into the yards, and originally probably across the yards to the barn. The identical square blocks at each end of the stable and cow shed blocks also contribute to an architectural aspect of which no tenant farmer, even if he were aspiring to the gentry class, need be ashamed. It is very difficult to know why this farm was singled out for such grandiose treatment. It was not one of the largest or the most fertile on the estate, nor was the tenant one who was particularly famous for his agricultural improvements. It was also too far from Holkham to be visited by the guests to the sheep shearings.

The Great Barn at Holkham (fig. 4.9) is probably the most famous farm building on the estate and it is surprising that there is no mention of it in the audit books. We do not even know exactly at what date it was built, but it must have been between Arthur Young's two visits to Holkham in 1784 and 1792. Its splendour was frequently remarked upon by visitors, especially those to the sheep shearings. The plan, redrawn as fig. 4.21, was originally drawn in 1844 for R. N. Bacon's *Agriculture of Norfolk*. It shows a layout very different from the usual design of a barn as one side of a rectangle. Instead, the barn is in the centre of the buildings. This appears to have been a very satisfactory arrangement and it certainly pleased the commentators of the period. Although the Great Barn, with its pond beside it, still survives, the cattle sheds have recently

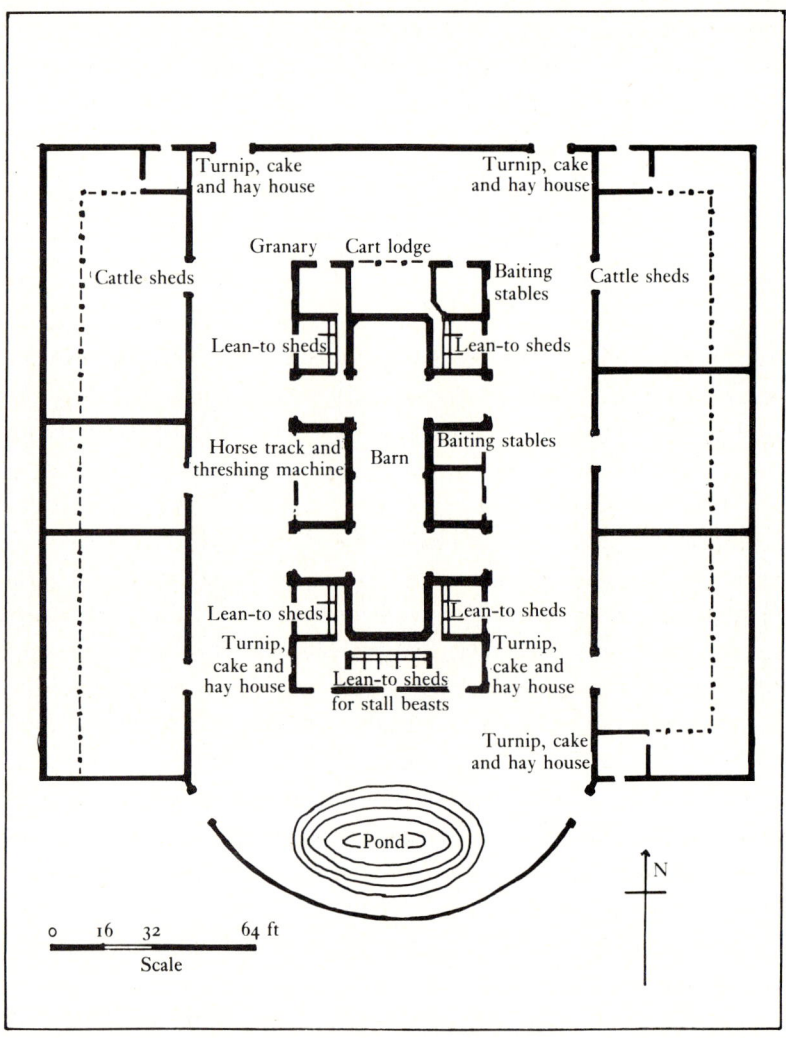

4.21 Plan of the Great Barn, Holkham.

been demolished. Two other barns were built by Wyatt in Holkham park but they have since been demolished and little is known about them.

When we come to look at the simpler farm buildings of the period, it is more difficult to tell if any were designed by Wyatt, as they lack a distinctive style. He was responsible for the sheds and the yards at Longlands and possibly for the cattle yards at Lodge Farm, Castle Acre, which contain the semicircular windows of which he was so fond and which we know were rebuilt between 1797 and 1800. The stables at High House Farm, Weasenham, and the barn at Abbey Farm, Castle Acre, also contain this feature, but there is no documentary evidence for building there at this time. It is clear that not all buildings during the period when Wyatt was working for the estate were designed by him. The house at Burghwood Hall, Mileham, was built in 1793, but it is of an entirely different design.

Samuel Wyatt was primarily a country house architect and his main contribution to agricultural buildings at Holkham was to introduce an architectural quality to functional buildings. His buildings have lost their vernacular appearance. Welsh slate and yellow brick was often used in preference to the traditional red brick and pantiles. Detailing was classical rather than local in style, and Wyatt did not develop the layout or operational design of farm premises. Wyatt worked for the Holkham estate until his death in 1807. His only other work in East Anglia was at Hurts Hall, Saxmundham, which was built in 1803.

Blaikie arrived at Holkham at the end of the Napoleonic Wars, just as depression set in, and he described both the tenants and their farms in his survey of 1816. His descriptions show us the degree of improvement which had been achieved during the boom years of optimism and rising rents. Work had just begun at Longham and John Hastings' pessimistic state of mind has already been cited. Blaikie's comments on the plain functional buildings at both Grenstein and Waterden are favourable, but with these two exceptions he was not enthusiastic about the recent improvements, particularly the fancy work of Wyatt. He himself considered large expenditure on farm buildings wasteful. Of Tithe Farm, Weasenham, rebuilt between 1814 and 1816, he said, 'New farm house and premises, but nothing to be said in favour of either.' Again he commented on one of the Wighton farms: 'Farm buildings undergoing considerable but injudicious and expensive alteration.' There is a further criticism of extravagence in the description of Hall Farm, Warham, rebuilt between 1810 and 1815. Blaikie said that the buildings were 'too expensive and too extensive for the extent or the rent of the farm'. Considering Blaikie's attitude to expenditure, it is surprising that so many farms were rebuilt during this period of his management between 1816 and 1832. Perhaps even Blaikie had to give way to pressure from both tenants and employer. Blaikie found most of the buildings in good repair. He described twenty-six as being in 'complete repair', ten were in 'tolerable repair' and ten were 'in need of repair'. The state of repair of the rest was not mentioned. Because Blaikie's descriptions of individual buildings were not detailed we cannot say how many farms had a specific type of building in 1816. Dairies, cow houses, stables, piggeries, barns, granaries, cart houses, waggon lodges, field barns, straw houses and out-buildings were all mentioned. There was also a single reference to a turnip house, showing that, although not as yet common on all farms, some were storing root crops for feeding to stock on the farmstead. A reference to 'mangers in the open sheds' shows that shelter sheds, probably placed around open yards, were being used for intensive winter feeding of cattle.

From the general descriptions of Holkham farms written by Blaikie and the more detailed ones by Keary, plus the evidence of surviving plans and often of the buildings themselves, it is clear that the sums of money which the audit books shows as being spent on individual farms between 1790 and 1820 were used for extensive and substantial improvements which brought many of the Holkham farms up to the standards of the advocates of progress.

Farm building, 1820–42

The end of the Napoleonic Wars and the onset of depression seems to have made little difference to the amount of building going on at Holkham. Although Blaikie disapproved of expensive building programmes, many continued, and between 1820 and 1842 seven farms were completely rebuilt and many other major improvements were undertaken. In 1827 five farms were being rebuilt and throughout the period there was always at least one farm undergoing improvement.

Most of these building programmes were very similar to many of those of the previous thirty years. The farmsteads were of simple functional design. The barn at Manor Farm, Tittleshall (fig. 4.22), is an example of this style. It has no elaborate porticoes, simply one threshing floor and a pair of double doors through which waggons could be driven and which could be opened to create a through draught for winnowing. It was built as part of the improvements between 1828 and 1831, and the initials T.C. can be seen at the ends of the tie beams. Brick was still the main building material used on the estate.

But the end of Thomas William Coke's life, a change in the estate's

4.22 Barn, Manor Farm, Tittleshall.

policy towards the type of farm building erected was becoming apparent. The last new barn to be built was at Rose Farm, Tittleshall, in 1837, and a shift in emphasis towards the providing of more cattle accommodation can be seen. Coke is supposed to have said to his tenants, 'If you will keep an extra yard of bullocks, I will build you a yard and a shed free of expense.'[59] Holkham farmers were still undecided between the comparative merit of yard and box feeding and only two buildings on the estate were described as loose boxes in 1851. They were at Panworth Hall, Ashill, and Manorhouse Farm, Tittleshall. Dunton Farm was rebuilt between 1834 and 1838. The new premises provided sheds for fifty cattle, built around four yards. As well as this accommodation at the home premises, a field barn could house fifty more. The only other farms which had sheds for more than fifty cattle in 1851 were Waterden Farm and Godwick, rebuilt between 1843 and 1847. As well as the provision of increased livestock accommodation, when entirely new premises were built, the audit books record new yards and sheds at nineteen other farms during these twenty years.

Between 1790 and 1842, twenty-three farms on the estate were

[59] Stirling, *Coke of Norfolk*, vol. 1, p. 269.

4.23 Stable and horse yard, High House Farm, Weasenham.

completely rebuilt. In 1851 they were all described by Keary. Nineteenth-century plans of many of them survive and many of the buildings are still intact. It is therefore possible to reconstruct the sort of farm that was being built by this progressive estate under the direction of the first earl.

Of the twenty-three farms rebuilt, seven were over 1,000 acres. Egmere, the only other farm of this size, was reconstructed a little later, in the 1850s. The rest are all over 400 acres. Nearly all of them received a generally favourable report from Keary. Minor complaints included the 'bad English timber' in one, and a few cases where the roofs needed repairing. There was one example of insufficient cattle and implement accommodation. Another farm needed more yards. Harpley Dam Farm was the only one of the new farms of which Keary disapproved. He found it 'ill-arranged and inconvenient'.

Keary described four of the twenty-three farms as well placed, while three were badly placed. The premises at Harpley Dam were at 'one end'. Tithe Farm, Weasenham, had a badly sited homestead and the buildings at Manor Farm, Tittleshall, were in 'the extreme corner of the land'. The fact that this was also the nearest point to both the village

and the public road was no compensation. It was thought that farm premises should be in the middle of their land, so that all the fields were easily accessible. Stephens wrote,

> We know of a large steading which is thus inconveniently placed for the sake of a good road and the command of water power; but these advantages were obtained at the additional expense of maintaining a man and a pair of horses with their implements to work in the more distant fields of the farm. Better make a good farm road to the turnpike from the centre of the farm, and erect steam power than have the farm in the extreme corner.[60]

All the rebuilt farms had at least one barn. They all had carthorse stables for anything from thirteen on a 469 acre farm to twenty-five on an acreage of 1,209. Cattle yards varied in size from those housing twenty to those for fifty. All except three of the farms had piggeries and there were only three farms which did not have cow sheds and yards. Dairy farming was not an important part of the farming economy and cows were kept only for domestic use. All but one farm had at least one waggon lodge, often with a granary over it. Nearly all the farms had riding horse stables and a gig house, while only three had smith's or carpenter's shops.

[60] H. Stephens, *The Book of the Farm* (3rd edn, Edinburgh, 1876), p. 317.

The Holkham planned farm of the early nineteenth century was nearly always in the centre of its land, with a good road to it. Within the farmstead the barn was usually in a central position. It was usually built of brick, although it might be of flint, carstone or chalk blocks. Some of the barns incorporate earlier structures, as at Peterstone where a medieval abbey wall and doorway are part of the barn. Others were entirely rebuilt in the early nineteenth century and these have a much more regular layout. Both pantile and thatched roofs are common, although Samuel Wyatt preferred to use Welsh slate from Penrhyn where his brother was agent. The barn was used for storage of sheaves of corn, as well as often housing the chaff and straw. It also contained one or more threshing floors. Around the barn, usually on the sunny side for warmth, were the cattle sheds. These were sometimes built as separate units and were sometimes adjacent to the barn. As the chaff and straw were often housed in the barn for use in the stables and cattle sheds, the nearer the yards and carthorse stables were to the barn, the less cartage would be involved. The stables were often arranged around a horse yard, where manure was allowed to collect (fig. 4.23) in the same way as in the cattle enclosures. Piggeries, hen houses and other minor buildings were often in a range nearer the house, as it was the kitchen scraps that were used for their feed. The cow houses were usually in a small yard somewhere near the cattle sheds. The gig house and riding horse stables were again near the house. Waggon lodges, cart lodges and implement sheds faced outwards, towards the driftways leading to the land, or out on to the public road. The few carpenter's shops and smithies were usually near the implement sheds. Many of the waggon lodges had granaries above them. Although the normal building material in the early nineteenth century was brick, Keary occasionally commented on 'new buildings' being built of 'round stones with brick jambs'. This type of flint and brick building became more usual in the second half of the century. As the flints were picked off the fields it could be cheaper to use them than to build entirely of brick. White brick was used as a facing on houses and also on some of the finer barns. The house was always very much part of the farm, usually being to one side of the buildings. This is the sort of farm layout we would expect on a progressive estate and was one much advocated by improvers of the period. R. N. Bacon, when discussing farm buildings in Norfolk, said,

The main object of the construction and erection of all agricultural buildings ought to be centralisation, convenience, accommodation and economical arrangement of all yards and offices which should be placed as much under the master's eye as possible. In the arrangement of the yards for cattle, attention should be paid to keep them dry and warm and as free from disturbance as possible.[61]

These considerations were obviously all taken into account by the Holkham estate.

The price of remodelling a farm seems to have changed very little between 1790 and 1842, and varied between £1,000 and £3,000 throughout the period. From the plans and the remaining buildings it is difficult to see why some farms should have cost three times as much as others. The simplest explanation is that more items were supplied directly by the estate for the building of the lower cost farms than for the higher. Where costs of remodelling were given in the descriptions of farm improvements in journals such as the *J.R.A.S.E.* they were usually within this range, and improvements on the Stafford estates in the early years of the nineteenth century normally cost just over £2,000.

By spreading the cost of improvements over several years, it was possible to have work going on at various farms at once. Thus while there was very heavy expenditure at South Creake in 1793 and 1801 there were only two other large-scale building schemes in progress. At a later date, when the rebuilding of Longlands as an estate workshop between 1853 and 1859 cost £9,775, there was little other large-scale expenditure. However, in periods when the cost of improvements was being spread over a number of years, as between 1823 and 1840, it was possible for large-scale improvements to be going on consecutively on as many as five farms. Although these patterns can be seen among the larger sums spent over the period, it is not surprising that no real pattern emerges from among the smaller sums of between £100 and £400 per annum. Little of this money went into major improvements and was presumably used for repairs as and when they were needed.

Although plenty was written on how to improve farm buildings, it is clear that well arranged premises were not to be found everywhere in England. John Grey of Dilston wrote in 1843,

No one can have travelled much in the rural districts of England, even in those which are comparatively well cultivated, without being struck, if he has any sense of neatness and order, with the illmanaged patchwork appearance of many of the farm buildings,

---

[61] Bacon, *Agriculture of Norfolk*, p. 394.

which are often placed in relation to their different parts, in utter defiance of the economy of labour in the case of cattle; and what is worse, with little regard to the production and preservation of manure, the dry parts of which may be seen exposed to the winds and the liquid part carried off without being applied to any beneficial purpose.[62]

All this enthusiasm for new building needs to be seen against a background of optimism amongst farmers who believed that, aided by reason and science, progress was inevitable; but the new farmsteads were built by practical men for practical purposes. They were convinced of the value of neatly arranged buildings with good cattle yards, aimed at saving labour and preserving manure. Good cattle yards were essential, as manure was basic to cultivation. Sheep might appear cheaper to keep as they require no buildings, but they only manured the pastures they were grazing, which reduced their value to the nineteenth-century cultivator. We may question the wisdom of the enthusiasm for symmetry and neat arrangement of farm buildings, and perhaps some new building was unnecessary, but then, as now, it was often cheaper to rebuild entirely than to convert old premises. This is particularly true where old buildings were of poor materials. 'Old mud and thatch sheds' are mentioned in descriptions of Holkham. It is no more expensive to build well arranged premises than it is to build inconvenient ones, and a lot of farmstead work consists of moving materials and animals. The advantage of well arranged buildings to animal production, storage and processing must have been very real. Certainly a well arranged farm would have been easier to let.

William Keary surveyed the Duke of Norfolk's south Norfolk estates in 1861 and was very critical of the farm buildings he found. Many were old and dilapidated. Lack of expenditure on the part of the landlord may have meant that he kept a greater percentage of the rent, but on the other hand rents had not risen. As a result, a lower calibre tenant than those to be found at Holkham farmed there. They were neither intelligent nor enterprising and the land was only 'indifferently' farmed. Keary was convinced that holding back expenditure did not pay off in the end and concluded his survey by saying, 'The time has come when a considerable outlay must be made if this property is to be raised to a condition worthy of its hereditary owner.'[63]

The Select Committee on Agriculture reported in 1833 that the state

---

[62] J. Grey, 'On farm buildings', *J.R.A.S.E.*, vol. 4 (1843).
[63] H. W. Keary, 'Description of the Duke of Norfolk's Norfolk estates' (1861), N.R.O.

of farm buildings in the county was continually improving. 'Mr Coke owns so large a proportion of the whole, and his are in such excellent condition.' The example of Coke was said to have encouraged other landlords to improve their farms. From my visits to the farms of the Raynham and Cholmondeley estates it is clear, that, although most of the farms had good barns, few had cattle yards, and instead the farm buildings were often either scattered or haphazardly grouped around a large central yard.

It would seem, therefore, that the large sums of money spent on improvements by the Holkham estates were well spent. Some of the earlier work, such as that at Wicken Farm, Castle Acre, and at South Creake, may have been unnecessarily expensive, but later schemes lacked such architectural embellishments and their plain functional character suggests that they were built as economically as possible.

There can be little doubt that in 1842 the buildings and layout of the Holkham farms were among the best in the country. The dominance of the barn may have lasted longer at Holkham than on some other estates, such as those of the Duke of Roxburgh, but the importance of stock and also of the manure produced was fully appreciated and the appropriate buildings provided.

On the death of the first earl, the estate passed to his eldest son, who was born in 1822 when his father was sixty-eight. Thus the second earl, like his father, was a young man when he inherited and he had his father's enthusiasm for estate improvement and agriculture. Although he had little interest in politics, he was influential and respected in the county, especially where agricultural matters were concerned.

After a sudden and dramatic fall in expenditure during the first eight years of his earldom, investment in farm improvements reached a new peak. Building involving an unprecedented scale of expenditure was undertaken in the 1850s. In 1851, William Keary was promoted from manager of the home farm to estate agent and it was under his guidance that these expensive schemes were carried out. Expenditure declined in the late 1840s, but by the mid 1860s it was rising and by 1871 was again 20% of rents collected. Until 1884, expenditure continued to be higher than it had been during the first half of the century, and then it dropped to the level of the Napoleonic Wars. Rents were also falling and so this lower expenditure was still over 10% of rents collected.

The appointment of William Keary as agent in 1851 meant that there were several changes in office management. Less detail of individual improvements was noted in the audit books, while expenditure on draining and fencing was listed separately. Sums of money were shown as going to individual carpenters and buildings, while the tenant's name no longer appeared. It would seem therefore that Keary was taking more responsibility for the administration involved in carrying out repairs and improvements than had been usual on the estate.

Keary also made sure that leases made specific reference to the terms on which new buildings would be erected. A twenty year lease was granted to John Hudson of Castle Acre in 1855. This laid down that the tenant had to cart materials for new buildings and repairs as well as for drainage. He was to pay $7\frac{1}{2}\%$ interest per annum on the landlord's outlay when it was at the tenant's request. Interest of 5% was to be paid on land drainage. The landlord was to keep the buildings in repair, except where it was agreed that it was the tenant's responsibility, and was to find wood, brick, pipes and lime for repairs carried out by the tenant. The charging of interest on drainage, but not other improvements, was general on other English estates in the second half of the nineteenth century. The interest rate varied from 5% to $7\frac{1}{2}\%$. In this way the landlord was sure of an adequate return on capital invested within the duration of a lease. He did not have to wait until a lease fell in and then hope for a return from an increased rent.

After the burst of building by the second earl ending in 1857, little was done during the next ten years. When improvements were again undertaken on a large scale they were of an entirely different character. Up until 1857, the second earl was continuing the work of his father in completely remodelling farms; after the ten year gap, improvements and extensions to these earlier buildings were needed. The emphasis moved from the providing of complete farmsteads to the adding of cattle and implement sheds to already existing buildings. This type of improvement usually involved less expenditure than the entirely new farms of the first half of the century, and so instead of spreading the cost over a series of years as earlier, the work was paid for more quickly. Most improvements were paid for within two or three years.

The period between 1842 and 1909 can therefore be divided into three. In the first part, entirely new farms were being built, while after 1857 no new farms, except at Kipton Ash in 1891 when it was taken over by the Overman family, were erected. A gap in building of about ten years was followed by a new type of development involving extensive additions to farms that had earlier been rebuilt. It is interesting to see what improvements it was felt necessary to make to these 'model' farms to suit changing agricultural practice. These two distinct phases of investment will be considered separately.

New farms built between 1842 and 1860

Books on farm building design and articles in the *J.R.A.S.E.* show that interest in the improvement of buildings continued into the 1870s. This enthusiasm reach a peak in 1850, when as a result of a competition sponsored by the *J.R.A.S.E.* six sets of plans for new farmsteads were published. Each plan was accompanied by a short article by its designer and an introductory paper by H. S. Thompson summarised the recent developments in layout and design.[64] Most of the changes of this period were in the type of accommodation for livestock. Livestock farming was becoming increasingly important and cattle played a significant part in the agricultural pattern of the Holkham estate. Blaikie, writing from his retirement in Scotland in 1840, said, 'My theory has always been, if we are not recuperated by keeping cattle, we cannot grow corn.'[65]

The value of manure had long been appreciated at Holkham. Leases stated that manure produced on a farm should not be sold, but should be spread back on the land. Field barns usually had cattle sheds adjoining, so that manure was easily available for the more distant fields. Mrs Stirling quoted the Norfolk proverb, 'Muck is the mother of money.'[66] R. N. Bacon's statement that Coke would build a tenant a new bullock yard if he would keep more cattle has already been quoted. Caird wrote of Holkham in 1850, 'Ample though the expenditure on the erection of farm buildings was, accommodation for stock is now, with still heavier crops, found far from adequate and the outlay by the present Earl in repairs and additions on the estate was not much under £10,000 last year.'[67] David Spring quotes James Caird as writing to Robert Peel, 'It will be vain to drain the land and fit it for the culture of green crops, if no suitable housing is provided for economically converting these into

---

[64] H. S. Thompson, 'Farm buildings', *J.R.A.S.E.*, vol. 11 (1850), p. 186.
[65] A. M. W. Stirling, *The Letter Bags of Lady Elizabeth Stanhope*, 2 vols. (London, 1913), vol. 2, p. 168.
[66] Stirling, *Coke of Norfolk*, vol. 2, p. 253.
[67] Caird, *English Agriculture*, p. 166.

a marketable form, and for preserving and accumulating the manure.' Melbourne's agent, Fox, wrote to him about his Panshanger estate saying that the whole system of building farm premises was undergoing a change. Fox found a great deficiency of cattle accommodation: 'in many cases the main buildings are bad and inconveniently situated and must at a future time be removed'.[68]

Between 1850 and 1870, the position of livestock within the farming economy changed. The price of grain was not rising, but that of livestock was. Until the 1850s it was held that the cost of stall feeding oxen through the winter was not recovered by selling the fatstock in the spring unless the grain enterprises were charged for the dung which was produced by the beasts. Philip Pusey went so far as to say that cattle were machines for making manure.[69] This must have been an extreme view which probably would not have been shared by Norfolk farmers who had long recognised the cash value of their livestock. By the 1850s oil cake was being fed to cattle on a scale which could not be justified simply by increased output of manure. Cattle were more generally recognised as profitable in themselves. By the mid-1860s this change in emphasis was widely accepted and by the 1870s grain production had to be 'given' manure to pay its way.[70]

It is not therefore surprising that the plans in the *J.R.A.S.E.* show an increasing emphasis on stall and yard feeding. The barn suggested on John Hudson's plan (fig. 4.24) is minute compared with that on earlier farms. Thompson wrote in his introductory article, 'In all the plans now published, the old method of building round a rectangular area, and using the enclosure as a stack yard has either been given up or very much modified.' Instead this area was usually filled with covered cattle sheds. There was some controversy over the relative merits of open and closed cattle sheds. C. S. Read wrote in 1858 that covered yards were not numerous in Norfolk and that sheds with open yards were still the most general.[71] These yards were usually small and held between ten and twelve beasts. On two sides of the yard were warm open sheds. 'Cattle thrive in them, but in a community of a dozen a few will be tyrants so the rest must be slaves.' He was an advocate of individual box feeding,

---

[68] D. Spring, *The English Landed Estate in the Nineteenth Century* (Baltimore, 1963), p. 117.
[69] E. L. Jones, 'The changing face of agricultural prosperity, 1853–1873', *Agricultural History Review*, vol. 10 (1962), pp. 102–19.
[70] *Ibid.*
[71] C. S. Read, 'Recent improvements in Norfolk farming', *J.R.A.S.E.*, vol. 19 (1858), pp. 265–311.

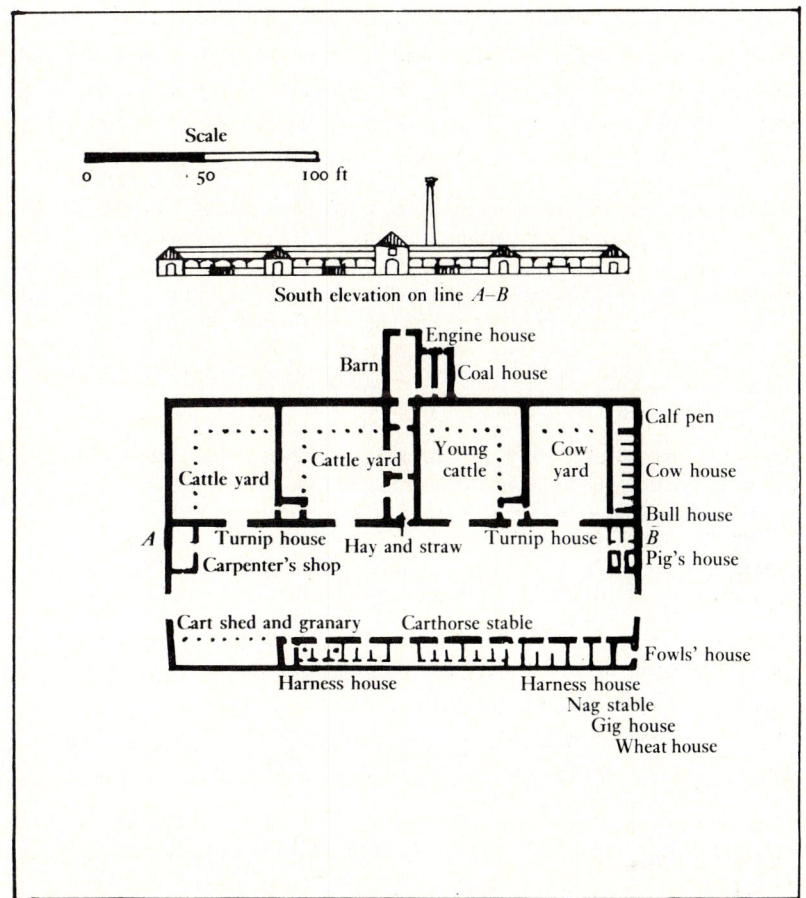

4.24 John Hudson's model farm plan (1850).

which was just being introduced on the Holkham estates. Significantly the only plan submitted to the *J.R.A.S.E* competition which showed open rather than closed sheds was one by the Holkham tenant, John Hudson of Castle Acre (fig. 4.24).[72]

Other developments which Thompson noted included the increase in the intercommunication between buildings. This was mainly because of the development of more sophisticated feeding techniques, such as the mashing and boiling of food, which involved the moving of food from storage to food preparation rooms before it was fed to cattle. More thought was also given to the grouping of buildings. The stables were

[72] J. Hudson, 'On the construction of farm buildings', *J.R.A.S.E.*, vol. 11 (1850), p. 282.

surrounded by everything pertaining to the food and work of the horses. Other changes were brought about by the increasing use of machinery. For instance, the development of the stationary steam engine for agricultural use meant that many farm plans now included a steam engine house and chimney next to the barn.

> There are doubtless many who are not either convinced of the advantage of thrashing by steam, box feeding or other modern practices, or at any rate are not prepared to introduce them on their own farms at the present moment; but there are probably very few of those who would be satisfied with any plan which was not capable of being adapted to such a system whenever it might be thought desirable to commence it.[73]

The eminent agricultural scientist, Philip Pusey, also felt that farm buildings were going through a period of change.

> Notwithstanding the really excellent plans of farm buildings we have recently published, I, for one, certainly should be puzzled; because farm buildings, like certain countries, are really in a state of revolution. Our old ideas about them are unsettled, our new ones undetermined. Their form must depend upon the management of manure.[74]

This spirit of change can be seen in many of the farm buildings both designed and built during this period. Not only were the architects aware of new developments in design, but many landlowners were adventurous enough to try them out in practice.

Various comments on the state of farm buildings and the merits of their own plans were made by the designers of the premises published in the *J.R.A.S.E.* Sir Thomas Tancred noted the great contrast between the types of farm buildings recommended and those usually to be seen.[75] Mr Ewart was at pains to point out that the providing of good farm buildings was a profitable exercise for the landlord. 'Numerous instances might be adduced of farms without adequate accommodation in buildings having been losing concerns of the occupiers, but on the deficiency of buildings being supplied, having proved profitable undertakings at an advance of rent equal to $7\frac{1}{2}\%$ or indeed 10% on the cost of the new buildings.[76] In the most mechanised sets of premises published, tramways were provided to take the chaff and other animal feed from the barn to the cattle sheds and then to take the manure from the cattle sheds to the dung houses from where it could be carted to the fields.[77]

---

[73] Thompson, 'Farm buildings', p. 186.
[74] P. Pusey, *What Ought Landlords and Farmers to Do?* (London 1851), p. 35.
[75] T. Tancred, 'Essay on the construction of farm buildings', *J.R.A.S.E.*, vol. 11 (1850), p. 192.
[76] J. Ewart, 'Farm buildings', *J.R.A.S.E.*, vol. 11 (1850), p. 215.
[77] W. C. Spooner and J. Elliot, 'On the construction of farm buildings', *J.R.A.S.E.*, vol. 11 (1850), p. 270.

John Hudson of Castle Acre wrote, 'The supplying of extensive buildings by the landlord encourages high farming.' In his plan, the cattle are accommodated in yards about sixty-four feet square, including the shelter sheds which were sixteen feet wide. Each yard would hold twelve to fifteen cattle. He commented that some of the sheds could easily be converted into loose boxes for individual feeding if required.[78] All the published plans include a steam engine house beside the barn, which, although still central and easily accessible from the rest of the farmstead, was losing its dominating position.

To discover what sort of farm buildings were actually being erected in the 1850s it is necessary not only to look at the model plans published, but also at some farmsteads that were built. In 1863 J. B. Denton published a collection of plans and drawings of farmsteads that had recently been built in England. He included none from the Holkham estate, but the farms that are illustrated show that many of the principles advocated by the *J.R.A.S.E.* were being put into practice. Not all builders were convinced of the value of closed yards, and open ones were usually erected on the Bedford estates.

Other than Samuel Wyatt, the only architect of national repute who worked for the Holkham estates was G. A. Dean, who planned both the new buildings at Egmere and the estate workshops at Longlands. Unlike Wyatt, Dean was primarily an agricultural engineer and was the author of several books on agricultural matters. In *The Land Steward*, published in 1851, he wrote:

> We have been surprised by the great want of accommodation and arrangement in farm buildings: we have found them unsuited, almost without exception, to the improved system of farming now pursued...A compact and well arranged steading is of immense importance to the farmer; it is there his livestock are sheltered and fed a great portion of the year, it is there the produce of his farm is manufactured and consumed, and it is there he collects the means of enriching his lands and of increasing the quantity and improving the quality of his crops. There is scarcely a farmer of stability throughout the country who would not be willing to pay an additional rent of from seven to nine or in some instances ten per cent upon the cost of a first rate homestead rather than put up with such a miserable one as farmers are now compelled to put up with.

Dean thought that buildings should not be crowded, but rather there should be plenty of room for conversion and extension. Animals should be well housed, 'as such an animal requires less food in the winter than the one exposed to the cold'. Farms should have adequate implement

[78] Hudson, 'Farm buildings', p. 282.

4.25 Farm premises, Egmere Farm. (a) Cattle sheds, interior of north-west yard, looking north. (b) Cattle sheds, exterior, looking south. (c) Loose boxes, interior.

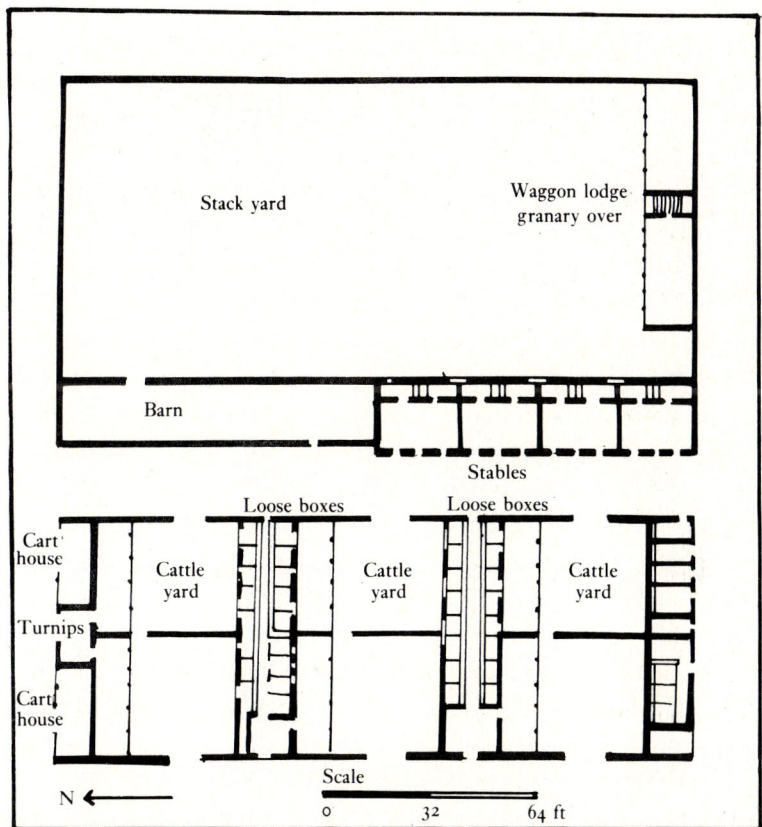

4.26 Plan of Egmere Farm.

sheds, as more wear and tear was caused to implements by leaving them outside than through actual work. Finally, his aim when designing a set of farm premises was: 'there ought not to be the smallest convenience on a farm, down to a pigsty, that is not so precisely in the right spot, that to place it anywhere else would be a loss of labour and manure'.[79]

Egmere Farm was the last complete set of farm buildings to be built on the Holkham estate in the nineteenth century (fig. 4.25). It was built at the height of agricultural confidence and the optimism of both landlord and farmer seems to be reflected in the grandeur of the building. Between 1850 and 1856, £5,458 was spent on the premises and repairs to the house. This included the fee of £200 paid to Dean. This makes Egmere the most expensive as well as the last rebuilding. In view of the

[79] G. A. Dean, *The Land Steward* (London, 1851), *passim*.

importance of this farm, we are lucky in having both the plans drawn by Dean and also the buildings themselves, complete and with only a few alterations.

The plan shows a very regular layout of buildings (fig. 4.26). The barns, stables, waggon lodges and granaries were in a block separate from the extensive cattle yards. This allowed the horses to be placed between the barn, where the straw and chaff for their bedding and food was produced, and the waggon lodges, where some of the vehicles they pulled were kept. The cattle yards and turnip houses stood near the barn and stables across a roadway. Straw from the barn went into the cattle yards, but their main food was stored in the turnip houses adjoining the yards. These buildings served a large farm of 1,222 acres and, considering its size, it may seem surprising that there was only one barn. Fifty years earlier there would certainly have been more. However, there is a large stack yard, which was an unusual feature for a Norfolk farm, and behind it a waggon lodge block with granary over. There is much more accommodation for cattle than there was on the earlier farms, and for the first time we have a surviving example of the much advocated method of feeding cattle in loose boxes. These allowed for the individual feeding of the cattle. The boxes were built in two rows between the yards, with a feeding passage dividing the rows from which the feeding troughs either side (dotted on the plan) could be easily filled (fig. 4.25c). The animals stood heads inwards and the manure drained out of the boxes into the open yards, where it could easily be collected for use in the fields. There was accommodation for thirty-three cattle in loose boxes as well as over seventy youngstock in the six open yards. It is surprising, however, to find that, in spite of Dean's remarks quoted earlier about the necessity of implement sheds, he did not provide any at Egmere.

At Egmere we see the logical development from the earlier type of building with its large barns, built when corn was king and showed every sign of remaining so, to premises dominated by livestock accommodation equipped for intensively fattening up cattle for market, and with store rooms for the feeds that not only helped in the fattening-up process, but also enriched the manure. The barn no longer needed threshing floors and the corn was being stacked outside. The barn now provided cover for the dressing, winnowing and threshing gear that was part of a modern farm. The size of the barn is not an indication of the decline in the importance of grain – the great extent of the granaries shows that this was not so – but rather an indication of a change in technique with the introduction of barn machinery. These premises were ideal for the improved agriculture practised by John Hudson and his type of farmer. After the rebuilding, Egmere was taken on by one of the members of the exemplary Overman family, who no doubt put the premises to good use.

The buildings at Egmere differ in many details from the locally designed buildings found elsewhere, and if we did not know that the architect was a professional from outside, we would suspect it from looking at the buildings. The finishing details such as the cornices are not of a local style. Cast iron columns supporting the roofs of the shelter sheds are not found elsewhere on the estate and the buildings seem to be an example of the standardisation of building style which was part of the industrialisation of the nineteenth century.

Buildings were erected at Longlands between 1853 and 1859, transforming what had been no more than a home farm into a huge estate workshop (fig. 3.2). Waggon lodges with great grain stores above, implement sheds, carpenter's shops, smithies and workshops were added to the late-eighteenth-century barn, stables and yards. A steam engine was installed to power the saws, bellow and lathes. These buildings did not maintain the entirely functional appearance of Dean's buildings at Egmere. They were faced in yellow brick, while red brick is used at Egmere. The fashionable Italian influence is typified by the style of the clock tower in the central workshop area. The old estate workshops were situated near the lake and would have been visible from the house and it was thought desirable to hide them from view. The new ones were far more extensive and elaborate than the old and so more materials needed on the estate could be prepared at Holkham. The new workshops at Longlands were on a scale comparable with those at Woburn, where the sixth Duke spent £12,800 in 1846. When Sir Robert Peel visited Woburn in 1849 he commented, 'I am full of wonder at the extent of the establishment. One part of it – that in which materials for buildings are prepared – is more like a dockyard than a domestic office.'[80]

The only other complete rebuilding of this period was that at Inn Farm, Holkham, where £1,382 was spent in 1853 on 'building a new farm'. These buildings were also somewhat decorative. They are faced in yellow brick and built around neat yards and an Italian style is again

[80] Spring, *The English Landed Estate*, p. 45.

apparent. However, there is no evidence that these buildings were designed by Dean.

It is interesting to compare the costings given in the audit books with those for model farms described in the 1840s and 1850s. None of the published designs were for farms of over 1,000 acres, such as Egmere, so it is not surprising that none of them was as expensive. John Hudson's plan cost £1,500 and was for a farm of 250–300 acres. Similarly, Elliott's plans were for a 300 acre farm and also cost £1,500. Pusey thought that a landowner who had set aside £3,000 for a new set of farm premises would have a wide selection of plans from which to choose.[81]

Even though the buildings at Egmere were built for a much larger farm, it must be realised that the cost per acre of providing buildings went down as the acreage increased. It would thus seem that the buildings at Egmere were very expensive, especially if the materials were provided by the estate and therefore not accounted for. Inn Farm premises, for a farm of only 125 acres, were expensive at £1,382, but this is probably accounted for by their rather ornate style. This provides additional evidence for the suggestion that the audit book figure must account for nearly all the expense involved in erecting buildings. To add another two thirds to this figure would produce an unrealistically high cost.

We are very fortunate in having the description of the Holkham farms made by William Keary when he became agent in 1851. By this date the first phase of improvements on most farms had been completed and the buildings were adequate until the second phase of improvements which began in the late 1860s. In his description Keary listed the buildings on each farm and from this information it has been possible to compile fig. 4.27. This shows the total number of each kind of building mentioned in Keary's description.

Nearly all the farms had a barn, and most of them had waggon lodges. Only fifty-five of the seventy had carthorse stables. Oxen were still used by farmers on the Holkham estate, as is shown by the answers to Bacon's questionnaire of 1844.[82] Possibly very few horses were kept on some of these farms. Cattle sheds, piggeries and granaries were all essential buildings and were to be found on all well equipped farms. However, it is surprising that there is no mention of these types of buildings on about a third of the farms, even although these are always the smaller

---

[81] Pusey, *What Ought Landlords to Do?*, p. 35.
[82] Bacon MS 4363, N.R.O.

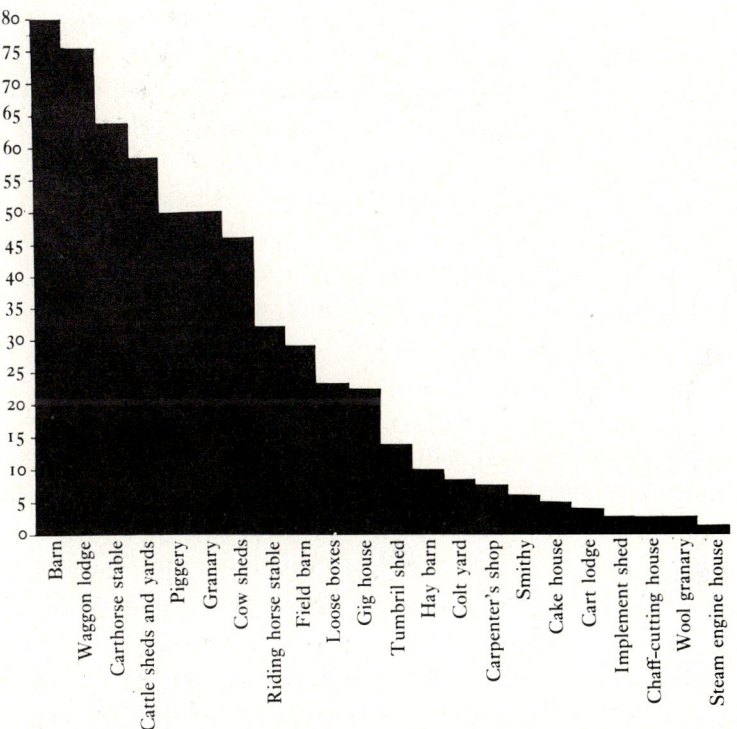

4.27 Number of buildings on the Holkham farms at the time of Keary's report (1851).

ones. Cow sheds were found far less frequently than cattle sheds. This emphasises the fact that cattle for beef were more important than cows in the high farming system of agriculture. There was no nearby market for milk and so one would not expect cows to be numerous in this area in the first half of the nineteenth century. Mr Overman was unusual in that he produced dairy goods, especially cheese. Less than half the farms rose to the dignity of a separate stable for riding horses and even fewer had a gig house. Most of the larger farms had field barns. Many farms already had the more modern loose box accommodation for cattle, although few had houses specifically for storing cattle cake. Unlike the model farms illustrated in agricultural journals, there were few stationary steam engines build on the Holkham estates. Keary only mentions the one at Lodge Farm, Castle Acre, while a few years later one was installed in the new estate workshops at Longlands. Labour was always cheap in Norfolk and the difficulties of obtaining coal before the establishment of the railway network probably provide the explanation for this. Coal which cost 18 shillings a ton at Kings Lynn was 28 shillings a ton at Swaffham and 30 shillings in Dereham. This situation was changed by the opening of the Lynn–Dereham line in 1848, but most Holkham farms were some distance from a railway.[83] The farms near Holkham could probably have obtained sea coal direct from Wells, but there are no accounts of this happening. There was little accommodation for implements and not many farms had their own smithies. In the period after 1865 we see some of these shortages being remedied as the types of farm improvement undertaken changed to suit changing farming techniques.

The extension of existing premises, 1865–80

As cattle came to be valued not only for their manure but also for meat, it became more important to find a way of keeping them so that they fattened up while consuming as little food as possible. It was therefore necessary to keep them warm and prevent them using up energy in exercise. Manure remained a very valuable by-product and its conservation was still all important. By 1842 Loudan was advising the housing of all cattle.[84] By the late 1860s the controversy about open and and closed sheds was nearly over and most improvers were advocating closed sheds. The entries for the *J.R.A.S.E.* farm plan competition in 1879 all emphasised the importance of covering both stock and manure. The plans for the building of a 300 acre arable farm, called somewhat improbably 'Experimentia', showed an almost completely enclosed steading. Two advantages of this system were pointed out. First, the servants attending the stock at night and in stormy weather could do so in comfort and, secondly, the dung was protected.[85] By 1879 the barn formed only a very small part of the whole building complex. Farmers at Holkham, however, were not impressed by these plans and remained loyal to the old system of small yards holding about twelve cattle, as described by C. S. Read in 1858. For the final fattening-up of cattle for market, loose boxes, such as those at Egmere, were used. A set of loose boxes was built at West Lexham in 1855 at a cost of £100 to the estate, and improvements of the 1870s often included the provision of this

---

[83] D. I. Gordon, *A Regional History of the Railways of Great Britain: Eastern Counties* (London, 1968), p. 14.
[84] Peters, *Farm Buildings in Staffordshire*, p. 132.
[85] J. Bailey Denton, 'Report of the judges of farm plans', *J.R.A.S.E.*, second series, vol. 15 (1879), p. 796.

means of individually feeding stock in closed boxes where they had little freedom of movement. The appearance of the loose box with two rows of cattle facing inwards on the Holkham estates in the 1850s corresponds with the earliest date at which Peters found them in Staffordshire.[86]

One of the main developments of the period was therefore in the type of livestock accommodation provided. Large cattle yards were divided into smaller ones, allowing for great subdivision of stock, and loose boxes were built for the fattening of beasts for market.

Secondly, from the mid nineteenth century, more elaborate farm implements were being developed. Sale catalogues for the 1870s show that a wide range of different types of ploughs, harrows, horse hoes, rakes, rollers, seed drills, reapers, self-binders and turnip cutters were needed on a large farm. The sale at Lodge Farm, Castle Acre, in 1877 included 124 lots of implements alone. This more sophisticated equipment was expensive to buy and needed to be sheltered from the weather to prevent deterioration. Many of the implements were used only at one time of year and so were idle for the rest. It is therefore not surprising to find an increasing provision of implement sheds in the second half of the nineteenth century.

The use of more implements, and especially of more iron implements, justified the building of more smithies on farms. These smithies might be used by the local blacksmith when he paid his regular visits to the farm or, more rarely, a blacksmith, often doubling up as a carpenter, would be employed by the farm. At Lodge Farm, Castle Acre, a wheelwright, a carpenter and a blacksmith were all permanently employed on the farm and so all carts, waggons and harrows were home-made in the 1860s[87]

In contrast to the development of stock farming and the use of more machinery on the land, the development of machinery to harvest and prepare the grain did not involve the provision of new buildings. The barn lost its pre-eminence as threshing machines were introduced and no new barns were built on the Holkham estate after 1837, when £180 was spent on a new barn at Rose Farm, Tittleshall. Dr Peters quotes Parkinson as saying, 'The first expense [of a threshing machine] will be over-balanced by the saving in building barns, as one barn of a moderate size will be sufficient, where it is now necessary to have two or three

[86] Peters, *Farm Buildings in Staffordshire*, p. 160.
[87] Jenkins, 'Lodge Farm, Castle Acre', p. 473.

TABLE 4.2. *Farms with two phases of building, one before 1850 and one 1860–83*

			£	
Bintry Hall	1	New houses and premises,	1,482	1794–1800
		New bullock sheds, cow houses and granary	1,971	1834–40
	2	Sheds and yards	1,116	1879–82
Lodge Farm, Castle Acre	1	New house and premises	2,664	1797–1800
	2	Yards, etc. (including the infilling of the earlier yards with smaller enclosures)	1,439	1876–9
Panworth Hall, Ashill	1	New house and premises	2,006	1813–18
	2	Yards, etc.	1,858	1871–4
Tithe Farm, Weasenham	1	New house and premises	1,696	1814–16
	2	Four new yards	1,212	1876
Beck Hall, Billingford	1	New house and premises	1,053	1822–7
	2	Two yards, sheds and stables	2,096	1879–81
Manor Farm, Tittleshall	1	Addition to house and premises	1,034	1828–31
	2	Four yards, waggon lodge, carpenter's and blacksmith's shops	1,422	1873–5
Dunton Farm	1	New house and premises	3,376	1835–8
	2	Yards etc.	1,195	1883
Wicken Farm, Castle Acre	1	New house and premises	4,247	1797
	2	Four sheds and yards	1,850	1868–70

Source: Holkham MSS, audit books.

of great extent.'[88] That this policy was approved of by at least one progressive tenant farmer on the Holkham estate is shown by the comment of Hudson: 'In this improving age, it will be unwise to recommend the building of large expensive barns.'[89] From 1851 portable threshing machines were available and so threshing could be done in the open. The barn became more of a feed store for the increasingly important livestock. With the slump in grain prices in the 1870s this change to livestock became more pronounced and the building which followed the negotiations for new leases in the 1870s always involved the improvement of cattle accommodation.

[88] Peters, *Farm Buildings in Staffordshire*, p. 86.
[89] Hudson, 'Farm buildings', p. 282.

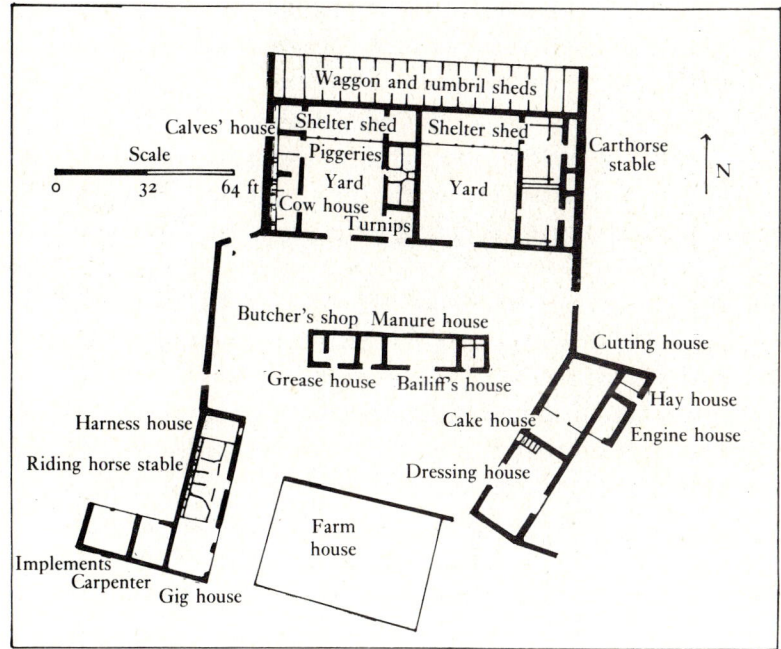

4.28 Plan of Hall Farm, Wighton.

Fig. 4.8 and table 4.2 show this change of emphasis in the type of building being erected. Between 1865 and 1880 at least twenty new sets of cattle sheds and yards were built. Eight new waggon lodges and several implement sheds were built, as well as four smithies.

If we look in detail at eight farms where over £1,000 was spent on a major improvement scheme both in the period before 1850 and in the period between 1865 and 1883, the differences between the earlier and later types became apparent (see table 4.2). The new farm houses and premises of the earlier period have already been discussed. The improvements of the second phase are those we would expect: cattle yards, implement sheds and blacksmith's shops. As early as 1851, Keary wrote that both Tithe Farm, Weasenham, and Manor Farm, Tittleshall, had inadequate livestock accommodation. However, his description of Panworth Hall shows that the cattle accommodation there was not increased by the improvements of the 1870s. As no plans of the farm before 1870 survive, it is impossible to know what the earlier layout was or how far the new buildings were a replacement along the same lines as the old. In the same way the building work done in the 1870s at

Waterden seems to have replaced old premises rather than increased their capacity.

The layout of the new buildings varied. Very often they involved the infilling of the original large yards with smaller ones, allowing for the greater division of cattle. This can clearly be seen at Lodge Farm, Castle Acre, where the contrast between the brick buildings of Wyatt's period and the flint and brick of the 1870s is very apparent. The same can be seen at Leicester Square Farm, South Creake, and Grenstein Farm, Tittleshall. In other examples the blocks of new buildings were built apart from the old premises. At Wicken Farm, Castle Acre, a range of four yards was built opposite the old barn.

The plan of Hall Farm, Wighton (fig. 4.28), shows the new cattle sheds and yards built between 1870 and 1875 as separate from the rest of the farm buildings. The rest of the buildings at Wighton are very scattered and the plan confirms the audit book evidence that there had been no concerted effort to improve the premises at Wighton Hall at an earlier date.

A very clear example of the type of rebuilding carried out during this period can be seen at Church Farm, Sparham (fig. 4.29), where a plan of 1880 shows a set of major modernisations which made this 220 acre holding into a stock farm. The old bullock shed and yard, which in Keary's days had housed ten cattle, was much enlarged. Three new yards were built and are dated 1882. Two small yards attached to pigsties are dated 1881 and one of the two barns mentioned by Keary was pulled down. A long narrow building containing two rows of loose boxes was built and is dated 1882. The audit books show £556 as being spent by the estate at Church Farm in 1881 and 1882.

During the nineteenth century there were many experiments in the use of new materials for building, and concrete was one of those tried. It was successfully used for docks by the 1860s, and in the 1870s articles in the *J.R.A.S.E.* were suggesting it should be used for farm buildings.[90] The earliest examples of its agricultural use were in Scotland in the 1860s. In England the eccentric agriculturalist, Robert Campbell, built a concrete barn on his highly mechanised farm at Buscot in Berkshire in the 1870s.[91] Other than this there were no known examples before 1900.

[90] G. Hunt, 'On concrete as a building material for farm buildings and cottages', *J.R.A.S.E.*, second series, vol. 10 (1874), pp. 211–31.
[91] Harvey, *History of Farm Buildings*, p. 123 and J. R. Gray, 'An industrial farm estate in Berkshire', *Industrial Archaeology*, vol. 8, no. 2 (May 1971), pp. 175–85.

4.29 Farm premises, Sparham. (a) Loose boxes. (b) Cattle sheds.

It is now clear that the second Earl of Leicester was also a pioneer in the use of concrete. In 1873 the estate paid £137 to 'Drake's Patent Concrete Co. for building apparatus'. Only two sets of concrete premises survive on the Holkham estate, both of them in the parish of Tittleshall. The earliest example is at Wicken Farm, where a waggon lodge of

4.30 Concrete sheds, Wicken Farm, Tittleshall.

concrete is dated 1876 (fig. 4.30) and a garden wall, 1875. In 1883 a range of two piggeries was built at Godwick Farm. Concrete cottages were built in several parishes on the estate in the 1870s. With a brick kiln at Holkham and plenty of flints to be found in the fields it can hardly have been worth making concrete. Concrete farm buildings suffered from the same structural defects as did concrete cottages (see chapter 5) and there is no indication that others were built. Unfortunately there is no correspondence in the letter books on this subject and the cost of the individual buildings is not given in the audit books.

Certain changes in the pattern of farm buildings can be seen between 1865 and 1880. No more complete sets of premises were built. Instead, buildings were being adapted to more intensive livestock farming. This often involved the spending of large sums of money over short periods instead of the staggering of expenditure over a number of years as before 1850. Tenants were not as often responsible for new buildings as in the earlier period and payments were usually made by the estate to the individual builders rather than to the tenants themselves.

There was little decrease in expenditure by the estate, or in rents collected, until 1880. This continuing expenditure, in spite of the pessimism pervading agriculture, is surprising and is not found on other estates. One explanation of this situation can be offered here. Several improvements after 1870 coincide with the renewal of leases and the putting of a farm in order was all part of the agreement made between the landlord and the tenant when the lease needed renewing. A letter concerning the new lease for Hudson's farm at Wighton, written in 1871, makes this point clear: 'and his Lordship has undertaken to make a new arrangement of the Creake gate road premises and to build some premises by the Holkham road and to make the house and home premises sufficient in his opinion for the size and requirement of the farm without any additional charge'. In a period when farming was depressed, it was necessary to keep the buildings in good order and to build new ones in order to keep both good tenants and high rents. This was an unprecedented situation on the Holkham estates, where in the past there had always been a waiting list of prospective tenants for the farms.

The effects of depression, 1880–1909

It was impossible for even a well run estate farmed by skilled tenants with capital and all the advantages of both land and buildings in good condition to avoid the depression for ever, and after 1880 rents fell rapidly. Expenditure on farm buildings also fell, but it still accounted for about 10% of the rents. Fewer building projects were undertaken and most of these were on a very small scale, involving expenditure of under £200 and usually being no more than miscellaneous repairs. Farm implements were continually becoming more sophisticated and two new implement sheds were built during this period. Ten schemes involved the building of new livestock sheds and yards and cost up to £400 per annum. Only five of these took more than a year to complete. Kipton Ash Farm was completely rebuilt in 1891, and although it is now very derelict it appears that the farm was similar to those of the 1870s. Very little was written in agricultural journals on the subject of farm buildings and, with the lack of landlord interest and often a lack of capital, no major improvements in farm building design were suggested, although covered yards increased in popularity. W. J. Moscrop explained how covered yards had come to be fully accepted by landlord and tenant alike. 'I had much difficulty in carrying the tenant with me in the first yard I roofed over, but now in letting a farm, almost the first thing asked is "Will you cover the yards?".'[92] Although no covered yards survive on the

[92] W. J. Moscrop, 'Covered cattle yards', *J.R.A.S.E.*, third series, vol. 1 (1890), p. 473.

Holkham estates, Rider Haggard wrote in 1902 that he visited a farm near Holkham where the buildings were very fine and the cattle were kept in large covered yards.[93] Large-scale mechanised farming was carried on by Keith at Egmere, but this was achieved with only the addition of a small waggon lodge, workshop and smithy to the original buildings designed by Dean.

The Royal Commission on the State of Agriculture reported in 1891 that Norfolk farms were well furnished with houses and buildings and that expenditure on repairs was being kept up. Every Norfolk farm had a straw yard and yards for fattening bullocks, some being wholly covered and others partially so. Some of the best farmers said they preferred partly open yards so long as they were well sheltered. Most of the farms had been so well equipped in the more prosperous times that expenditure could be curtailed without very serious effects. 'Where landlords now build, they often do so less substantially and permanently than before.'[94]

The farms of the Raynham estates were much improved in the later years of the nineteenth century. Although there are no date stones and no documents which can help, the style of building suggest that they were erected after 1870. In his report for the Royal Commission on Agriculture, Henry Rew said that the Marquis of Townshend had spent £40,000 on his estates between 1880 and 1895; £8,000 of this had been used for the improvement of cottages and the remaining £32,000 for the farm.[95] Some large older barns survive and this later expenditure must have been partly for repairs to existing buildings and partly for building new cattle yards.

By the last twenty years of the nineteenth century investment in farm improvements had slowed down considerably on most of the great estates, including Holkham. Only necessary repairs were carried out and few new cattle and implement sheds were erected. Most of this work coincided with the granting of new leases.

Conclusions

Through these detailed studies of types of building erected on the Holkham estates between 1790 and 1909 it is possible to see how far the improvements made by two generations of Cokes followed the theoretical

---

[93] Haggard, *Rural England*, vol. 2, p. 471.
[94] Parliamentary Papers (1896), (c.8021), XVII, Henry Rew, *Report on Norfolk*, p. 35.
[95] *Ibid.*

plans published, and to what extent they led national trends. Many of the planned farms of the first half of the nineteenth century were very much like those advocated by the designers, and the second earl continued to follow closely the work of the agricultural engineers. It is particularly interesting to have an example of Dean's work on the estate, showing that one of the best known farm architects of the time was employed to build the estate workshops and the only farmstead that was completely rebuilt. The result was the show pieces of Longlands and Egmere. Later, the estate tried building in concrete at a time when the technique was still at a very experimental stage.

By the 1870s the estate was less attracted by the theoretical plans published. Highly mechanised farms with covered yards, steam engines, tramways and special buildings for boiling and preparing animal food were not built at Holkham. Very few seem to have been built at all, and those there were were built for owner-occupiers rather than tenants. The cost was frequently not justified by increased efficiency. Instead of expensive complete rebuilds at Holkham, the farmsteads of the early nineteenth century were later adapted for a more intensive animal husbandry, while the barn became a less important building in the farm layout.

The pattern of expenditure was also changed over the period. The tenant played a less important part in carrying out improvements and expenditure was not staggered over a number of years as it had been previously. In the last years of the century improvements were more often linked with the renewal of leases.

Having considered both the financial and architectural aspects of farm building on the Holkham estates it is now valid to ask whether the large expenditure on farm building improvement was profitable to either the tenant or the landlord, and whether farming was in fact over-capitalised by the middle of the nineteenth century.

The farms of the Holkham estate in the 1860s usually provided no more than that which was needed by a progressive and intensive farmer practising a system of mixed agriculture. He would have used all the buildings and, except for some of the more extravagant designs of Samuel Wyatt, there was little unnecessary embellishment. Henry Rew pointed out that, because the buildings had been kept in order in better times, they would not suffer for a few years when landlords could not afford to invest in their estates. If the money had not been spent in earlier years, then the effect of the depression would have been much greater. There is the specific example of Egmere, which was able to remain a profitable and highly mechanised farm using buildings unaltered since the time of their erection half a century before. Certainly one of the reasons why Holkham tenants suffered less than many others during the depression was that by the 1870s they leased farms well equipped for the intensive livestock farming that alone remained profitable.

5
The landlord and the labourer

The life of most villagers was affected directly or indirectly by their landlord. Estate villages had a focus that the more diversified open villages did not. The control of the squire had a unifying influence on the inhabitants.

This control could make itself felt in several ways. First and most directly, the landlord was an employer. Not only did he employ agricultural labourers, he also needed servants to run his house, gardeners and gamekeepers in the grounds, stable hands, grooms and coachman to look after the horses and carriages, and an agent and his staff to administer the estate. The estate probably had its own brickyard with its own employees, its own plantations needing woodmen and foresters and an estate workshop with bricklayers, carpenters, waggoners and wheelwrights. In Holkham village, 162 of the 240 employed men were working directly for Lord Leicester in 1851.

However, the landlord indirectly influenced the lives of his cottagers before they reached an employable age. Usually before the 1870s, schools were only built where they were sponsored by him. He, or his wife and daughters, might well visit the school regularly and from a very early age children would come to treat him with the respect he thought due to him.

The religious side of village life was also under his influence. Very often he was patron of the living, and how much control he could exercise over his incumbant varied from place to place. The classic study by Professor Chadwick analysing the relationship between Sir John Boileau and his vicar at Ketteringham shows just how much control some landlords felt they had a right to exercise.[1] The spread of non-conformity might also be influenced by the views of the squire, and chapels built only where he tolerated them. Sometimes he might even give a piece

[1] O. Chadwick, *A Victorian Miniature* (London, 1960).

of land for the purpose; more often the building was some distance from the main village, often in a hamlet less under his control.

Politics were almost entirely controlled by the landlord. Before 1832 it was only the landowners who could vote. The first and subsequent reform acts gave an increasing number of tenants the right to vote as well, but their vulnerability to eviction meant that before the introduction of the secret ballot in 1872 they must have voted as their landlord wished.

At a later date the landlord could effectively prevent the setting up of unions on his estates, often using the threat of eviction from their cottages to union men. The autobiography of George Edwards, a farm labourer in the 1870s and 1880s and later an M.P., clearly shows this happening in Norfolk.[2] We have seen, however, that Lord Leicester was not against unions and that he hoped to protect labourers from eviction by farmers by letting cottages directly rather than through the farmer.

Finally, the landlord's power was felt through his control of cottage building and conditions. He was responsible for the upkeep and repair of his cottages as well as for their letting. The living conditions of many of the villagers were thus directly governed by him.

It is clear from articles in the *Norfolk News* in the 1860s, describing cottage conditions, that the mood within a village was affected by the attitude of the landlord to his social duties. In parishes where the landlord took little interest in the well-being of the inhabitants, labourers were sullen or morose, with a deep-seated dislike of the wealthy owners of broad acres, or desperately rebellious, not caring about themselves or others. In other parishes where the squire's presence was more obvious, where the cottages were well looked after and a good village school was frequently visited by the squire, his wife and daughters, morale was much higher.

The role that the landed estate was expected to play in the local community changed little during the nineteenth century. By the end of this period some of its duties were being taken over by the state, and the decline in rents meant that many estates were curtailing their philanthropic activities, but the Duke of Bedford was at pains to point out that this was not true at Woburn,[3] and some of Lord Leicester's most generous gifts were also made after 1875.

By the late nineteenth century, the hereditary system of landownership

---

[2] G. Edwards, *From Crow-scaring to Westminster* (London, 1922).
[3] Duke of Bedford, *The Story of a Great Estate* (London, 1897), p. 109.

was being openly criticised and great landowners were having to defend their position by stressing their important and valuable role in the community. One reason why the Duke of Bedford wrote *The Story of a Great Estate* was to show that 'none of the responsibilities generally regarded as inseparable from the position of a great landowner had been evaded'.[4] in spite of the 'Great Depression'.

One of the arguments for the hereditary system was that landowners took their traditional responsibilities seriously. Running an estate was more than a business where profits alone counted. The well-being of the estate and those dependent upon it was also important to the hereditary landowner.

> Abolish primogeniture, compel either by law or by the weight of opinion a sub-division of landed property; it will still be bought up and held in great quantities, but it will be held by men of business, who being no longer able to look forward to permanence of occupancy and therefore having no motive for securing the good will of the people around them, will regard their possessions from a money point of view, and will aim at attaining the largest possible amount of profit and pleasure for themselves.[5]

This statement of Froude's is quoted by the Duke of Bedford who obviously approved of the sentiments it expressed. In fact, the landowning community had always had its ranks swelled by businessmen who often brought new management techniques with them. The established landowners learnt from them, but the newcomers also took on the traditional philanthropic duties which were necessary if they were to become respected members of their local community.

These responsibilities, which the landowner accepted and which he felt justified the hereditary system, were many. He usually saw himself as more than a rent collector. The comfort of the cottagers as well as the state of their homes was his concern. The motives for these philanthropic activities were mixed. 'Philanthropy and religious feeling coincided with a desire to protect the establishment.'[6] The sense of duty of the aristocratic class combined with a desire to control all aspects of life on the estate and preserve the deferential society and habitual respect of the landed class which was basic to their way of life.

The Holkham estate was large, and direct contact with the community was difficult. Here the personal initiative was often taken by the larger tenant farmers who would suggest worthy projects to the landlord for

---

[4] *Ibid.*, p. 7.
[5] *Ibid.*, p. 8, quoting J. A. Froude, *Short Studies on Great Subjects*, vol. 3, p. 424.
[6] F. M. L. Thompson, *English Landed Society in the Nineteenth Century* (London, 1963), p. 4.

his financial support. In this way, 'even the more distant villages on the estate looked to the great house for the upkeep of local charities the schools, for repairs to the church and for feasts and merrymaking on great occasions'.[7]

In a Holkham village, as in any other in the nineteenth century, the variety of employment was far greater than in the same community today. In the large village of Tittleshall (population 615 in 1851) there was a grocer, more than one butcher, a shoemaker, a baker and a draper. The craftsmen represented included bricklayers and brickmakers, a thatcher, blacksmiths, wheelwrights (one employing eleven people), hurdle makers, a miller, a basket maker, a tailor, a fisherman and a 'dog breaker'. Just over half the employed population of 215 were agricultural labourers, but in only 55 of the 124 dwellings was the head of the family an agricultural labourer. At the same date Keary lists fifty cottages in the village as owned by the Holkham estate, but not all of these were occupied by agricultural labourers. A carpenter, two hurdle makers, a blacksmith, a tailor, a shoemaker and the parish clerk were all tenant cottagers. The only occupier who would have been directly employed by the estate was a woodman, presumably working on the Tittleshall plantations. Flitcham is the only Holkham parish where as many as half the houses were owned by the estate. In Weasenham it was a third, in Warham about 40% and in Wighton 30%.

The farm labourers themselves fell into various categories, each having a different degree of security. The most secure were those who cared for livestock. The shepherd, the (cattle) yardsman and the (horse) teamsman were always hired by the year and usually provided with a cottage on the farmstead. Annual hiring fairs had been an important part of rural life in the eighteenth century. Newspaper advertisements show that there were twenty-five in Norfolk in 1762. This had declined to three by 1822 and coincides with the decline of annual hiring, except for certain specialised tasks. Other labourers might be provided with cottages, but were only hired and paid by the day. They had no security of work or tenure. In fact, when cottage rentals on the Holkham estate are studied, it is clear that some cottages stayed in the same family for more than a generation. In Weasenham about half the cottages changed hands every ten years. Four families stayed for over eight years and six for between fifty and eighty years. Most agricultural labourers would be

[7] G. E. Mingay, *English Landed Society in the Eighteenth Century* (London, 1963), p. 16.

doing a variety of different tasks from season to season. As well as the regular group of workers, most farmers would hire gangs to help with various seasonal tasks. Members of these gangs might be the children and wives of regular workers, or more often were recruited from neighbouring non-estate villages. All three types of labour, those hired annually, those hired daily and gangs, could well be employed on the same farm.

Most farmers also employed women and boys. Fourteen boys in Tittleshall between the ages of five and fourteen were permanently employed, while many more, described in the census as 'scholars', would have helped with seasonal tasks. Only four girls under the age of fourteen were regularly employed. Twenty-two women were listed as field workers and supplied some of the all-important cheap labour for the farms. Victorian morality disliked the idea of women and children working the fields and Lord Leicester gave his views on the subject to a Royal Commission in 1867. His attitude towards juvenile labour seems to have been similar to that of other employers, and certainly not ahead of his time. He thought that boys of ten ought to work, although he claimed that he would support a law prohibiting the employment of children under ten. If there was such a law 'he need not succumb to the solicitations of parents'. Similarly he would have liked to prohibit the employment of women under twenty in field labour, 'but female labour cannot altogether be dispensed with in this neighbourhood'.[8] There was no concern shown at this date for the plight of elderly labourers. In the days before pensions, men worked for as long as they could find an employer, and in Tittleshall there were four agricultural labourers in their seventies and one of eighty-two.

Wages on the Holkham estate were very similar to those elsewhere in Norfolk. In 1840 they varied between 9 and 10 shillings a week for men and about 2 shillings a week for boys and 4 to 6 shillings for women. Teamsmen often earned about 2s. 6d. more. On top of this, harvest money amounted to between £5 and £6 per labourer, as well as extra earnings for the other members of the family working on the harvest field. There was an added monetary bonus for those working directly for the Earl of Leicester, who did not give harvest beer or provide a 'harvest frolic' for his labourers. Instead he gave 10 shillings in place of beer and

---

[8] Parliamentary Papers (1867), (510), XVI, *Royal Commission on the Employment of Women and Children in Agriculture*, p. 165.

5 shillings in place of the 'frolic'. 'Some of the best labourers do not drink beer at all; they do their work on coffee or cocoa.'[9]

If wages in Holkham villages were no higher than elsewhere, it does seem that cottage rents were lower. It was generally agreed that cottages on a large estate were better, and were let at lower rents than those put up by speculators in the open villages. The Holkham rents were between £2 10s. and £3 and Lord Leicester claimed that rents in the open villages were between £4 and £5.[10] These figures can be supported from other evidence. It was generally accepted that the market value of a cottage costing £50 to build was £5 per annum. However, most of the big landowners let at a lower rent. 'Cottages were rented low to allow low wages to be paid.'[11] Some cottagers found it difficult to pay even low rents and so it was deducted from the harvest money before it was paid.[12]

If cottages were let with the farms and then sub-let by the farmer then he could certainly subsidise wages himself by letting at a low rent. At Holkham where the cottages were let directly by Lord Leicester it would seem that he was subsidising the tenant farmer.

Unlike farm rents, those for cottages rose only slowly through the nineteenth century. In the early years they varied from £1 to £2 12s., while by 1900 they were mostly about £2, with a few as high as £4 per year.

There is some scattered evidence that Lord Leicester supported the allotment movement, and between 1888 and 1902 he let small parcels of land in several parishes to either the Guardians of the Poor or the parish council to be used for that purpose. However, as he claimed that all his cottages had good gardens, there may have been little need for allotments as well. Landlords and farmers were often against the granting of allotments, as they felt that men who dug their own land for a couple of hours before or after work had little interest or energy left for their employers.

School building

The suggestion has been made that, as the century progressed, landlords lost some of their importance as benevolent fathers to their community. It is argued that industrialisation meant that the limited philanthropy

---

[9] Ibid.   [10] Ibid., p. 142.
[11] F. Clifford, 'The Labour Bill in farming', *J.R.A.S.E.*, second series, vol. 11 (1875), pp. 113–17.
[12] Ingham and Threxton farm accounts, N.R.O.

of landowners was not sufficient to cope with the needs of the new society. In rural areas political reform meant that landowners were no longer dominant in government and slowly other organisations such as school boards and Boards of Guardians took over some of these functions. Agricultural workers were beginning to resent the paternalism of the landowners.

By the end of the century, the new county councils may have played a more important part in the lives of the community than the landlords, and the decline of the landlords' influence can be seen particularly in education. In 1800, the provision of village schools in England was very limited. Those there were, were the result both of endowments and the charity school movement. There were a few schools supported by landowners and also a variety of fee paying 'dame schools', which were often very impermanent and sometimes offered little more than baby-minding services. The situation in Norfolk follows this pattern. In 1819 there were one hundred endowed non-classical schools. A typical endowment was that for a school in Wighton, where Sarah Charles left money to teach six girls to read, knit and sew, and to learn the church catechism. Charity schools were set up in the early eighteenth century and thirty-four schools were opened in Norfolk, providing for 570 boys and 223 girls by 1750. However, there was little expansion after 1730, possibly because of the limited curriculum. Children were to be taught humility and the acceptance of their status. Instruction in reading, particularly the Bible, writing and arithmetic was provided. Where possible children were made fit for service or apprenticing. Many schools degenerated into schools of industry and children were set to work. By 1787 the schools in Norwich were said to be in decline because the children were given no earnings.[13]

There was obviously much scope for improvement and the nineteenth century saw the foundation of many schools, some privately financed by landlords and others supported by one of the two national societies. The National Society for Promoting the Education of the Poor in the Principles of the Established Church was founded in 1811, and the British and Foreign School Society was founded in 1814. The returns of the Select Committee appointed to enquire into the education of the poor show that in 1816 there were 344 Norfolk parishes with schools for a total population of 212,830. 17,869 children were attending day

---

[13] M. F. Lloyd Pritchard, 'The education of the poor in Norfolk, 1700–1850', *Norfolk Archaeology*, vol. 33, no. 3 (1964), pp. 321–31.

schools and 8,457 Sunday schools.[14] Figures quoted by Bacon cover only church schools, or those affiliated to the church. They shows that, in 1840, 14,185 children went to day schools and 10,797 to Sunday schools. Writing in 1844, he adds, 'since this report was published, an addition of from 4–5,000 under education in connection with the church has been made'.[15]

The only schools on the Holkham estate which were built and entirely supported by the Coke family independent of any society were at Holkham. Schools for boys and girls were erected in Holkham village in 1821 and were thus the earliest to be founded on the estate. These buildings were replaced in the 1880s by one still standing near the Victoria Hotel gate to the park. It is a lofty single-storied two-room building typical of many country schools of that date. As a privately financed school, much of the administration was carried out by the estate. In 1852, the agent wrote to the Secretary for Education asking for the payment of £4 12s. for books at Holkham school. The estate ledgers show that in the 1850s and 1860s the salary to the master, which included an allowance for coal, was £65 per annum. In 1854–5 he received an extra £5 7s. 0½d. for teaching adults at evening school. In the 1870s his salary rose to £80, which was paid by the estate. Allowances for coal were also paid and amounted to £4 per annum. By the 1870s a salary of £13 a year was paid to a teacher at the infant's school at Holkham and £10 8s. to the mistress of the new infant's school in New Holkham. The girls' school teacher received £15 8s. The schools were made over to a school board in the 1880s and at that time were attended by sixty children. There is no correspondence connected with the schools surviving and the log books have been lost, so we know little else.

The only other interest the Earl of Leicester took in education at Holkham was shown in the building of a village reading room and library in 1886 at a cost of £1,500 (fig. 5.1). Nothing is known about the administration of the library or the librarian. There is no record of a salary being paid to a librarian; perhaps it was the responsibility of the school master. It would have been interesting to know what sort of books were in the library and who paid for them, but there are no records or personal memories which help here.

Founded in 1821, Holkham school is the earliest on the estate. A

[14] *Ibid.*
[15] R. N. Bacon, *Agriculture of Norfolk* (London, 1844), p. 159.

5.1 Holkham reading room.

national school was set up by the rector of Tittleshall in 1836 and another in Castle Acre in 1839. In 1843 the Earl of Leicester donated £30 to a school in Billingford. In 1852, £20 was given to Bawdeswell and Foxley schools. The 1850s saw the founding of several schools on the Holkham estate, but none of these was initiated by the earl. Sparham school was founded by subscription in 1852, and thereafter the earl reguarly paid £5 to the fund. In 1854, the rector founded a school at Wellingham. The earl did not contribute to the school until the 1880s, when he occasionally paid a subscription of £4 and in 1885 gave £10 towards the building of an extension. In 1859, Lord Leicester gave the site for a school at Weasenham and in the same year contributed £200 to John Hastings' fund for building a school at Longham. He also allowed Hastings to dig brick earth for making bricks for building the school. The school was to be run on a voluntary system with Lord Leicester contributing a share based on the rateable value of his property in Longham.[16] Longham school was built as a one-roomed school with a master's house attached. A Holkham date stone is inserted in the gable wall. Lord Leicester also paid an annual subscription of eight guineas to Longham and £10 to Weasenham school. In 1855, the total sum paid out in school subscriptions was £46.

[16] Holkham MSS, letter books, vol. 2 (1859), p. 435.

In the 1860s a new infant school was begun by the rector of Tittleshall and a new school was opened in Warham, but there were no other new schools on the estate. Schools at Castle Acre and Billingford were added to the list of those receiving subscriptions from the earl, and by 1865 this sum had risen to £73 11s.

This very limited interest in school building up to 1870 is typical of estates in many parts of rural England. However, the 1870 education act galvanised many landowners into action. The alternative to a school financed and controlled by the estate was one run democratically and along non-denominational lines by a school board, and this was not usually favoured by landlords.[17] Thompson illustrates this point from the Wilton estates, where the annual payments to schools made by the Earl of Pembroke rose in the 1870s from £600 to £1,000. Eventually, however, voluntary schools could not compete with the standards of the board schools. 'The struggle was slowly conceded and landlords' contributions fell away.'[18]

Holkham conforms to Thompson's pattern of higher expenditure on schools in the 1870s. In 1875, 'the parishioners and Lord Leicester' built a school at Flitcham, Lord Leicester contributing £193. The school at Wighton was built by subscription in 1872, Lord Leicester giving £100. Some schools needed enlarging if they were to reach the standards required by the school board. In 1873, the earl gave very small sums (£3, £2, £6) towards the enlarging of Burnham Thorpe, Sporle and South Creake schools. Other schools received more substantial help. North Creake school was endowed with £388. The total donated to schools in the 1870s was £1,059; however, none was built entirely by Lord Leicester, and it is clear that there must have been plenty of support from other sources. By 1875, the earl subscribed to eighteen schools at an annual cost of £330. This is the highest expenditure on school subscriptions for the period studied.

Lord Leicester's performance is lamentable when compared with that of the Duke of Bedford and the Earl of Pembroke at Wilton (Wiltshire). Even though the timing of this increased expenditure at Holkham does conform to the Wilton pattern, the motive was not that described in the study by Thompson. Lord Leicester was not against school boards, but was quite prepared to share the responsibility for school building with

---

[17] Thompson, *English Landed Society*, p. 208.
[18] *Ibid.*, p. 209.

other ratepayers. He was well able to maintain his influence over the new school boards, as they consisted mostly of his tenants. The Wells Board School opened in 1875 with Lord Leicester's agent, Samuel Shellabear, as chairman of the board.

An example of the earl's encouragement of school boards can be seen at Castle Acre. In 1871, Lord Leicester wrote to John Hudson saying that he was not prepared to do anything about a school in Castle Acre as he thought that a school board including Newton and South Acre should be set up.[19] Shellabear was instructed to negotiate with the Board of Education and other landowners around Castle Acre to find a way of setting up a school board there. In June he wrote to the agent of the neighbouring Fountaine's estate, 'I was in Castle Acre yesterday and had a consultation with Messrs Leeds and Hudson upon the subject of the school there.' It was then agreed that an arrangement should be made between Newton, South Acre and Castle Acre and this was discussed with a government inspector, who was also at the meeting. Shellabear suggested that Castle Acre should pay two thirds and the other parishes one third of the costs. 'Usually in a school of this size the Government grant and the children's pence pay the salaries, therefore the amount required annually would be small.'[20] There followed a lengthy correspondence between Hudson and Leeds, the two largest Castle Acre tenants, and Shellabear who undertook the correspondence with the Board of Education in London, filled in the appropriate forms requesting the setting up of a local school board, and then sent them to Hudson and Leeds to sign and send off. Eventually the board was set up. The existing national school, built in 1839, was to become an infants' school and a new school was to be built. A school master was to be employed and paid £40 per year, and a school mistress, £20. Shellabear provided the plans for the school, Holkham brick was to be used, and Lord Leicester would convey the school and its site on trust. The school board of 1872 consisted of the vicar of Castle Acre and the vicar of South Acre, Thomas Moore Hudson and Thomas Leeds, both farmers of Castle Acre, Thomas Matthews, farmer of Newton, and John Love, a doctor. The professional and farming community dominated school boards and, from the limited evidence available for this area of Norfolk, there does not seem to have been any working class participation. Evidence for

[19] Holkham MSS, letter books, vol. 7 (1871), p. 87.
[20] Castle Acre School Board MS, lent to the author by Mr R. D. Everington of Blakeney, Norfolk.

Derbyshire shows the same situation. The school boards 'had a sameness about them; a member of the local gentry, a clergyman or manufacturers, depending on the district'.[21] There was some criticism of the number of Lord Leicester's tenants on Castle Acre school board. Shellabear wrote in answer to these criticisms, 'As Lord Leicester will pay most of the expenses, through the rates, then he should be represented on the Board, "Taxation without representation is tyranny."'[22]

At Castle Acre we see the initiative for the school coming from the tenants, while dealings with the Board of Education were carried out by the estate office. Although the actual sums donated to school building were small, much help in kind was given. The land and building materials were given by the estate and, as the principal ratepayer, Lord Leicester would be the main contributor to the upkeep of the school.

The interest of tenant farmers such as Hudson, Leeds and Hastings in the building of schools is surprising. Contemporaries frequently recorded the antipathy that farmers had towards education: 'The farmers and the squire are no friends to elementary education. They associate depression and high rents with compulsory education and grudge to pay for that teaching which deprives them of servants and furnishes their labourers with wings to fly from the parish.'[23] Norfolk evidence also shows this attitude. 'Farmers preferred boys young and boys ignorant, for an educated man was discontented, independent and more fond of reading newspapers than work. It is difficult for school masters and clergy to combat this strong farming influence.'[24] A Derbyshire farmer reporting to the Royal Commission on the Employment of Young Persons and Women in Agriculture (1867) said, 'The business of a farm labourer cannot be thoroughly acquired if work be not commenced before 11 or 12.' Boys were usually employed at the age of seven or earlier.[25] Answers to Bacon's questionnaire of 1844 show that the employment of young boys was common in Norfolk as well. In their attitude to education the Holkham tenants seem to be in a class apart from other farmers. They took the initiative in the setting up of schools and the estate would then negotiate with the appropriate authorities and provide a substantial proportion of the funds.

[21] M. Johnson, *Derbyshire Village Schools in the Nineteenth Century* (Newton Abbot, 1970), p. 136.
[22] Holkham MSS, letter books, vol. 7 (1872), p. 852.
[23] R. R. Sellman, *Devon Village Schools in the Nineteenth century* (Newton Abbot, 1967), p. 65.
[24] L. Marion Springall, *Labouring Life in Norfolk Villages, 1834–1914* (London, 1936), p. 68.
[25] Johnson, *Derbyshire Village Schools*, p. 110.

Few records for schools on the Holkham estate survive, but an application made for a grant by Castle Acre school in 1873 gives a few details. The school consisted of three rooms, one for the infants, one for the boys and one for the girls. The infant school had been built in the 1830s, but the rest was new. The school had no endowments but collected £41 in school pence. The children of tradesmen paid 4d., and of the labouring class 2d. for the first child, 3½d. for two and 4½d. for three children. There were fifty-four boys, forty-nine girls and forty-seven infants in the school.[26]

The only log books remaining for any school on the Holkham estate are those for the school set up by the rector of Tittleshall in 1867 and are in the Education Department at County Hall. They do not give a detailed picture of the day-to-day running of the school, but they mention special events and also give the level of absenteeism. The school was run by the rector, who was the manager. He, his wife and his daughters visited the school and also taught in it regularly. Tenant farmers and their wives only rarely visited the school, while two visits from Lady Ann Coke and one of Lady Margaret are recorded. The school nearly always received a favourable report from both the diocesan and Her Majesty's inspectors. Numbers on the registers varied between fifty and eighty, but absenteeism was always high. Entries such as 'Numbers greatly decreased by some of the children leaving to go to work' are typical of all rural schools of this period. The school staff consisted of two teachers helped by two monitors drawn from among the older pupils. The picture given in the log books is very much that which we would expect of a small rural church school in the second half of the nineteenth century. The lack of interest of tenant farmers in this church school contrasts greatly with their attitude elsewhere on the estate.

There was really little need for farmers to worry about losing labour. Although many young people were moving away from the countryside by the end of the century, it was the low wages and agricultural depression that were responsible rather than education. The schooling provided was very limited and was usually aimed at teaching subordination rather than encouraging ambition. If attempts towards compulsory education were to be made it was better, from the farmers' point of view, that they should be in charge rather than anyone else. There is no

---

[26] Castle Acre School Board MS, as note 20.,

evidence that the school boards made any efforts to force compulsory education.

Plans for various schools built on the estate survive among the estate archives. The existence of these plans at Holkham suggests that the estate office may have helped in their design and allowed its drawing office facilities to be used. They include plans for the new Holkham School (1881), Longham School (1862), North Creake School (1896), Dunton School (1872), Weasenham School (plan undated), Castle Acre School (1871), Billingford School (1874, 'converted from Millatt's barn'), and Tittleshall Infants' School (1894). Longham and Billingford schools were both one-roomed schools. Longham is the only one on the estate which includes a house for the master. The other school plans are more substantial, providing two or three rooms. They are all simple buildings with no architectural pretensions, but they probably provided adequately for the standards of the time.

Expenditure on school subscriptions and building dropped in the 1880s (£198 in 1885). There was only one donation of £5 for the alterations to Elmham school master's house. By 1895 the subscriptions paid had dropped to £126 as more schools were taken over by school boards. Subscriptions were replaced by school rates. In 1903, the Norfolk County Council set up its education committee and many schools on the estate were leased by Lord Leicester to the county council. These included those at Holkham, Flitcham, Wells, Longham and Warham.

By the late 1870s every parish on Lord Leicester's estates had a school and he had contributed in some way to them all. At Bintree, Weasenham, Longham and Castle Acre he had given a site, and sometimes, as at Longham, he had given permission for the digging of brick earth on his estate. The sums of money which he contributed were always small and his help seems to have been in kind rather than in money. The estate office often helped the local residents in applying for grants and drawing up plans.

The amount spent on schools by Lord Leicester is very small when compared with the expenditure of the Bedford or Wilton estates. Only the school at Holkham was entirely supported by him, while other local landowners seem to have done far more. The Cholmondeleys of Houghton were responsible for founding schools at Harpley, Bircham and Massingham, and the Townshends supported the Raynham and Helhoughton schools.[27]

Lord Leicester's contributions to both the building and running costs of schools are minute when compared with the cost of cottage or farm repairs, and it seems that he had little interest in school building beyond that which duty demanded. The initiative for new schools always came from outside the estate office, usually from tenant farmers, who were often school managers or active members of school boards.

Lord Leicester was not afraid of handing over the control of education to the non-denominational school boards and he did much to help in setting them up. This also seems to have been the attitude of the Duke of Bedford, although Thompson points out that it was not true of the Earl of Pembroke on the Wilton estates. Thompson believes that the Wilton situation is more typical of England as a whole, but the Bedford and the Holkham estates must stand out as two notable exceptions.[28]

Religious activities

We know very little about the religious life of labourers in Holkham villages, or the landlord's influence over it, but they do seem to have had plenty of denominations to choose from by 1851. The religious census shows Baptists, Wesleyan, Primitive and Reformed Methodists, Ranters, Independent and Latter Day Saints, as well as the Church of England, holding well attended services in Holkham villages. Every estate village, except for Holkham itself, had at least one non-conformist chapel by 1870 and so it seems that Lord Leicester did nothing to prevent the establishment of non-conformity in his villages. There is one reference to the earl paying a subscription to the Walsingham circuit. About half of the estate population attended a religious service on the Sunday of the census, which shows that Holkham villages differed very little from the national average. A third of those attending were in chapel rather than church, which is rather lower than the national average of a half. The church was usually stronger in the countryside than in the towns. The Earl of Leicester was patron of Billingford, Holkham, Flitcham, Castle Acre and Tittleshall churches. Many of these are some

---

[27] W. White, *Norfolk Directory* (London, 1881).
[28] Thompson, *English Landed Society*, p. 100.

distance from Holkham and it is doubtful whether his influence over the direct running of church affairs would be felt. At Holkham, however, he could have had more influence. Lady Elizabeth Stanhope's description of Christmas in 1847 shows that all those at the hall were too exhausted by Christmas day to attend church and it seems as if few villagers were there either. This rather suggests that little interest was taken in church affairs. Holkham church was a long way from Holkham village and this could have discouraged the potential congregation. A chapel was built at New Holkham in 1888, which could have been attended by the scattered population to the south of the park.

Lord Leicester's interest in church restoration was very limited. It was a popular activity of the landed gentry in the nineteenth century. In the 1870s, Sir Tatton Sykes, one of the most famous church restorers, either restored or rebuilt about twenty churches in the parishes around Sledmere, his Yorkshire seat.[29] Antiquarianism was fashionable and Sir John Boileau's improvements to Ketteringham church in Norfolk were typical of the period. He built a children's gallery, made the pews for the squire and his family more dignified and whitened the church walls. His pride in these achievements was satisfied by inscribing on the gallery, 'Erected September 26th 1841 by Sir J. P. Boileau Bart'.[30]

Lord Leicester's attitude to church restoration was similar to his attitude to school building. He did not take the initiative, but acted in support of his tenants. In 1873 Leeds and Hudson were in communication with the estate about the restoration of Castle Acre church, and in 1876 the estate thought that £44 was a reasonable estimate for the repair of the vestry roof.[31] After consultation with Leeds and Hudson, the estimate for paving the church floor and for new gates was also accepted by the estate.[32] A total of £2,450 was paid by Lord Leicester for extensive restoration work to Castle Acre church in 1875. Similarly, John Hastings corresponded with Lord Leicester on the subject of rebuilding the chancel of Longham church, and the earl agreed to do this over the years following 1867.[33] The resulting building was in plain flint work with an estate date stone inserted in the east wall. In the chancel there is a monument to John Hastings, praising his services to Longham.

[29] N. Pevsner, *The East Riding of Yorkshire*, The Buildings of England (Harmondsworth, 1960), passim.   [30] Chadwick, *A Victorian Miniature*, p. 75.
[31] Holkham MSS, letter books, vol. 8 (1873), p. 12.
[32] Holkham MSS, letter books, vol. 9 (1874), p. 133.
[33] Holkham MSS, letter books, vol. 5 (1867), p. 96.

The church restoration in which Lord Leicester was most involved was, not surprisingly, at Holkham parish church, where between 1868 and 1871 the considerable sum of £7,931 was spent on repairs and enlargements. The inspiration behind this work was the earl's wife, Juliana, who was responsible for employing James Colling as architect for the work. The east end was entirely rebuilt and the pulpit, font, reredos and stone staircase in the tower were all designed by Colling.[34]

In answering the 1851 religious census, the vicar of West Lexham complained, 'We are a very small parish of not more than 22 poor cottages. The church is in a wretched condition. There is one large residence, the only one, occupied by one farmer who rents the entire parish', and unlike Longham, no interest in restoration emanated from there. In 1881 the church was restored on the initiative of the vicar. The work involved entirely rebuilding the nave and the chancel. The estate's contribution of £551 covered the cost of new gates to the churchyard, new pews, windows in the nave, buttresses, a tiled floor and a new roof. The tenant of West Lexham Farm was still not involved and Lord Leicester had to write to him to ask if he would supervise and check that no damage was done to existing fabric.

In all, £15,000 of the estate income was spent on church building. This is an appreciable sum, especially when compared with the figures for cottage building. Between 1850 and 1880 there was more spent on restoration at Castle Acre and Holkham churches than on cottage building.

Many local charities relied heavily on the landowners for support, but Lord Leicester seems to have given them very little. Altogether about £560 was subscribed to local funds between 1840 and 1890. Donations went to Holkham clothing club, the Wells benevolent society, 'Tittleshall poor via Mrs Forby', Wells clothing club and Castle Acre soup kitchen. Contributions went to help in the aftermath of specific catastrophes, such as Thorpe accident fund, Norwich inundation fund, widows and orphans, and Wells lifeboat catastrophe. The earl regularly paid subscriptions to Weasenham Friendly Society and the Leicester Lodge of Oddfellows at Wells. The Weasenham Friendly Society may have been similar to the club in Tysoe (Warwickshire), which provided both companionship and security in times of sickness or unemployment. It

---

[34] N. Pevsner, *North-west and South Norfolk, The Buildings of England* (Harmondsworth, 1962), p. 200.

was sponsored by the vicar and was run by trustees drawn from the honorary members who paid a guinea subscription. Through the club the trustees, who were nearly always gentry or employers, exercised control over the labourers.[35]

Almshouses and estate pensions

Most estates had some system whereby pensions were paid to retired employees and accommodation was provided for those who needed it. The Holkham almshouses were founded in 1757 and endowed with the income from Holkham Staithe Farm and small estates at Tittleshall and Weasenham. The almshouses stand to the left of the Victoria Hotel gate to the park and they housed between six and thirteen pensioners. In 1804 there were six pensioners receiving a pension of 4 shillings a week. In 1812 this rose to 5 shillings and, in 1822, 6 shillings. It rose to its highest of 7 shillings in 1865 but was reduced to 6s. 9d. in 1885. In addition, pensioners received clothes, medical aid and coal. In the early part of the century the almhouses cost about £100 a year to run. This was less than the income from the endowment. By the 1880s it had risen to about £190, which meant that, even allowing for rent increases, the endowment only just covered the running expenses. Little was spent on the upkeep of the almshouses. In 1818 repairs cost £46, but no other maintenance costs appear in the accounts.

Very few estate workers received regular pensions. The ledgers recorded that, in 1855, four received 3 shillings a week, and six, 30 shillings a month. In 1865 fifteen were receiving 30 shillings a month and this number remained fairly constant for the rest of the century. The standard pension remained at 30 shillings a month. Help was also occasionally given for nursing and medical expenses and the cost of transport to the Norfolk and Norwich Hospital.

Early household accounts, and the ledgers after 1850, show a few small incidental donations being given to individuals under special circumstances. In 1802 a sailor from Wells who was injured by a boat falling on him received £1 10s. An entry in Crick's accounts for 1804 reads: 'To Alice Large of Thornham who has lost two cows, £1 10s.' In 1855 £1 3s. 9d. was paid to cover the expense of moving William Stimpson

---

[35] M. K. Ashby, *Joseph Ashby of Tysoe, 1859–1919. A Study of English Village Life* (Cambridge, 1961), pp. 70–1.

TABLE 5.1. *Holkham Almshouses accounts for 1854, from account book, 1804–90*

11 pensions of 6s. per week	Men's clothes £1 6s.
Coal £8 5s.	Funeral expenses £9 3s.
One year's surgeon's attendance £12	Nurses £12 12s.
Women's clothes £5 7s.	

to the Norfolk and Norwich Hospital. In 1865 nurses' fees for a pensioner for sixteen weeks, amounting to £16 9s., were paid by the estate.

By the 1830s, emigration was seen by many as the answer to the poverty of the overcrowded countryside. In 1836 and 1837, Lord Leicester contributed to schemes helping the poor to emigrate. In 1836 his share of the expenses of the Fulmodeston emigrants was £150 and in 1837 he gave £9 10s. to help emigrants from Warham.

The number of pensioners on the Holkham estate is very low when compared with the Bedford estate, which was of a similar acreage. There, in 1896, £1,469 was paid in pensions to two clerks, one gardener, one bailiff, one dairyman, one dairy woman, three foremen, one watcher, one lodge keeper, thirty-two labourers and nine widowers. The size of pensions varied between 2 shillings a week for labourers' widows to £266 a year for a former chief clerk.[36] The Duke of Bedford also claimed that 'Looking at the list of Thorney [Lincs.] men now actually in Peterborough Workhouse, only one can be regarded as being remotely connected with the Bedford estates. Few parishes of a purely agricultural population of nearly 2,000 can boast of such freedom from pauperism.'[37] Without a list of those employed at Holkham or the workhouse admission books for Docking and Walsingham union, it is impossible to discover whether this would be true on the Holkham estate or not, but twenty-eight people living in Holkham in 1851 are described as 'paupers'. The only other evidence available is Rigby's not necessarily reliable statement that Holkham Workhouse was pulled down because it became superfluous.[38] Wighton Workhouse, however, existed in the early years of the nineteenth century and received a yearly subscription of £3 18s. from Thomas William Coke.

The amount spent on estate pensions and allowances on the Bedford

---

[36] Bedford, *The Story of a Great Estate*, p. 107.
[37] *Ibid.*, p. 110.
[38] E. Rigby, *Holkham and its Agriculture* (3rd ed, Norwich, 1817), p. 79.

estates varied between £472 and £3,824 in the years 1856–95.[39] The figure for Holkham seems so low in comparison that it is possible that the amount recorded in the ledgers does not represent the full sum.

We know little of the charitable activities of the first earl, and little, other than the stories recorded by Rigby and Mrs Stirling, about his influence on the local community. For the second earl we have some statistics, but little else, and it would appear that he probably performed adequately the duties of a landlord as cottage, school and church builder and supporter of local charities. He was most generous in the large sums he gave to hospitals, over £52,000 in his lifetime, and in this way he benefited a far larger community than that of his estates. Perhaps he saw his role more on a county basis than a purely local one.

Cottage accommodation

It was in the provision of cottages that many landlords failed most seriously in their duty. The problem of providing houses for agricultural labourers was made more acute by rural population growth which began in the mid eighteenth century and increased most rapidly in the years immediately following the Napoleonic Wars. The greatest intercensual increase was between 1811 and 1821, but between 1851 and 1861 the population of Norfolk declined by 2% and thereafter the population of the county, excluding the large towns, changed little until the First World War.

The problem of a labour shortage worried farmers. Rider Haggard discussed the problem with farmers he met in Norfolk and included their comments in his survey published in 1902. The agent at Holkham told him that the supply of labour was short and that young men were going away. The population of Whissonsett, a small village in west Norfolk just outside the Holkham estates, had declined by a third since the 1880s and there were thirty empty cottages.[40]

Very few labourers owned their own cottages. Joseph Arch, a cottage freeholder in Warwickshire, was always aware of the advantages ownership gave him, particularly in his political career, but also points out its rarity.[41] Instead, cottages were put up either by large landowners who often owned entire villages, or by 'speculators' who relied heavily on

---

[39] Bedford, *The Story of a Great Estate*.
[40] H. Rider Haggard, *Rural England*, 2 vols. (London, 1902), vol. 2, p. 467.
[41] J. Arch, *The Story of his Life, Told by Himself* (London, 1898).

cottage rents for an income. Some of the worst cottages visited by the *Norfolk News* reporters in 1863 were owned by cottage speculators or poor widows, one of whom had even built her cottages on common ground. Both types of landlord came under criticism in Smallborough where 'poor cottages were to be found by the dozen...A few belonged to people as poor as the occupants themselves but most of them were the property of Mr Postle about whom the poor folks bitterly complain...A stranger cannot enter the village without being struck by its wretched and desolate condition.'[42]

Much was written during the late eighteenth and nineteenth centuries about cottage conditions, and plenty of advice was available in print for landowners who wanted to improve the conditions in which their labourers lived. Nathaniel Kent's *Hints to Gentlemen of Landed Property*, published in 1775, pointed out that a gentlemen's dogs and horses were often housed better than his tenantry.[43] Kent's cottage plans were simple and less decorative than many others.[44] The smallest consisted of a living room twelve and a half foot square with a pantry and cellar adjoining. Above were two bedrooms twelve and a half by eleven feet and twelve and a half by seven feet. This would cost £66 to erect if built of brick. However, the production of this type of plan did not mean that even these very small cottages were actually being built. In 1795, the steward of the Marquis of Bath, Thomas Davies, wrote, 'Humanity shudders at the idea of the industrious labourer, with his wife and five or six children, being obliged to live or rather exist in a wretched damp gloomy room without a floor; but common decency must revolt at considering that over this wretched apartment there is only one chamber to hold all the miserable beds of the miserable family.'[45] Arthur Young, who was familiar with East Anglian conditions and farmed in Suffolk, wrote in 1805, 'Cottages are perhaps one of the greatest disgraces to this country that remain to be found in it.'[46] He thought that cottages should have three bedrooms as well as a dairy and a main room. The front door should open into a porch.

Books, pamphlets and articles on the subject of cottage improvement

---

[42] 'The cottage homes of England, 3', *Norfolk News* (31 Oct. 1863).
[43] N. Kent, *Hints to Gentlemen of Landed Property* (London, 1775), p. 207.
[44] *Ibid.*, pp. 224–30.
[45] T. Davies, 'An address to the landowners of this Kingdom, with the plans of cottages for the habitation of labourers', *Communications to the Bath and West Agricultural Society* (1795), pp. 294–309.
[46] A. Young, 'Idea of a cottage cheap to build and warm to inhabit', *Annals of Agriculture*, vol. 42 (1805), p. 284.

continued to be written in great numbers throughout the nineteenth century and, by 1851, the situation was such that Andrews could write, 'Scarcely any subject has had more attention bestowed upon it than the social condition of the labourers and the external and internal accommodation of their cottages.' However, 'nine tenths of the books are utterly useless for any practical purpose'[47] and certainly, in spite of the flood of literature, there seems to have been little actual improvement. The highly ornamental rusticated and neo-Gothic plans that were contained in most of the publications were far too expensive for most landlords to build and their implementation was usually restricted to the entrance lodges of large estates. When we look at the Holkham estate cottages of the first half of the nineteenth century, it is clear that a much simpler and more practical plan was adopted here.

Cottage conditions in Norfolk, 1790–1840

Evidence for cottage conditions in Norfolk at the beginning of the Napoleonic Wars is rather scanty. There is no reason to assume that they were better than elsewhere and they may well have been worse. The materials available for building cottages in Norfolk were not good. In much of the county, clay lump was used. Although this is fairly satisfactory as long as it is kept dry, it must be regularly retarred. In the area of the Holkham estate flint was also available and this was a much better material. Carstone occurs in the extreme north-west of the county and was used by the estate when building cottages in the Flitcham area. However, other than this, there is no building stone within the county and this must have adversely affected the standard of cottage building. Conditions improved during the nineteenth century and, by 1884, those in Norfolk were said to be in advance of the West Country.[48]

It is very fortunate that the description of the Houghton estate compiled by Samuel Hill in about 1800 contains not only details and sketches of the individual farms, but also of the cottages. These are perhaps the most interesting buildings illustrated as so little other evidence for cottage conditions survives.[49]

---

[47] G. H. Andrews, *Rudimentary Treatise on Agricultural Engineering* (1851), p. 117.
[48] Parliamentary Papers (1884–5), (c. 4402), xxx, *Royal Commission on the Housing of the Working Classes*, minutes of evidence, pp. 588–90.
[49] Houghton MSS, S. Hill, 'A survey of the Norfolk estates of the Marquis of Cholmondeley' (c. 1800).

5.2 Cottages on the Houghton estate, c. 1800.

An example of each of the main types of cottage illustrated has been redrawn in a simplified form in fig. 5.2. The first thing to notice is the amount of dilapidation. Three of these cottages had to be held up with some sort of primitive shoring. Others not illustrated here had decaying thatched roofs and sagging roof ridges. In one pair of cottages one half was inhabited while the other half was in ruins. This is the sort of disrepair that is described in many contemporary accounts of the shacks and hovels in which farm labourers lived. The top three cottages appear to have only one storey. This is against the ideas of the cottage improvers, who nearly all advocated a sleeping room upstairs as being less damp, more convenient and providing more accommodation. The cottages in the second and third row have some sort of room in the roof, lit by a dormer window. This upstairs room would have been very low indeed and many examples of this sort of cottage survive (fig. 5.3). Again, it is not a type that was advocated by improvers and no such plans were published in the agricultural journals or books on the subject of cottage improvement.

The materials of which the Houghton cottages were built are not always clear from the illustrations. Brick would be the most likely material in the area round Houghton and the cottages redrawn in the fourth row of fig. 5.2 are obviously of brick and flint. Most of the cottages were thatched, although the right-hand terrace in the fourth row was pantiled. This terrace contained three or four cottages with low attic rooms upstairs, at least at the two gable ends. Because the left-hand building has only one chimney it is unlikely to have been more than one house. The right-hand pair of cottages on the bottom row were the only ones illustrated, other than those in Houghton village, with a second floor. Houghton village was begun in 1729 and consists of two rows of five houses each. It stands at the south gates of Houghton Hall and was built as a show piece. The cottages were up to the standards advocated by the end of the eighteenth century and were a great contrast to the others on the Houghton estate.

The normal cottage of the late eighteenth century appears to have been either single storey or with a dormer window in the roof. Downstairs there was only one room, usually no more than fifteen foot square, and sometimes with a lean-to behind. Many cottages of this type survive, so they were certainly not all replaced in the nineteenth century (fig. 5.10).

5.3 Cottages at High House farm. Weasenham.

The earliest documentary evidence for the size of cottages on the Holkham estate is contained in an inventory of tenants' fixtures, made between 1816 and 1820. In it the fixtures owned by tenants are listed room by room. If a room contained no fixtures it would not be mentioned, so the inventory does not show exactly how many rooms a cottage had. Only in a few cases is the number of bedrooms given. However, if a tenant had two grates in 'chambers' he must have had at least two bedrooms. Of the sixty-two cottages listed in Holkham village, all have a kitchen–living room, but eleven had no pantry. In five cottages a sitting room as well as a kitchen is listed. Six had cellars and eight, privies. Five bakehouses and six 'offices' are also mentioned. Twelve cottages seem to have had no bedroom and in one a step-ladder is classed as a fixture, which suggests that it provided the only access to a loft used for sleeping.

Cottage building at Holkham, 1790–1840

Interest in the improvement of labourers' cottages began to increase from the end of the eighteenth century and one of the projects designed by Samuel Wyatt for the Holkham estate was the village of New Holkham, built between 1793 and 1795. The cottages were replaced in 1913 and there is no record of the appearance of Wyatt's dwellings. Old maps show that there were fourteen cottages arranged in an elaborate nine-faceted semicircle. Other cottages were built from 1801 onwards in Holkham Staithe, but all the earlier ones, except Octagon Cottage just inside the park, were replaced in the nineteenth century.

One of the earliest cottage plans to be published was that of 'New cottages built at Holkham by Thomas William Coke, Esq.' in the *Annals of Agriculture* for 1793 (fig. 5.4).[50] This early set of model cottages was of an interesting design in that it contained four cottages, back to back. The facade is plain, but it has certain architectural features, such as the blank windows, the obedience to the rules of proportion in the differing size of the upstairs and downstairs windows, the band of relief between the two floors, the moulded bricks around the top of the end gables, and the semicircular windows on the end walls, which are all characteristic of Samuel Wyatt's work at Holkham. Although they have been altered internally, these cottages are still standing near Holkham Hall and are known as Rose Cottages (fig. 5.5). They are built of yellow Holkham brick with slate roofs. In spite of the problems of ventilation that must have existed in this back-to-back plan, these cottages do have certain features that would have recommended them to the improvers. A front door that opened into a porch rather than straight into a main room was considered an advantage, as it reduced draughts. The provision of a pantry and cellar as well as the kitchen was commendable. There is no plan of the upstairs, but it must have contained one bedroom, the other being downstairs, across the passage from the living room. If privies and wash houses were provided, they must have been in a separate block. A two-bedroom cottage was the ideal design towards which the improvers were working. Waistell, writing in 1827, said, 'Every cottage ought at least to have a kitchen, wash house and a closet or pantry with two bedrooms' and he recommended the building of cottages in pairs.

[50] *Annals of Agriculture*, vol. 20 (1793), pp. 488–9.

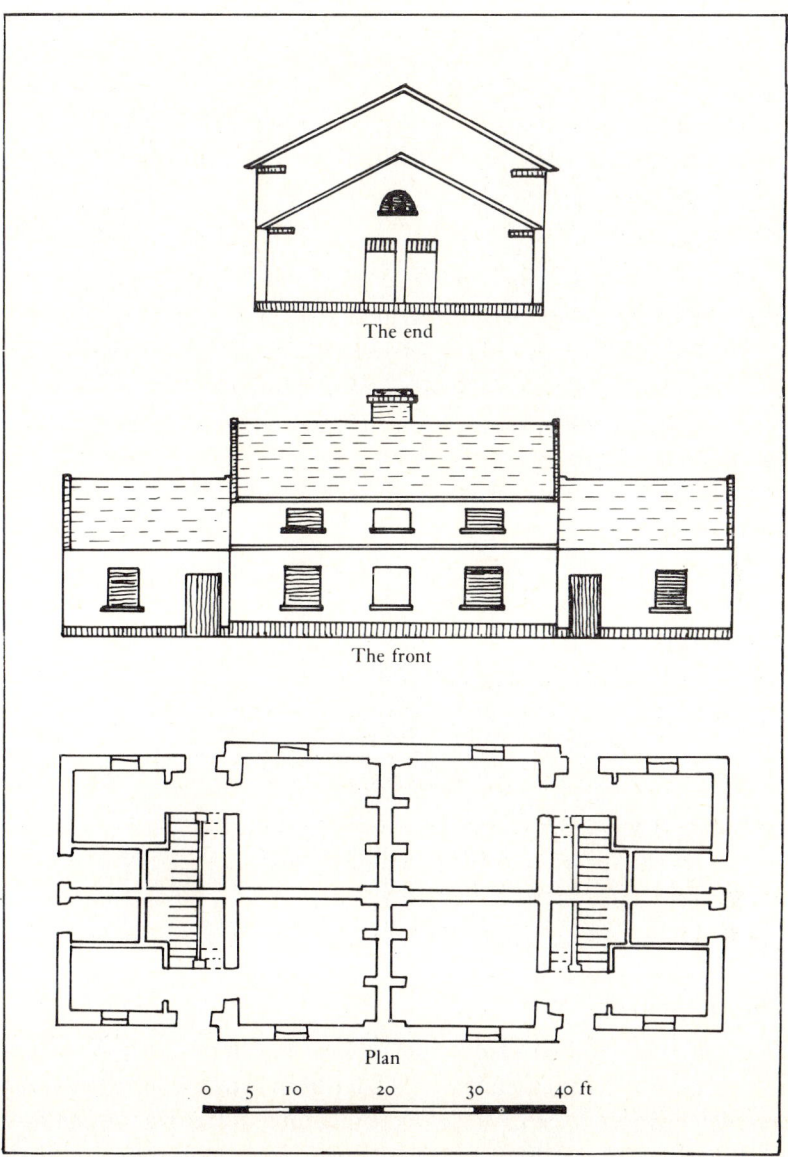

5.4 New cottages built at Holkham by Thomas William Coke.

5.5 Rose cottages, Holkham.

5.6 Cottages, Holkham Staithe.

The kitchen should be twelve foot square and the wash house should be in a lean-to.[51] Although it would have been better to have the second bedroom upstairs, Rose Cottages were undoubtedly far better than many on the estate.

The earliest dated cottages on the Holkham estate are at Holkham Staithe where at least one terrace of either two or four houses was built each year between 1817 and 1821 (fig. 5.6). Each house contained one main room and a scullery downstairs and two or three bedrooms upstairs. Unfortunately the audit books do not say how much they cost. There

[51] C. Waistell, *Designs for Agricultural Buildings* (London, 1827), p. 80.

5.7 Cottages, Flitcham, 1833.

is a similar pair at Grove Farm, Warham, dated 1817. A steward's house built into the corner of a stable block at Quarles is dated 1819, but other than this there are no dated cottages until the 1830s. They are all of a simple style and were probably designed in the estate office. Although no costings are given for these cottages in the audit books, a new cottage at Kempstone cost the estate £58 in 1794 and another £63 in 1814. All the surviving Kempstone cottages are very small with low ceilings and dormer windows upstairs. This shows that not all new cottages came up to the 'model' standards. Another cottage built at Sparham in 1814 also cost the estate £63. Figures of between £50 and £70 were usually quoted for the building of the simpler cottages for which plans were published. This confirms that the audit book figure is about correct.

Date stones show that, in the 1830s, three pairs of cottages were built at Flitcham (fig. 5.7). Only the pair at Harpley Dam field barn are mentioned in the audit books and cost £224 to build. the photograph shows a pair of cottages uncluttered by the neo-Gothic embellishments, but of a more spacious design than many of the cheaper types recommended by the improvers. Each had three bedrooms upstairs with a living room and scullery downstairs. The amount of accommodation is more than in Rose Cottages. The main disadvantage is that the upstairs windows are partly in the roof and therefore the rooms are not full height.

In building these cottages at Flitcham, it seems that the estate was very belatedly taking some of the advice given by Kent in his survey made for the estate in the 1790s. When writing about Harpley Dam Farm, he said,

> it would likewise be prudent in my opinion to erect two or three additional cottages upon so large a tract of land, adding about three or four acres to each to enable the prospective occupiers to keep a pig or a cow... There are always sufficient numbers of industrious men to be chosen as proper objects for receiving this encouragement and it must be a pleasure to every gentleman to do all the good he can in his station. I think it is as necessary to provide plain and comfortable habitations for the poor as to provide comfortable and convenient buildings for cattle, although the farmer will never stipulate for the former, yet he will for the latter. The gentleman therefore in this situation should act as a chancellor between them and decree what is necessary and suitable. In point of policy, the landlord will ultimately find his advantage in this measure, for these sort of cottagers will tend to enhance his property, for they will be permanently fixed to the soil and having some interest in their dwellings and possessing comforts superior to those who have not the same advantages will be the last men to risk them by joining occasional tumults, but will, on the contrary, be the best props a farmer can lean upon in case of any such calamity and will be the least likely to become a burden on the parish.[52]

The cottages built at Harpely Dam in the 1830s had the usual garden in which vegetables could be grown, but no cottages on the estate ever had the large plots advocated by Kent.

The audit book evidence for cottage building is very sketchy. Often only the total sum for an improvement scheme which included the building of cottages is given and it is impossible to know how much a cottage cost, although we do know that one was built. Some but not all cottages have date stones. Sometimes there is no entry for a dated cottage in the audit books. Between 1790 and 1842 the audit books recorded the building of about thirty cottages. To this can be added a further twenty with date stones which are not otherwise recorded. There are two surprising entries in the audit books, both for the parish of Dunton, where in 1802 and 1810 £65 and £40 were spent on moving cottages. It is strange that it was worth moving them when a new one could be built for very little more.

Between 1790 and the death of Thomas William Coke in 1842, over fifty cottages were built. The earlier ones provided more cramped accommodation than the later ones and the cost varied between £60 to just over £100. Even the less spacious ones provided accommodation far superior to the many small and dilapidated cottages available at the time.

---

[52] Holkham MS, N. Kent, 'Holkham estate evaluation of sundry farms, estimated progressively as leases expire and are renewed from Michaelmas 1789'.

Building on the Holkham estate, 1842–1900

During his long career the second Earl of Leicester showed a great interest in cottage improvement. The earliest evidence we have for cottage conditions during his time as earl is contained in William Keary's report in 1851 (appendix 5). When Keary had described the farms in a parish he then listed all the cottages which were let directly by the estate, with the name of the tenant and the rent. Finally he described very briefly the condition of the cottage. Comments such as 'a most wretched thatched cottage', 'small, but comfortable cottage', and 'rain comes in' are typical. He also gave the number of inhabitants per cottage and the number of rooms. This information provides ideal evidence for the degree of overcrowding and will be discussed later. Cottages let with individual farms are described in a similar way. Keary's survey covers over 300 cottages; 128 are described as being let directly by the estate and 105 were let with farms. Six cottages were described as new, but of these, four were defective in some way. Three at Tittleshall were entirely rebuilt in the summer of 1850, but were 'small and inconvenient'. Each had only 'one bedroom, one living room and a sort of closet'. At Sparham a new cottage should have been comfortable, 'but the rain comes in'. It had two bedrooms on the ground floor and was very damp. The other new cottages, one in Holkham and one in Castle Acre, were good, roomy homes. It is clear from these descriptions that not all new cottages were of good design. Of the older ones, many were not kept in repair. Keary considered that ninety-two of them were in disrepair, while only sixty-nine were well kept up. He said of a row at Dunton, 'Though they are not by any means what labourers' cottages should be, there are numbers on the estate in worse condition.' Most of the cottages were small. Only 2 had more than three bedrooms, 138 had two, 98 had one and 8 had only one room.

Keary noted only a few cottages with no privy, which suggests that where there was no comment the sanitary arrangements were of a standard acceptable at the time. In one case the privy was 'in a bad state', and elsewhere one privy was shared by four houses. A cholera epidemic in Tittleshall was attributed to bad drainage. Keary wrote in 1851,

and when the defective state of the drainage of the village is observed, the late mortality during the visitation of the place by cholera may be easily accounted for and fairly attributed to pestilential causes near home. It is however gratifying to observe that through the exertions and by the directions of the Board of Health which now sits monthly in the parish, steps for thorough and efficient drainage round all the cottages are in progress and there can be little doubt that the causes which occasioned the late dreadful mortality will be removed.

Keary felt that the cleanliness of the houses and the state of drainage around the cottages was a parish and not an estate concern. Even if the cottages were provided with adequate privies by the landlord, this did not automatically ensure a healthy environment.

The general picture given by Keary's report is of poor cottages. Many were in bad repair. Some were described as 'unfit to live in', while others were 'very small and bad'. The roofs of many leaked and Keary blamed the poor pantiles. The cottage building of the late earl had by no means solved the housing problem and much remained to be done.

The first earl's work had mainly been confined to the show village at the gates of his hall, and to some nearby farms. This is made clear in Keary's description, as on the whole he found the cottages near Holkham in a better state than those in the more remote parishes. However, during the second half of the nineteenth century, more money was spent and more successful attempts made to ensure that the labourers on the estate were better housed.

An interesting type of cottage is described by R. N. Bacon in his prize-winning report to the Royal Agricultural Society in 1844. At Mr Overman's farm in Weasenham, he saw a large cottage occupied by the farm foreman or bailiff. It was a three-bedroomed cottage with two living rooms and the farm labourers were boarded in it. Bacon said that this system of boarding labourers was usual on the large farms of west Norfolk,[53] and it is implied by Keary at South Creake and Weasenham, where farm servants were boarded with the steward or yardsman. No other evidence can be found and there was no large cottage at Mr Overman's farm when Keary visited it. Instead he mentioned two cottages which were comfortable dwellings in good repair. Possibly the bailiff's house had been divided into two cottages.

It is during these middle years of the century that interest in improvements was at its height. Plans for improved cottages were being published through the 1840s, 1850s and 1860s. Articles and plans appeared regularly in the *J.R.A.S.E.* and interest was so great that, in 1853, a competition for cottage design was run by the society and the

[53] Bacon, *Agriculture of Norfolk*, pp. 156–7.

prize-winning plans were published in 1854. After this there was a decline in interest until the 1870s. Locally, a collection of cottage plans was published in the *Norfolk News* in 1862. It is against this background that we can consider the work of the second Earl of Leicester.

Some of the designers of the 1840s allowed for very few comforts in their plans. The Reverend Copinger Hill wanted to show that cottage building could be a sound investment and could bring in a reasonable return. His plans therefore kept costs to a minimum and he produced a two-bedroom cottage for £60. Perhaps his most revealing comment on the subject of cottage design was, 'The window should be near the fireplace so that the housewife has the advantage of the declining light for as long as possible while seated at her needle.' Both the oven and copper were in the living room, as there was no scullery.[54] The cottages proposed by John Grey, agent for the Greenwich Hospital estates in Northumberland, were even more humble than this. He did not feel that a staircase was necessary and built small cottages with ladders instead. He did think that a cottage needed more than one room and that preferably it should have two floors. For £61 each he built cottages with one large room twenty-two and a half by fifteen feet, a lean-to pantry and a bedroom upstairs.[55] Cottages well in advance of these plans were being put up at Holkham by the 1840s.

More progressive plans were being suggested in the *J.R.A.S.E.* by the end of the 1840s, and Henry Goddard's plans, published in 1849, were more typical of the sort of ideal aimed at by the improvers. His cottages contained a living room and scullery downstairs and three bedrooms upstairs. Often the front door was protected by a porch. He estimated that these cottages built in pairs would cost £220 a pair to erect.[56] Arnold's prize-winning design in the 1854 *J.R.A.S.E.* provided similar accommodation. He thought that, in spite of the cold draught downstairs, it was an advantage to have the staircase going straight up from the living room to allow warmth from the living room to circulate upstairs.[57]

There is a certain sameness about the plans of the 1850s and 1860s. By this date it was generally accepted that the aim must be a

[54] C. Hill, 'On the construction of cottages', *J.R.A.S.E.*, vol. 4 (1843), pp. 356–68.
[55] J. Grey, 'On the building of cottages for farm labourers', *J.R.A.S.E.*, vol. 5 (1844), pp. 237–45.
[56] H. Goddard, 'Construction of a pair of cottages for agricultural labourers', *J.R.A.S.E.*, vol. 10 (1849), pp. 230–46.
[57] G. Arnold, 'Prize plan of a double cottage for farm labourers', *J.R.A.S.E.*, vol. 15 (1854), pp. 455–9.

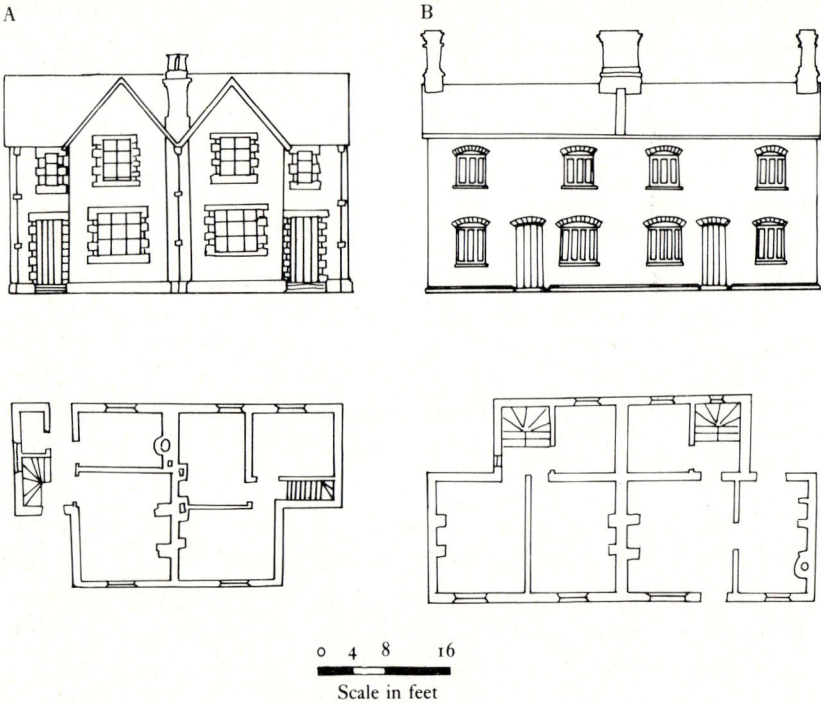

5.8 Cottage plans published in the *Norfolk News*.

three-bedroom cottage with a pantry, scullery and living room and, if possible, a porch. Variety was only possible if the landowner wanted a more decorative structure and was prepared to pay the necessary extra cost. Isaac in 1857 believed that a simple cottage could be built for £85. He thought that Gothic gables were not only expensive, but also impractical as they usually leaked. Money should be spent on giving every cottage three bedrooms, rather than on ornamentation. No bedroom should be either wholly or partially in the roof, or of less than fifty square feet.[58] The designs in the *Norfolk News* in 1863 are very similar (fig. 5.8). The most expensive cost £260 a pair and had been erected by J. H. Gurney at Northrepps. Other prices varied between £170 and £245 a pair. On the right of fig. 5.8 there is one of the *J.R.A.S.E.* prize plans, and the *Norfolk News* thought it one of the best plans among the set it published. These two designs are reproduced here as examples of the better sort of cottage planning of the period.

[58] T. W. P. Isaac, 'On the construction of labourers' cottages', *J.R.A.S.E.*, vol. 17 (1857), pp. 494–512.

One of the problems of using these numerous plans as evidence for the types of cottages provided is that often we do not know whether any of them were ever built. The Duke of Bedford was one of the landowners who was improving living conditions on his estates by building better cottages and he described the sort of cottages he was actually erecting.

> The arrangement and design of a cottage are matters of supreme importance. If there are two doors to a dwelling house, there is a tendency amounting in some cases to practice, to leave one unused. It is found also that if two dwelling rooms of the same size are provided, one is often kept idle as a parlour where china dogs, crochet anti-macassars and unused tea services are maintained in fusty seclusion. This idle parlour adds nothing to the comfort of the cottages. The best plan is to divide the ground floor into one good living room, one kitchen, one back kitchen or scullery and one spacious and airy pantry. There is a growing inclination among the rural population to avoid single cottages as being lonely and cold. For a pair of cottages a joint wash house is sufficient, but a partition wall dividing the court is desirable.[59]

The Duke of Bedford complained that the importance of the pantry had often been ignored and that 'in this respect there is a good deal of leeway to be made up'. He thought it was better to have a wash house outside and so, on the Bedford estates, indoor wash houses were being converted into pantries and wash houses moved out into a disused bakehouse. 'The bake house is a thing of the past. In England bread is almost universally procured from the baker.'[60] Certainly at Holkham a few bakehouses are mentioned in the inventory of tenant's fixtures at the beginning of the nineteenth century, but there are no later references. All cottages should have a porch to protect the main door from draughts and the two larger bedrooms should have fireplaces, both for ventilation and in case of sickness. The Duke also gave the cost of building cottages that came up to these standards. Those built in the 1850s and 1860s cost £135 and £158 each, while those built later were more expensive. However, it is clear from the Royal Commissions of the late nineteenth century that the Duke of Bedford was not typical of cottage proprietors in the country as a whole, and very few of them copied the many plans for model cottages that were published.

Conditions in Norfolk were generally far below those desired by the improvers. The *Norfolk News* commented in 1862, 'We have recently seen a farm where thousands have been expended in magnificent stalls and outbuildings for horses and cattle and within a few hundred yards

---

[59] Bedford, *The Story of a Great Estate*, p. 86.
[60] *Ibid.*, p. 88.

stand miserable huts through the roofs of which the stars may be seen at night.' From the autumn of 1863 to the spring of 1864, this newspaper continued its agitation about cottage conditions by publishing a series of articles entitled 'The cottage homes of England'. For each article the cottages of a different landlord were visited. Although the names of the various proprietors were not mentioned, their identity was only thinly disguised, and it is possible to tell who came under scrutiny in each article. The Earl of Leicester was not one whose property was visited. Nearly all the articles tell of dilapidation and overcrowding very similar to that found by Keary around Holkham. Many landowners were not providing enough cottages and labourers were walking long distances to work.

However, there were some estates where conditions had already begun to improve. Lord Walsingham's estate of between 11,000 and 12,000 acres received some favourable comment. Cottages were overcrowded, but mostly in reasonable repair. Some of the most overcrowded and wretched were being demolished and replaced by larger dwellings or, as a local labourer put it to the *Norfolk News* reporter, 'My lord ha' just been flitting some of them where they lay a bit too thick.'[61] Some of Sir Proctor Beachamp's cottages on his 6–7,000 acre estate were described as 'capital' while others were derelict. The model landlord seems to have been Mr Brampton Gurdon, whose Norfolk estate covered 4–5,000 acres. His cottages were well thatched and whitewashed with good gardens and at least two bedrooms. The two villages on his estates had schools and there was a Sunday school run by Mrs Gurdon and her daughters, to teach those who could not attend the day schools. The daughters of the squire were to be seen about the village 'engaged in errands of mercy'.[62]

All the estates visited were small ones below 12,000 acres and the report admits that some of the worst cottages were in fact owned by cottage speculators rather than by the estates. Cottages in west Norfolk were generally better than those in the east and south of the county for several reasons. Firstly, the building materials in the west were better. The traditional clay lump of the south was often not properly maintained and this led to really appalling conditions, while the flint and carstone of the west meant that far more substantial cottages were built. Secondly,

[61] 'The cottage homes of England, 6', *Norfolk News* (21 Nov. 1863).
[62] 'The cottage homes of England, 5', *Norfolk News* (14 Nov. 1863).

5.9 Cottages, Great Bircham. (a) Unimproved cottage (b) Late-nineteenth-century cottages.

conditions on large estates were generally better than on small ones. Both the report *On the Employment of Women and Children in Agriculture* (1867–8) and the Royal Sanitary Commission of 1869 refer to the work of the Marquis of Cholmondeley and the Earl of Leicester in building new cottages on their estates. On the Marquis' estates, cottages with a sitting room, scullery and three bedrooms were built for not less than £120.[63] These brick cottages, built in pairs, still dominate villages such as Great Bircham on the Cholmondeley estates (fig. 5.9b). The Royal Commission on the Housing of the Working Class (1884) was told that cottages in the west of Norfolk were far better than those to the east because of the example of both the Earl of Leicester and the Marquis of Cholmondeley.[64]

If the cottages of the Holkham estate were of a high standard by 1880, there must have been considerable investment in improvement during the preceding thirty years. Various sources are available for the study of the pattern and quantity of this investment. They also show how far cottages were brought up to the standards accepted by the improvers of the time. First we have the evidence of Lord Leicester himself. A speech made 'recently' to the Norfolk Agricultural Association is quoted in the Children's Employment Commission report of 1866. When describing the standard of living of cottagers on his estates, he said,

> They live in good houses and I may say with hardly an exception owing to the energies of my late agent, Mr Keary, and my present agent, Mr Shellabear, they live in decency and comfort. They almost all have good gardens... I much doubt whether the cottages I have built since 1863 can in any way be surpassed. They are not ornamental and cost between £100 and £115 to build.

The carriage of materials was done by the farm tenant and so was not included in this sum.[65] The earl's personal views obviously need supporting from other sources, but they are worth bearing in mind when examining the more objective evidence.

The audit books show a great increase in cottage expenditure between 1850 and 1880, when a total of £6,824 is recorded. These figures can be broken down for each ten year period as in table 5.2. The building of forty-three cottages is specifically mentioned as well as repairs and

---

[63] Parliamentary Papers (1867), *Royal Commission on the Employment of Women and Children in Agriculture*, pp. 589–90, and Parliamentary Papers (1868–9), (4218), XXXII, *Royal Sanitary Commission*, minutes of evidence, p. 359.
[64] Parliamentary Papers (1884–5), *Royal Commission on the Housing of the Working Classes*, p. 594.
[65] Parliamentary Papers (1867), (3796), XVII, *Childrens' Employment Commission*, sixth report, p. 142.

TABLE 5.2. *Expenditure and number of date stones for ten year periods, 1850–80*

	Expenditure £	No. of date stones
1850–60	2,044	12
1860–70	1,123	12
1870–80	3,657	26

improvements to many more. In addition, there are fifty cottages with date stones, suggesting they were built during this period, but which are not mentioned in the audit books. The number of date stones for the same ten year periods are also shown in table 5.2. This shows a great increase in cottage building during the last ten years of the period, in spite of the fact that the population was actually decreasing at about this time. It will be argued that the main reason for this interest in building was the repealing of the Settlement Laws in 1865, which removed the incentive to keep down the number of labourers resident in an estate parish. The audit books show that 1850–60 was a period of high expenditure, while there was a lull between 1860 and 1870. The explanation for this may be that, following the compiling of Keary's report on cottage building, much was spent on remedying the worst ills that this revealed.

It is probably not an exaggeration to say that at least one hundred cottages were built in the thirty years after 1850. This is far more than were built during the previous sixty years. It is clear that the audit books do not include all expenditure, and if the average cost of building a cottage was between £100 and £115, then the total expenditure, not including repairs to existing cottages, could be about £10,000, or 0.7% of the estate rental over the period. The figures given by the Earl of Leicester and Henry Rew show that over two hundred cottages had been built between 1867 and 1895. It is impossible to calculate accurately how much this would have cost. By the 1890s the cost of building a cottage had risen to £300; two hundred cottages must therefore have cost between £20,000 and £50,000, or between 1% and 2.5% of estate rental. All these percentages show that a very low proportion of the total sum spent on improvement went into cottage building.

5.10 Cottages, Harpley Dam, Flitcham.

To decide how effective this investment was we must look at the cottages themselves. Many of the cottages built during this period still survive, although most have been considerably modernised. In addition, a selection of plans, probably of the better cottages, were collected into book form under the title 'Holkham estate, farm premises and cottages, 1856–'. This unfinished book is kept in the Clerk of Works' Office at Holkham (see figs. 5.11 and 5.12). That these plans represent the best that was being built is shown by some inferior cottages of this period that still survive. A row of single-storey cottages at Flitcham, recently sold as two for conversion into one, was probably built as four cottages in 1872 (see fig. 5.12). Each would have contained a larder, one small bedroom and a living room. Later they were converted into two, so that each gained a wash room and second bedroom. This bedroom was inconveniently placed, as the only way to the scullery, other than through the outside door, was through this bedroom. It seems unlikely that the house was originally planned in this form. It is possible that the date stone, which along with two dated bedroom fireplaces is our only evidence for the date of the building, was put in at the time of the conversion and that the cottages are older. If that is the case, then a form of improvement which would have been more in keeping with the better standards advocated would have been to add a second storey. The standard of these Flitcham cottages is not such that Lord Leicester would have liked them publicised. However, these are the only dated one-storey cottages of this period and so cottages of the type illustrated in the book were probably more typical of the new building of the period.

The landlord and the labourer

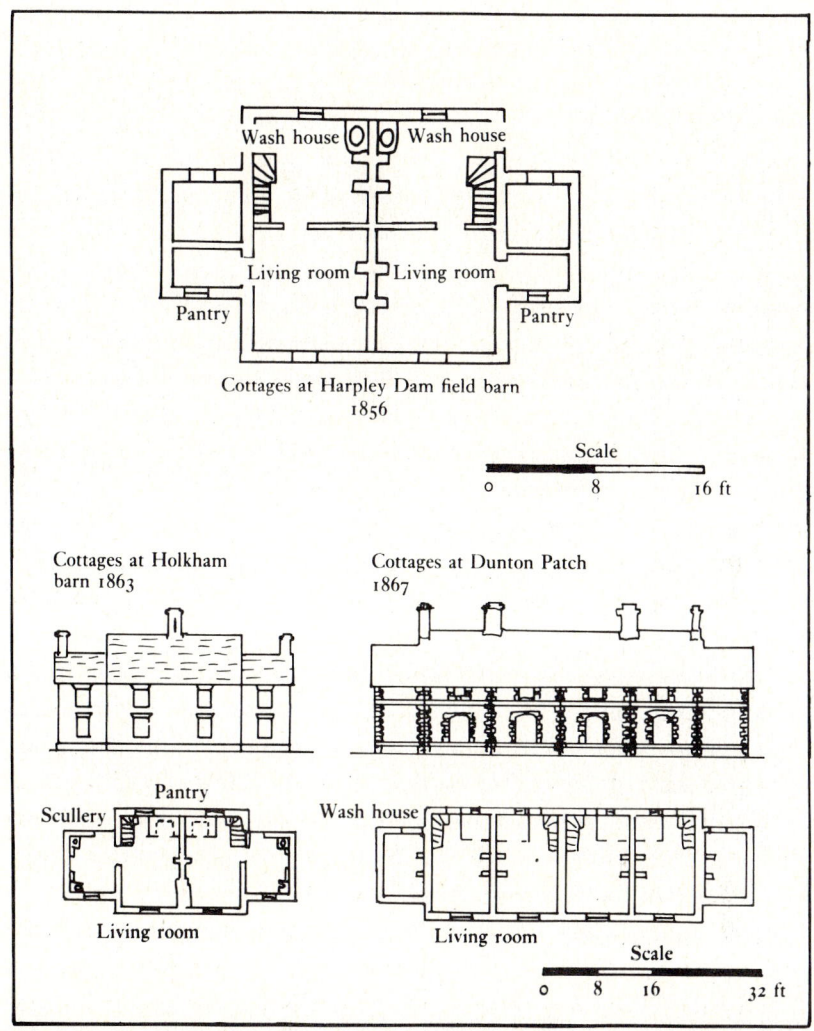

5.11 Cottage plans, 1850–70.

The two pairs of cottages at Harpley Dam field barn serve as a good example of the development of cottage design on the estate at this time. They are both dated, and were built twenty-five years apart (1831 and 1856). They show certain differences in design which illustrate the improvements made over a quarter of a century. The left-hand one in fig. 5.10 is the earlier of the two. The upstairs windows are of a semi-dormer type, which shows that the bedroom ceilings must have been low. In the later cottage these have been replaced by full-sized windows below the roof line. This means that the small gables are no longer needed and the much simpler style of the later cottage gives a roof which was easier to maintain. The later cottage is also larger as it has a small wing on each gable end. Fortunately the plan of the 1856 cottages is in the book of estate designs and it is reproduced here (fig. 5.11). From this plan we know that the wing contained a porch and pantry downstairs and a third bedroom upstairs. Although the 1831 cottage also had three bedrooms, they were all much more cramped than in the later one. The earlier cottage had no porch and the front door opened straight into the main room. In the later design the staircase was still in the scullery rather than in a hall. Many cottages of this design are still standing on the Holkham estate. Although the arrangement of the rooms differed, and some cottages had porches while others did not, the accommodation provided was always similar. All of them had three bedrooms, a living room, pantry and scullery and were very similar to the many published plans. Sometimes the staircase went up between the two rooms, but more usually it ascended from the living room or scullery.

Lord Leicester's plans were usually of a standard as good as those recommended, but not any better. The fact that not all had porches and none had staircases in a hall showed a degree of economy which prevented the building of the best type of cottage. Most of these cottages were built in pairs, although there were a few cases as at Dunton in 1866 (fig. 5.11) and Sparham (early this century) of cottages built in fours. The report *On the Employment of Women and Children in Agriculture* (1867–8) quoted Lord Leicester as having given much thought to the problem of the number of cottages that should be built in a block and deciding that the best number was four. 'He builds his newest cottages in blocks of four, the two interior with two bedrooms and the two exterior with three.'[66] The problem was how the two middle ones should have back access to their gardens and in fact it seems that, even if this was a cheaper method of building, it was not used for long.

An interesting experiment in building techniques carried out in the 1870s showed that the estate office was well abreast of modern ideas and prepared to try new methods, especially if they might cut building costs. As early as 1867–8, Mr Nicholl had suggested that concrete could be used for building cottages. He claimed that it would halve the cost of

[66] Parliamentary Papers (1867–8), *Employment of Women and Children in Agriculture*, p. 590.

building in brick or stone, that it would have greater strength, greater resistance to the damp, and if the cottages were built with cast iron joists and concrete floors they would be fireproof. As concrete is a bad conductor of heat they would be warm in winter and cool in summer.[67]

In 1874 this idea was followed up by an article in the *J.R.A.S.E.* in which G. Hunt pointed out that there were problems attached to the use of concrete.[68] Where bricks or stone were easily available concrete was not always cheaper. Great care was needed in selecting the right materials for making a strong concrete. Straight concrete was not attractive and a little ornamentation would be desirable. The method of construction recommended by Nicholl and Hunt was to build the walls within shuttering. The first concrete cottages on the Holkham estate were already erected when Hunt wrote his article. Cottages at Egmere were built in concrete in 1873, 1874, 1875 and 1877 (see fig. 5.12). Unfortunately there is no reference to any of these in the audit books, so we cannot know how the prices compared with more conventional building materials. There is also a block of three cottages at Dunton built of concrete, but undated. As the concrete experiment was short-lived, we can assume they were erected in the 1870s. There are audit book entries for cottages at Dunton in 1873 (£349) and 1874 (£361). As there are no other cottages at Dunton to which these sums can refer, most of this £710 must have been spent on these three cottages, although some may have been used for repairs to older ones. However, a cost in the region of £200 each makes the concrete cottages an expensive proposition. It is probable therefore that because of expense this new method was dropped.

The present Clerk of Works' assistant at Holkham has given other reasons which make concrete unsuitable for cottage building. As the concrete dried it shrank. This meant that door and window frames no longer fitted. The concrete cottages were also damp. Finally, the concrete is now so hard that alterations are difficult and the cottages are almost impossible to knock down. Thus the problems created by an experiment one hundred years ago are still troubling the estate. The final pair of concrete cottages was built at Crabbs Castle, Wighton, in 1878.

Many copies of the Egmere-type plan were printed and are still in a

---

[67] *Ibid.*, p. 155.
[68] G. Hunt, 'On concrete as a building material for farm buildings and cottages', *J.R.A.S.E.*, second series, vol. 10 (1874), pp. 211–31.

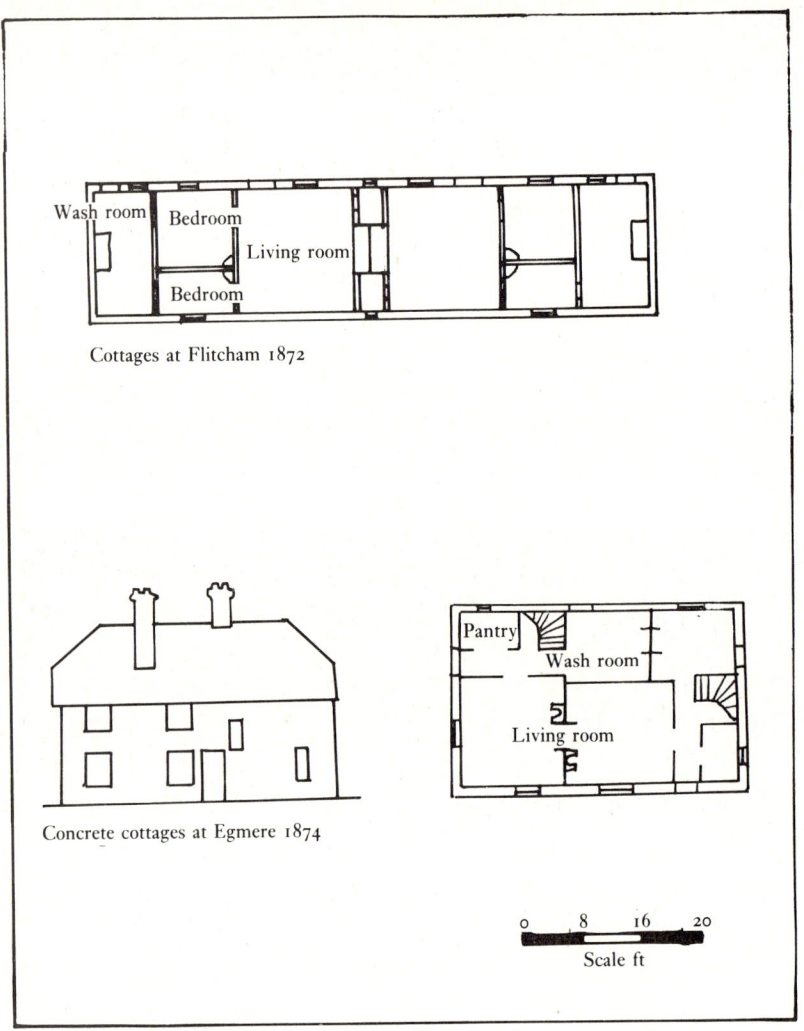

5.12 Cottage plans, 1870s.

roll at Holkham. It looks as if it were intended that a number of these cottages should be built. The words 'to be built of concrete' are printed on the plans, but this had been crossed out and 'to be built of brick' inserted in pencil instead. There are several examples of this type of cottage built in brick or brick and flint (fig. 5.13). The Egmere plan shows a three-bedroom cottage with a living room, pantry and scullery–wash house downstairs (fig. 5.12). The front door opened into a small hall and an improvement on earlier designs is the staircase which goes up from

5.13 Cottages, Sparham.

5.14 Cottages, Holkham Staithe.

the hall. Each cottage had a separate privy and wash house. This is a design that was in every way up to the standard of the improvers.

Through the thirty years from 1850 to 1880 there was a development in cottage style on the estate which meant that by the end of the period accommodation of a high standard was being provided in the new cottages. Economies resulting in the lack of a porch or a stairway in a hall were less common. Nearly all new cottages had three bedrooms and were built in pairs rather than in longer rows.

New cottages continued to be built until 1900, but in smaller numbers.

The houses on the left-hand side of the road from the Victoria Hotel to the hall were rebuilt in the 1880s in a late Victorian style (fig. 5.14). Elsewhere there are only five dated cottages during the last twenty years of the nineteenth century. Cottage expenditure recorded in the audit books for this period amounted to only £2,856. This is a time when income from rents was declining, but this still only represents 0.3% of income. With the depression, interest in cottage conditions subsided. The national journals no longer contained articles or plans for improved dwellings. With rural population declining, the pressure on existing housing was not so great and the only literature on improvement was confined to a few articles on cottage sanitation.[69] The Earl of Leicester thought that the only way to keep a good supply of competent young men as farm labourers was to provide them with good cottages, and he told Rider Haggard in 1902 that he was still building several cottages every year.[70] Mr Beck, agent for the Sandringham estates, told the Royal Commission on the Housing of the Working Classes in 1884 that cottage building was still going on, but at different rates on different estates.[71] Henry Rew, reporting on Norfolk for the Royal Commission on Agriculture in 1895, said that by this date there were 730 cottages on the Holkham estates. He stated that they all had good gardens and modern sanitary arrangements, which had necessitated considerable expenditure.[72] Except for the addition of sanitation, the plans of the later cottages differed very little from those of the 1870s. This three-bedroom plan with a good scullery, living room and pantry could be little improved upon.

Of more importance than the building of new cottages during the last twenty years of the nineteenth century was the improving of old ones. Plans still survive, both in the estate workshops at Longlands and at the hall, which show these improvements. They also show how long much substandard property had survived on the estate. Some two-bedroomed cottages were made into three-bedroomed ones by adding a small wing containing a washroom downstairs and a bedroom upstairs. Other one-storey cottages had a second storey added. In 1884 a row of cottages at Fulmodeston was given a second storey. Previously there had been three cottages, each with a bedroom and living room downstairs and

[69] H. M. Wilson, 'Cottage sanitation', *J.R.A.S.E.*, third series, vol. 3 (1892), pp. 631–50.
[70] Haggard, *Rural England*, vol. 2, p. 467.
[71] Parliamentary Papers (1884–5), *Royal Commission on the Housing of the Working Classes*, p. 590.
[72] Parliamentary Papers (1896), (c. 8021), XVII, Henry Rew, *Report on Norfolk*, p. 45.

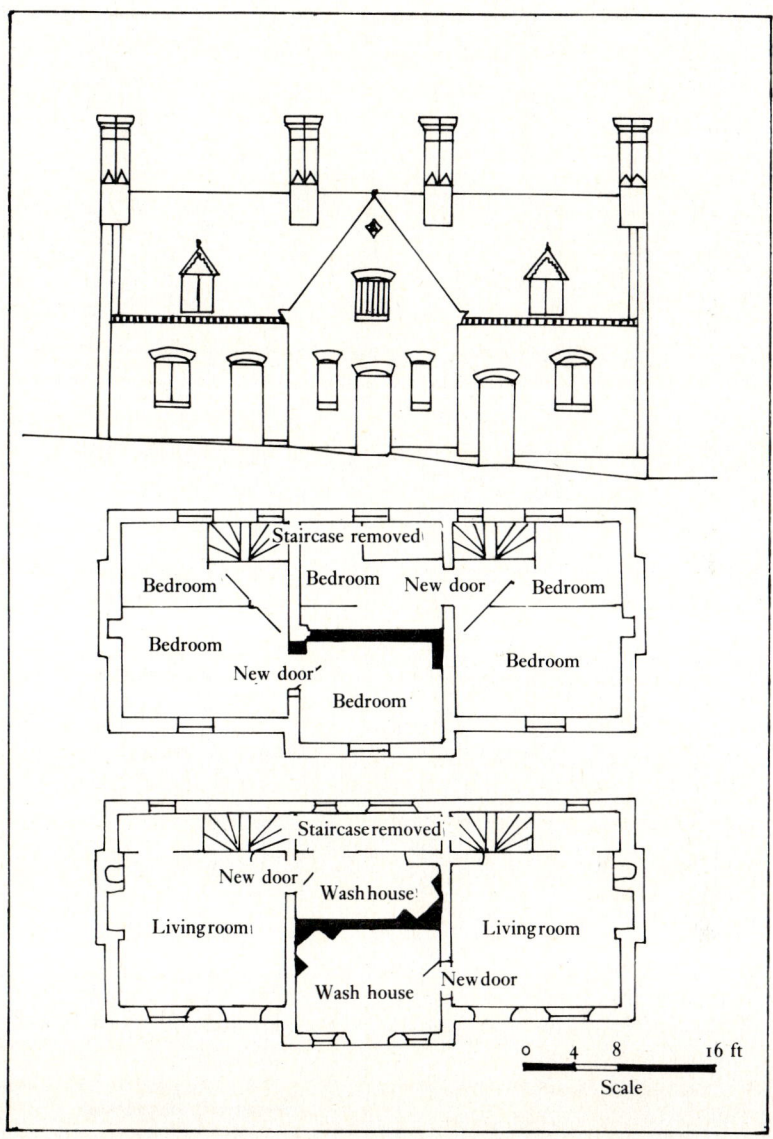

5.15 Improvements to cottages in the 1880s. New walls are shown blacked in.

possibly a small room in the roof. They were converted into two cottages, each with two bedrooms upstairs and one down, and also a shared wash room. About thirteen plans of these conversions are in the munument room at Holkham, but many more were carried out (figs. 5.15 and 5.16).

By 1900, therefore, many of the cottages on the Holkham estate

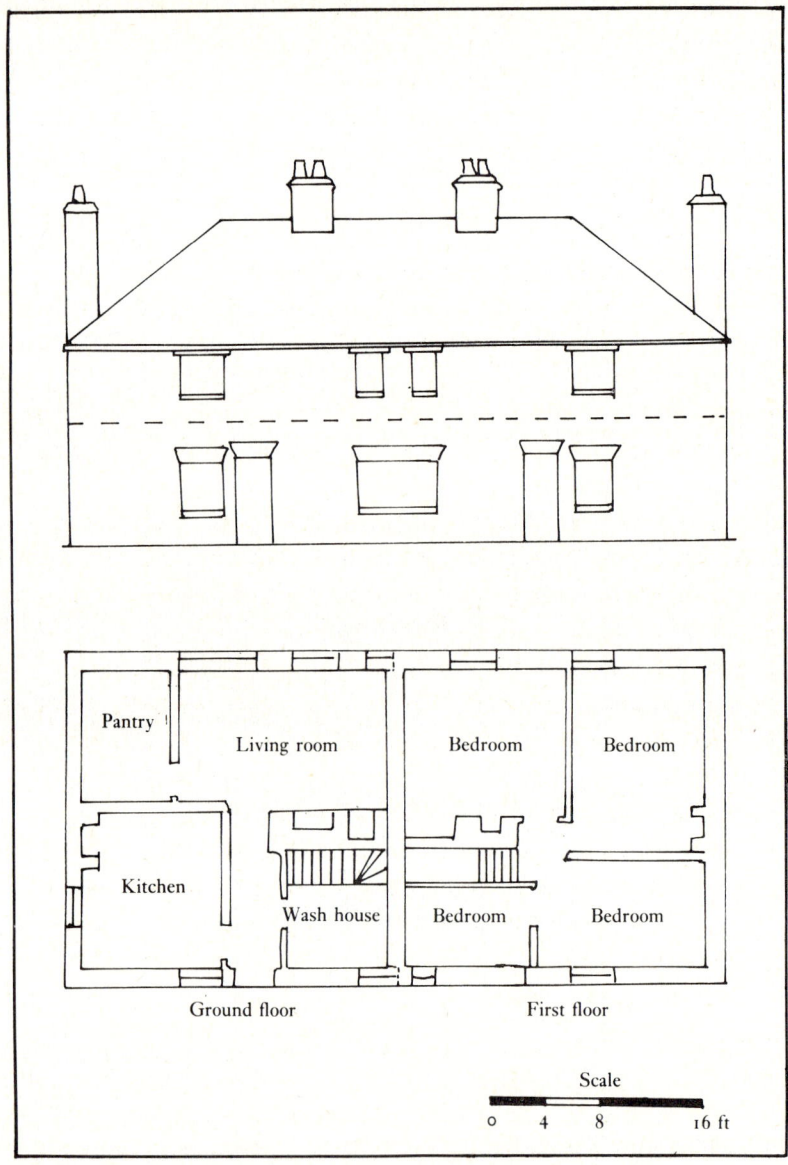

5.16 Addition of a second floor to cottages at Mileham, 1890.

complied with what Fussell described as the 'modern ideal of five or six rooms, and these rooms no smaller than those in many urban or suburban houses of more recent construction'.[73] These would mainly be the cottages built since 1860 and there were still plenty of earlier ones on the estate. There were attempts to improve many of these at the end

[73] G. E. Fussell, *The English Rural Labourer* (London, 1949), p. 117.

of the century, but by no means all of them were modernised by 1900. By that time, however, the majority of the Holkham cottagers were living in houses which were a great improvement on conditions fifty years before. This was not entirely due to the labours of the landlord. A contributing factor was the end of population growth in the area.

We can see throughout the nineteenth century a national movement for cottage improvements which reached its height about 1850–80. Published plans become more practical and also more spacious throughout the period. This is reflected in the improvements at Holkham. The back-to-back layout of the earliest plans was far less satisfactory than the cottages of the 1830s, and these in their turn were improved by the addition of an entrance hall and higher upstairs ceilings. The final stage of improvement was reached by the 1870s in the plans for concrete cottages, and dwellings of this type were built mainly in brick until the end of the century. There was some more picturesque building in Holkham village, where more elaborate cottages with tall ornamental chimneys were built, but this style was limited to the approaches to the hall.

As the standard of design rose, so did the cost of building, and this rise was accentuated by the inflation of building costs. The result was that, while in 1790 a cottage could be built for £60, the model cottages of the 1860s cost £100–£120 and by 1900 cottages cost £300 each.

Although only a very small proportion of income from rents was ploughed back into cottage improvements, by 1900 cottage conditions were far better than in the 1850s. This was mainly due to the increased rate of building new cottages until 1880 and the continuing improvement of old ones thereafter.

The problem of overcrowding

Before any assessment can be made of how adequate this very low investment was, it is necessary to consider how far it provided enough housing for the labour force needed on the estate. Not only were early-nineteenth-century cottages bad, they were nearly always overcrowded. Mr Clarke, the Norwich sanitary inspector, pointed out in 1863 the need not only to build good cottages, but enough good cottages.[74] Overcrowding was attributed to various causes, the most important being

---

[74] Samuel Clarke, 'Labourers' cottages', supplement to the *Norfolk News* (12 Sept. 1863), p. 1, quoting an article in *The Times* (9 Sept. 1863).

population increase, evictions resulting from enclosures, and the working of the Settlement Laws. The figures from the censuses show that rural population was increasing rapidly during the early years of the nineteenth century. Although there was a certain amount of enclosure left to be carried out in west Norfolk, by the nineteenth century it mostly involved the enclosure of common land rather than open fields. Although this deprived the poor of commoning rights, it resulted in few, if any, evictions. The Settlement Laws resulted in a general reluctance of landowners and tenant farmers to attract more residents to their parishes and this created serious problems in west Norfolk.

The question of 'open' and 'closed' villages in Norfolk was discussed by Naomi Riches writing in 1937, and her views have been unchallenged since then. Much of her evidence came from Arthur Young.[75] The seventeenth-century Settlement Laws made the ratepayers of each parish responsible for the poor born or claiming a settlement within the parish boundaries. Arthur Young explained the results of this system in places where a whole parish was owned by one landlord who then let it as one or two farms. 'The tenant pays the poor rate and perhaps as part of his agreement repairs the cottages. Here, therefore are two strong reasons why he should drive the people away and let their houses go to ruin or perhaps advise his landlord to pull them down. Firstly he eases himself of rates and secondly he rids himself of repairs.'[76] It was villages of this type that were known as 'closed'. In many of the parishes where Lord Leicester owned land he was in possession of most of the farms and cottages. There is no direct evidence for the deliberate pulling down of cottages on the Holkham estate, although Mr Blyth of Burnham wrote in 1848, 'I have myself known cottages taken down, avowedly to reduce the liability of maintaining the poor'.[77] The prospect of rising poor rates would certainly have discouraged new building.

Some recent work has produced more evidence to show how seriously the east of England, and particularly north-west Norfolk, was affected. The problem of 'open' and 'closed' parishes was most acute in the light soil regions of eastern England, especially the East Riding of Yorkshire, Lincolnshire, Nottinghamshire, east Leicestershire, north-west Norfolk, and also further west in the Cotswolds. Reports to the 1850 Government

---

[75] N. Riches, *The Agricultural Revolution in Norfolk* (London, 1967 reprint), pp. 143–6.
[76] A. Young, *Political Arithmetic* (London, 1774), p. 102.
[77] Parliamentary Papers (1850), (1152), XXVII, *Reports on the Laws of Settlement and the Removal of the Poor*, appendix 13, communication from Mr Blyth, Sussex Farm, Burnham, p. 70.

Enquiry show how badly Norfolk was affected. Proprietors were strongly opposed to building cottages and 'one Norfolk landlord admitted that he bought land in adjacent parishes to house his labourers'.[78] The Holkham evidence shows that there was a great lack of accommodation until the late 1860s. The parishes which were divided into very few farms and almost entirely owned by the Holkham estate would be the most vunerable. These include Dunton (two farms, 1,678 acres), Egmere (one farm, 1,122 acres), Kempstone (two farms, 729 acres), Waterden (one farm, 760 acres), and West Lexham (one farm, 1,131 acres).

The earliest reference we have to a shortage of cottages is contained in the letter books and it concerns the parish of Kempstone. One of the tenants of the Kempstone farms wrote to Francis Blaikie in 1816 asking if the estate would buy two cottages 'south of the pasture of Kempstone Lodge Farm'. He described the cottages as having mud walls, a roof of rotten thatch and a clay floor. They were derelict and in a terrible state. The tenant suggested that they could be rebuilt and, 'although they were derelict, the materials could be used again'. At this time they were inhabited by an old man, his wife and two daughters and they paid no rent. The purchase of the cottages was urged because 'we are sadly off for cottages for our labourers who belong to this parish'. The letter books do not say whether the purchase was made, but Keary described three cottages south of the pasture. He wrote that 'if they were in good repair they would be good cottages'. In 1851, there were six cottages in the parish.

Perhaps the most interesting aspect of Keary's description of cottages in 1851 is the evidence for overcrowding which it contains (appendix 5). In his account of the cottages let directly by the estate, Keary gave the number of rooms and the number of inhabitants. For the purposes of this discussion a cottage where more than three people had to share a bedroom is defined as overcrowded.[79] Out of the 227 cottages listed, 103 were overcrowded, some exceptionally so. Several cottages in

---

[78] B. A. Holderness, 'Open and closed parishes', *Agricultural History Review*, vol. 20 (1967), pp. 280–92.

[79] Recent housing acts define overcrowding in more precise terms. A bedroom of over 110 square feet is suitable for not more than two adults. A room between 90 and 110 square feet can be used by one adult and a child. Where a room has an area of between 70 and 90 square feet it can be occupied by one adult and a room between 50 and 70 square feet can be used for a child. A room below fifty square feet cannot be used as a bedroom. In many cases the second or third bedroom described by Keary would have an area of less than fifty square feet. Very few were over a hundred square feet.

Flitcham housed seven inhabitants, but had only one bedroom. One 'small bad cottage', where the rain came in, had one bedroom and nine inhabitants. There are similar examples in Tittleshall and a cottage at Wighton, surprisingly described as 'clean and neat', had one bedroom and ten inhabitants. The shortage of cottages was particularly acute where more than one family shared a cottage and also where lodgers were taken in. This point was made by the Norwich sanitary inspector in 1863. The fact that cottages were inadequate was shown when 'married men are living in cottages suitable only for single people and lodgers are taken in. These lodgers must be working on the land and therefore required by the estate, but no houses are provided for them. These lodgers are not a class that should exist permanently in a country village.'[80] Lodgers were recorded in thirteen cottages in 1851, often in dwellings already overcrowded. There is one example of three families occupying a three-bedroom cottage and fourteen examples of two families in one cottage, sometimes in only one bedroom. One single-bedroomed cottage, in Flitcham was occupied by two families and three lodgers.

The problem of overcrowding was not considered by Hunt when he discussed the question of labour productivity in the second half of the nineteenth century. In Norfolk both the wage rates and the productivity were among the lowest in England.[81] Perhaps the explanation for the low productivity could lie in the housing conditions. In these overcrowded cottages, no farm labourer could have had a good night's sleep, and the efficiency of his work would suffer. The lack of cottages also meant that men were walking a long way to work and therefore were tired before they started.

Even with this sort of overcrowding it was still not possible to find from the local cottages all the labour required by the few farms in a 'closed' parish. The alternative was to recruit labourers from further afield, possibly from a village where poor rates could not be controlled by one landlord, but instead ownership was split among many. These were known as 'open' villages, where cottage speculators gathered and built cottages, usually of a much lower standard than those of the great estates, and could take advantage of the shortage of cottages to demand a high rent. Castle Acre is an example of an open village which was

---

[80] Clarke, 'Labourers' cottages'.
[81] E. H. Hunt, 'Labour productivity in English agriculture', *Economic History Review*, second series, vol. 20 (1967), pp. 280–92.

providing labour for the neighbouring closed parishes. The Castle Acre system is described in detail by Mr Denison for the report *On the Employment of Women and Children in Agriculture* in 1843.

> Suppose a farmer in or near Castle Acre wishes to have a particular piece of work done, which demands a number of hands, he applies to a gang master in Castle Acre, who contracts to do the work and to furnish the labour. The bargain is made with the gang master, and it is then his business to make his bargain with the labourers. He accordingly gets together as many hands as he thinks sufficient, and sends them in a gang to their place of work... Castle Acre is what is called an 'open' parish, that is, in the hands of a considerable number of proprietors while the neighbouring parishes are owned by one or two or very few proprietors. These last, partly in order to prevent an increase of birth settlements and to keep down the rates, partly from an unwillingness to invest money in cottage property, not only allow no new cottages to be built but let the old ones fall into ruin. The resident population of these parishes is thereby gradually reduced as the labourers are forced to quit them and to reside in Castle Acre... The competition caused by these newcomers raises the house rent throughout the parish.[82] Mr Hudson of Castle Acre provided Mr Denison with the following list of inhabitants of Castle Acre:
> 1 Clergyman, 4 Farmers, 89 Tradesmen and Journeymen
> 49 Labourers with families belonging to Castle Acre
> 12 Poor Widows with families belonging to Castle Acre
> 103 Labourers with families belonging to other parishes

The figures from the 1851 census show a similar pattern. Only one man, William Long, is described as a gangmaster. The notorious Mr Fuller, a great gangmaster and drunkard who caused the downfall of many young girls, 'but now has become a methodist and reformed', was mentioned by witnesses to the 1843 commission, but seems to have disappeared by 1851. Nine people are described in the census as 'owners of houses', an occupation not found elsewhere, which suggest the existence of the speculative cottage owners so much complained about.

Of the population of about 1,500, 290 were not born in Castle Acre. This is a much higher proportion than that at Tittleshall. There were 264 people listed as agricultural labourers but only 132 were employed on the local farms; the rest were probably working some distance away. The average number of people per house is no higher than in Tittleshall, but here again there are examples of intense overcrowding. Lodgers are also occasionally listed. In one cottage there were sixteen people of whom three were lodgers. Twenty-nine of the 337 houses in Castle Acre were owned by the Holkham estate and perhaps they housed some, but

---

[82] Parliamentary Papers (1843), (510), XII, *Employment of Women and Children in Agriculture*, Special Assistant Poor Law Commissioner's reports, Mr Denison's report on Norfolk, Suffolk and Lincolnshire, pp. 220–6.

certainly not all, of the labourers working on the Holkham farms there. A few of these were in good repair. Three new ones had just been built in the meadow by the river. However, half of them were wretched and four of the worst were pulled down in 1870.

Gangs from Castle Acre worked in the many closed parishes in the neighbourhood and a list of farms on which gangs were employed is given in Mr Denison's report. Those owned by the Holkham estate were in Lexham and Castle Acre. In spite of severe overcrowding in the Lexham cottages, there were still not enough labourers on the spot. In his letter to the Poor Law Board in 1848, Mr Blyth gives other examples of labour being drawn from outside the parish to work on Holkham farms. Labourers for Waterden Farm came from South Creake.[83] Thirty-six men were employed on Waterden farm in 1851, but only three, one shepherd and two labourers, lived in the one cottage available. 'The two principal landowners in Burnham [one of whom was Lord Leicester] have not for their labourers more than two cottages each by their respective farm houses.' He quotes the owner of Amner parish as saying that he considered his estate to be valuable 'in proportion as he could keep it free from any increased liability'.

This lack of humane interest by the employer towards his labourers was very obvious to visitors from the north of England and in great contrast to conditions there.

> After the elaborate and we may say paternal methods pursued in the north, the Norfolk system of labour is not very attractive. There is no such thing as a yearly labourer, no boarding paid for by the farmer, and in short, no connection between master and man, except work on the one hand and payment on the other. The bailiff gets a guinea per week, the yardsman 14/6d., the engine driver 3/- per day and the ordinary farm labourer 10/- to 12/- per week. Lads are paid from 8/- to 10/- per week and boys 4/6d to 5/-. Women get from 10d. to 1/- per day. All the payments are made in money, there being no privileges in addition to the wages.[84]

The Laws of Settlement were finally repealed by the Union Chargeability Act in 1865. Some areas had already introduced their own Union Chargeability system. Docking union was classed as one parish for Poor Law rating purposes from 1847. This removed the economic incentive for keeping down the number of cottages and landowners suddenly recognised the advantages of having labourers near their work. Instead

---

[83] Parliamentary Papers (1850), *Reports on the Laws of Settlement*, communication from Mr Blyth, p. 70.
[84] H. M. Jenkins, 'Lodge Farm, Castle Acre', *J.R.A.S.E.*, second series, vol. 5 (1869), p. 473.

The landlord and the labourer

of fearing the burden of poor rates, prospective tenants now wanted to be sure of a reliable labour force. This gave a great boost to cottage building. However, there was much lost ground to be made up, and the need for gangs continued. They were still to be found in the Swaffham area in the 1890s,[85] and labour books for Lodge Farm, Castle Acre, show that they were employed there until 1895. Anne Digby argues that it was the labour-intensive agriculture of the agricultural revolution rather than the 'open' and 'closed' villages that created the need for gangs. As mechanisation was slowly introduced, gang work was no longer necessary.[86]

In 1866, Lord Leicester explained the situation on his estates to the Norfolk Agricultural Association.

> I am the owner of 521 cottages, supplying about 450 able-bodied labourers. I calculate that 950 labourers are required to cultivate my property. The home supply can always be relied upon. They receive wages of between 10 and 12 shillings per week... The other 500 who are needed for proper cultivation, may be living in cottages put up by speculative builders and paying rents of between £4 and £5 per year. [Holkham cottagers were paying £2 17s. 4d.] These houses are usually poor and hardly ever have a garden. The labourers have to walk three or four miles to work. They are less reliable and cannot rely on regular work... The time is not far distant when the first requirements of a farm will not be ample farmsteads, but sufficient cottages.

In an effort to cut down overcrowding the earl did not allow lodgers in his cottages and married children had to find their own homes. Such improved conditions would help keep the best agricultural labourers from emigrating or moving to the towns.[87]

Lord Leicester reckoned that two cottages were needed for every hundred acres cultivated[88] and Captain de Winton of the Gloucester Chamber of Commerce thought that there should be a law compelling this.[89] The Earl of Leicester admitted that the provision on the Holkham estate was well below this, but he said that he was building all he could afford each year. The building of large numbers of cottages in parishes such as Egmere, where in 1851 there were seven cottages for a 1,122 acre farm and, by 1877, twelve new ones in addition to four of the old ones,

---

[85] Parliamentary Papers (1893-4), (c.6894-1), XXXV, *Royal Commission on Labour*, minutes of evidence, p. 584.
[86] A. Digby, 'The operation of the Poor Law in the social and economic life of nineteenth century Norfolk', Ph.D. thesis, University of East Anglia, 1971.
[87] Parliamentary Papers (1867), *Children's Employment Commission*, p. 142.
[88] Parliamentary Papers (1867-8), *Royal Commission on the Employment of Women and Children in Agriculture*, p. 36n.
[89] *Ibid.*

emphasises the acute shortage which must have existed previously. No new cottages were built at Waterden Farm in the late nineteenth century, but at other small parishes, such as Kempstone and West Lexham, there were some developments. By 1895 there were 730 cottages on the estate. If an average of two per hundred acres was required, then Holkham needed a hundred more. However, as migration from the countryside continued, the estate probably had an adequate supply of cottages by the end of the century. This represents a great improvement on the 1851 situation. Not only were most of the cottages of a reasonable standard, but there were also enough of them. This seems to have been achieved by the investment of a very small proportion of the estate rental.

For example, we can see in Weasenham that as the number of Holkham cottages slowly rose through the nineteenth century, the amount of overcrowding declined. In 1820 there were thirty cottage tenants. This slowly increased to forty-one in 1850 and forty-six in 1860. By 1880 there were seventy-three and it is clear, from the list of names, that large families who had previously been living together were now splitting up. Where, at an earlier date, all the members of the Carr family had been living together, they now occupied three houses, and the Barnards were now living in four cottages. The number of cottages continued to increase until 1890, when there were eighty-seven cottages and for the first time three are listed as vacant. We can safely assume that by 1900 there were enough cottages in Weasenham.

In contrast, the total number of inhabited cottages was declining after 1851. Thus, while the estate owned one third of the cottages in the Weasenhams in 1851, the proportion had increased to two thirds by the end of the century.

This standard was certainly not achieved elsewhere. Conditions on the great estates were probably better than on the small ones. Royal Commissions praised the work of the Marquis of Cholmondeley alongside that of the Earl of Leicester and, further afield, the Duke of Bedford was also famous for his improvements. By 1884 there was far less overcrowding and the gang system was less common. However, there were still cases on the smaller estates of a man, wife and lodger living in a small cottage.[90]

In 1895, Henry Rew reported that on the large estates in Norfolk cottages were generally good, many having three bedrooms, but on the

[90] Parliamentary Papers (1884–5) *Royal Commission on the Housing of the Working Classes*, p. 590.

smaller estates they were inferior and there was still insufficient accommodation.[91] The worst cottages were still those of the small proprietors. Joseph Arch, writing of 1872, said,

> The cottage accommodation was a disgrace to civilisation; and this not only in Somerset, but all over the country. As many as thirteen people would sleep all huddled together in one small cottage bedroom. I think among the worst sinners in this respect I should name the class of small proprietors. Most likely they have not the money either to improve or enlarge the cottages they own, or to pull them down and build new and better ones, so the labourer is forced to live in one room.[92]

Seabohm Rowntree's enquiries into how agricultural labourers lived showed that there was still much overcrowding in 1913. Some cottages were falling down because it was not worth repairing them for the rent. The standard type of cottage outside the great estates in Norfolk, as elsewhere, consisted of a living room and small lean-to scullery downstairs and two interconnecting bedrooms upstairs. The second bedroom upstairs was always very small and one of Rowntree's informants told him, 'You fit into it as one day you will fit in your coffin.'[93] Very rarely was there a porch and the staircase led up from the living room, tucked in beside the chimney. The space on the other side of the chimney contained the larder. Not all cottages had even a lean-to scullery. Cottagers on the large estates were certainly better off than those whose cottages were owned by small proprietors.

Types of tenure

How well cottages were kept in repair often depended on the type of tenure under which they were let. In the first half of the nineteenth century a few cottages on the Holkham estate were let for life, but this practice ended after 1850. In 1800, six lifehold leases were granted. Some of these were for two or three lives rather than one. The cost of these varied between £15 and £60, and the subsequent rent was between 6d. and 10s. a year, with the majority between 2s. and 4s. In Weasenham before 1850 about one third of the cottages were let in this way. The system provided the tenant with security of tenure, but Keary thought that cottages let this way usually fell into disrepair. He wrote of 'a small,

---

[91] Parliamentary Papers (1896), Henry Rew, *Report on Norfolk*, p. 45.
[92] Arch, *The Story of his Life*, p. 127.
[93] S. Rowntree, *How the English Labourer Lives* (London, 1913), p. 330.

poor cottage in bad repair' at Lexham: 'This was a lifehold estate and fell in about two years ago in the very dilapidated state which lifeholds invariably do.' If cottages were let with a farm the tenant farmer was expected to keep them in repair. At least half the cottages let with farms were in poor repair when Keary visited them in 1851. The problem when letting cottages with farms was that of security of tenure for the cottagers. The labourer was at the farmer's mercy and could be evicted at his will. Henry Rew said in 1895 that more farmers were insisting on having cottages under their control in an attempt to break the agricultural unions.[94] It was very easy for a farmer to evict someone because he was a union man.[95]

A compromise system of tenure was developed at Holkham to cope with this situation where the farmers wanted their own cottages, but the landlord did not want to lose control. By the late 1860s all Lord Leicester's cottages were held directly from him, but the tenant farmers nominated the occupiers of the cottages near their farms.[96] These nominations were subject to the agent's approval. This was still the system in 1895 and seems to have been unique. It was commended by the Agricultural Commission because it protected the cottager from unfair eviction.[97] The system was not copied on other estates. The Duke of Bedford, for instance, let his cottages directly to farm labourers, and there was no nomination by farmers.[98]

Cottage building as a sound investment

There was much discussion during the nineteenth century as to whether cottage building could be a profitable investment. T. W. P. Isaac, in his article in the *J.R.A.S.E.* in 1857, said that no farm labourer could afford to spend more than £5 a year on rent and therefore, to be a profitable investment, cottages must be erected for less than £85.[99] Even £5 was a rather high rent on the Holkham estates, but most good cottages cost more than £85 to build. The authors of the series of articles on 'The cottage homes of England' in the *Norfolk News* wrote, 'We have high

[94] Parliamentary Papers (1896), Henry Rew, *Report on Norfolk*, p. 45.
[95] Edwards, *From Crow-scaring to Westminster*, pp. 43–5.
[96] Parliamentary Papers (1867–8), *Royal Commission on the Employment of Women and Children in Agriculture*, p. 37.
[97] Parliamentary Papers (1896), Henry Rew, *Report on Norfolk*, p. 45.
[98] Bedford, *The Story of a Great Estate*, p. 94.
[99] Isaac, 'On the construction of labourers' cottages', p. 494.

and practical authority for stating that pecuniary return may be secured for capital invested in improved dwellings for the humbler classes. Many experienced landowners have given their views on this subject and proved that a larger net interest than is usually got from land can be obtained with proper care and economy from cottages.'[100]

However, a Norfolk witness to the Royal Sanitary Commission of 1869 pointed out that speculators had to build poor cottages if they were to get any return and that good cottages could not be expected to be profitable.[101] The Duke of Bedford wrote, 'I know of no more satisfactory form of philanthropy possible for the owner of a great estate than the provision of good cottages.'[102]

Of the Holkham estates, Henry Rew said that new cottages were costing £300 to build in 1895 and on this outlay the earl made a $2\frac{1}{2}\%$ profit, which would hardly make cottage building a successful commercial venture. The earl did not expect cottages to bring in a fair return, but he did not believe in letting at too low a rent, because he thought low rents meant low wages.[103]

However, Lord Leicester was sure that good cottages increased the value of his farms. Where cottages were lacking they were a good investment because they were needed for the proper cultivation of the land, and he questioned whether

the existing rents for land can be maintained without further cottage accommodation, but I am satisfied that rents may be increased when there are sufficient homes for the labourer. During an existing lease there is not one tenant who is not willing to ensure me 5% upon any sum I may expend in providing homes for his labourers.[104]

This is a complete reversal of the situation in the period when the Settlement Laws were in force. The argument that cottages increased the value of farms was upheld by Captain Beck, agent on the Sandringham estate. In 1884 he said, 'They are not let with any idea of repayment in the shape of interest on outlay, but rather with reference to the advantage they confer on the rest of the estate.'[105] A less tangible advantage of good cottages was given by the Duke of Bedford: 'Good and comfortable cottages in which the decencies and dignity of human

[100] Clarke, 'Labourers' cottages', p. 1.
[101] Parliamentary Papers (1868–9), *Royal Sanitary Commission*, p. 358.
[102] Bedford, *The Story of a Great Estate*, p. 81.
[103] Parliamentary Papers (1896), Henry Rew, *Report on Norfolk*, p. 45.
[104] Parliamentary Papers (1867), *Children's Employment Commission*, p. 45.
[105] Parliamentary Papers (1884), (c.4402), xxx, *Royal Commission on the Housing of the Working Classes*, minutes of evidence, pp. 589–90.

life may be maintained generally imply that they are inhabited by good and efficient labourers.'[106]

From this we can conclude that the profits in the form of interest on capital were small, but that by the late 1860s cottage building was not the philanthropic exercise that the Duke of Bedford made it out to be. After the adoption of the Union Chargeability Act of 1865, cottage building was as necessary to keep up farm rents as was the building of farm premises.

The landlord was responsible for providing housing for the labourers on his estate, and it is clear that only a very small proportion of income from rents was ever spent on cottage building. The sums involved were always far less than those for farm improvements. Although expenditure was low when compared with the rather extravagant building on the Bedford estates, a great deal was achieved. The standard of design improved greatly throughout the century and by 1900 most of the cottage accommodation was adequate. This is very different from the dilapidation and overcrowded conditions of the 1850s described by Keary. The number of cottages also increased. Keary's report covered about 350 cottages, while in 1867 Lord Leicester owned 521 cottages. In 1895, Henry Rew said he had 730 cottages, or twice as many as forty years before. The fact that the rate of population increase had greatly slowed down meant that this level of cottage building was enough to end the acute shortage of accommodation of the mid nineteenth century.

It seems that the Holkham estate village was by no means the homogeneous community that we might at first sight expect it to be. Not all the houses, except in Holkham itself, were owned by the estate and many of those owned were not let to subservient agricultural labourers but rather to independent master craftsmen. As the century progressed and more cottages were built, more of the farm labourers were housed by the estate. The evils of overcrowding and the open and closed villages were much reduced and the fact that a few cottages were vacant by 1900 shows that enough had at last been built.

The population was also more mobile than we might imagine. Contemporary autobiographies often show labourers changing jobs and frequently moving on. This is borne out by the names in cottage rentals. Although some families remained in the same cottages for fifty years or more, others came and went with surprising rapidity.

[106] Bedford, *The Story of a Great Estate*, p. 82.

Unlike farm rents, those for cottages increased very little over the period. Between £2 and £3 was usual after 1851 until the end of the century, but there were more under £2 in the previous fifty years. This relative stability is surprising when it is realised that both building costs and agricultural wages were rising. During the Napoleonic Wars prices of between £50 and £70 were quoted in the published specifications for 'model' cottages, while by the 1840s some were just over £100 and by 1900 they could be in the region of £300. Wages rose from about 8s. a week in 1804, to 10s. a week. It has been shown that cottage standards did steadily increase throughout the century and this improvement is partly reflected in the rise in building costs.

Although a few cottages were built before 1850, and a certain number were built to rectify the worst conditions found in Keary's report of 1851, the majority were rebuilt after 1865. The total stock of cottages on the estate trebled between 1851 and 1895. Where more than two generations of a family had been cramped together in one house, they were now able to spread out. This increase was taking place in a period of population decline accompanied by a reduction in the number of inhabited houses. This meant that the proportion of cottages owned by the estate in any village increased considerably in the second half of the nineteenth century.

The influence of the earl in the local community probably changed very little during the period and would not have been affected by the agricultural depression. Cottage building continued until an adequate number of cottages had been provided. Education was the only traditional responsibility of the landlord which as yet received state assistance. School building declined after 1870 but the landlord's influence over school management remained great, as many members of school boards were his tenants.

The decline in rural population, which resulted from increased employment opportunities elsewhere and the less labour-intensive methods of the agricultural depression, helped to ease the pressure on cottage accommodation and must have reduced the control of the landlord over a labouring class who knew that they could seek a living elsewhere. Their increasing independence was also being shown in their interest in agricultural unions, although here their argument was usually with the farmer rather than the landlord.

Although the earl must have been a very remote figure to all except those in the immediate vicinity of the hall, his role in the community as a provider of funds and encouragement for such schemes as school building and church restoration, and also as the major rent collector, ensured that his influence remained important until the end of the nineteenth century.

6
Some conclusions: The landlord, the tenant and the landscape

This study has set out to provide an overall picture of a great estate and to view its impact on the community as a whole. Estate records are numerous, but evidence for the private life and financial affairs, particularly of the second earl, for the day-to-day running of the average farm, and for village life in general, is sadly lacking. Where written evidence fails, building evidence can take over. This is an attempt to combine documentary and building evidence and to show the value of this approach for research in such fields as agricultural, social and estate history.

There is very great danger in drawing general conclusions from the study of only one estate, and especially so when even contemporaries recognised that Holkham was unusual. However, the very fact that the Coke's management was set up as an example for others to follow makes this study worth while.

The landscape of a great estate always stands out in contrast to that of the smaller landholdings around it, and the Holkham area is no exception. There the villages are dominated by estate cottages; the school was usually built with estate funds and sometimes the church was restored at the landowner's expense. The area is crossed by wide, straight enclosure roads running through well laid-out, rectangular fields. Substantial farm houses with their premises beside them are evenly distributed about the fields. In areas where the medieval village had substantially decayed there is often no central nucleus to the parish. Instead, it may contain only a couple of large farms with a few cottages beside each of them. It is in these areas, where there were few freeholders to hinder the rationalisation of field systems and communications, that the influence of the landlord is seen most clearly.

6.1 Aerial view of estate landscape. (a) Coastal area between Holkham and Wells, showing 1856 drainage dyke, Holkham branch of the Wells and Fakenham railway, and the woodland belt around the park. Note the large regular fields of planned enclosure. (b) (*facing page*) Holkham park and house.

The park

At the centre of the estate was the great house, with its park and estate village. The building of country seats began in the sixteenth century. In Norfolk, houses such as that at East Barsham were built early in the century, while Godwick Hall, the home of Chief Justice Coke and now demolished, was dated 1586. Raynham Hall, the home of the Townshends, was built in the 1620s and Blickling Hall at about the same date. The civil war brought a temporary halt in country house building, but by the eighteenth century it had reached its peak. This included not

b

only the great halls such as Holkham but many smaller houses in more modest parks. Rebuilding and adding to houses, as well as the expansion of parks, continued throughout the nineteenth century until the end of the last wave of Victorian farming prosperity. Where money was coming from sources other than agriculture, building could go on much later. Sennowe Hall, the home of Thomas Cook, the travel agent, was built in 1908.[1]

More important to the landscape than the houses themselves were the parks in which they stood. Holkham Park covered 3,000 acres by 1850. The creation of rolling parklands with fine trees and artificial lakes is perhaps the most pleasing way in which the estates affected the English landscape. Holkham Park is typical of many, expanding from relatively small beginnings and doubling in size between 1770 and 1800 (fig. 6.2).

[1] N. Pevsner, *North-west and South Norfolk* and *North-east Norfolk and Norwich*, The Buildings of England (Harmondsworth, 1962).

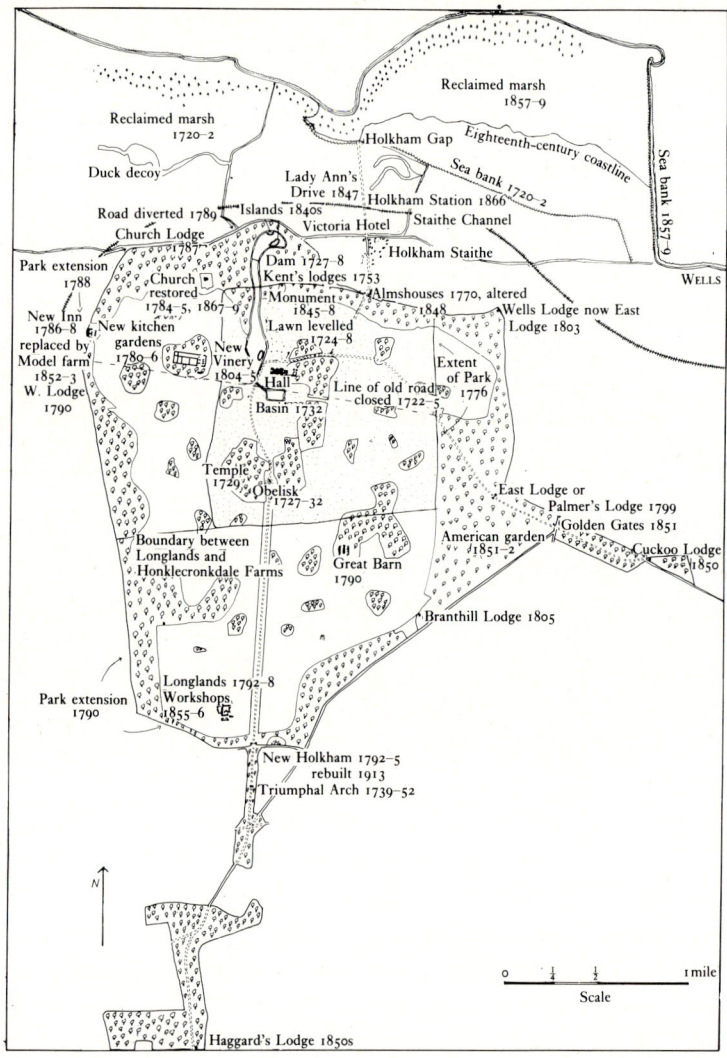

6.2 Plan of Holkham park.

Thomas William Coke made very few alterations to the house. When he inherited the estate it had been completed for only ten years and, although 'Capability' Brown had undertaken some initial tidying up of the surrounding land, there was still great scope for improvement. Contemporaries felt that the park fell far short of the splendour of the house. The lake itself was only a tidal creek which ebbed and flowed daily, leaving unsightly stretches of mud. There were very few trees in the park and little protection from the wind which seemed to blow continuously across this coastal area. The layout of the gardens, as set out by William Kent when he designed the house, was considered far too formal and old fashioned by the end of the eighteenth century, and so in the 1780s Coke set about improving his rather bleak surroundings (fig. 6.2). The general layout of the park was Coke's own: he employed professional landscape gardeners only for the treatment of details. Their services were required particularly for the lake; by 1806, 36,000 cubic yards of earth had been removed and it had been extended over an area previously occupied by a kitchen garden. A system of sluices was constructed to keep out the tide, the formal canal with its flanking pavilions designed by Kent was drained and the pavilions demolished. Entirely new kitchen gardens further from the house were built. The trees planted by Kent on the slopes leading up to the obelisk wood were thinned out, thus opening up the view and creating a spacious parkscape.

The park, and with it the home farm, was steadily enlarged. In 1788 Honklecronkdale Farm was taken in hand, the vinery and the new kitchen garden built and the rest of the land added to the home farm. The new six acre kitchen gardens were the work of Samuel Wyatt. They were enclosed and subdivided by high red-brick walls. Beside the garden is an elegant vinery, the front range of which is white brick and has two storeys. The upper floor was the dormitory for the apprentice gardeners. The fine porch has a delicate fanlight over a pair of supporting ionic columns. A contemporary visitor described it as a 'graceful little paradise'.

The final extension of the park to include Longlands Farm took place in 1790 and then the work of encircling the park with a continuous tree belt began, fifty acres being planted each year until the whole circuit of nine miles was completed. Finally, the wall surrounding the entire park was built between 1833 and 1839 to replace the temporary wooden paling.[2]

The enlarging of the park meant that the octagonal Kent lodges were now well within the outer perimeter wall and so five new ones were designed by Samuel Wyatt and built between 1780 and 1807. All except one were simple cuboid or octagonal buildings, but one on the east side of the park was more ambitious with two single-storey cuboid wings flanking a pedimental central arch between Tuscan colonnades.

[2] A. M. W. Stirling, *Coke of Norfolk and his Friends*, 2 vols. (London, 1908) vol. 1, p. 239.

The first and most striking change to the immediate vicinity of the house to be made under the second earl was the erection of a monument to his father. It was described by Elizabeth Stanhope: 'The monument is too near and *frightful*, the wheatsheaf looks like a vulgar evergreen flower on top.'³ The building of the monument involved the demolition of one of Kent's original lodges, which would have upset Elizabeth Stanhope.

The second earl himself was responsible for several alterations to the surroundings of the house. One of his first actions was to create two islands in the lake and to thin out the trees on the banks to allow better views from the house into the woods beyond. In the 1850s the stables, terraces and lawns to the north and the south of the house were rebuilt and a conservatory erected. The country house architect, S. S. Teulon, was employed and further afield several new lodges were built. These included the present main gates from Holkham Staithe, the Golden Gates with their lodge at the easternmost corner of the park, Cuckoo Lodge at the eastern end of the avenue leading to the Golden Gates, and Haggard's Lodge to the south. By the end of the 1850s the park had very much the appearance it retains today.

This work, of consciously creating 3,000 acres of parkland with its woodland and clumps of trees, lodges, model farm buildings and a lake, fundamentally altered the landscape surrounding the hall and resulted in a park larger than any other in the county.

It has already been shown that most of the houses at Holkham, including those in the park, those that acted as lodge houses, those at Holkham Staithe and in the marshes, and the village of New Holkham, were rebuilt, some between 1790 and 1820, some in the 1850s and some in the 1880s. As was usual with the cottages at the gates of a park, they were regarded as show cottages, built to model designs. The same is true of the farms near Holkham. They were often visited by those attending the sheep shearings. Half of the employed inhabitants of Holkham in 1851 worked for the estate, either in the house and park, at the brick kilns or in the estate workshops. Most of the others were agricultural labourers employed by Holkham tenants.

---

³ A. M. W. Stirling, *The Letter Bags of Lady Elizabeth Stanhope* 2 vols. (London, 1913), vol. 1, p. 216.

Further afield

Further from the hall, the influence of the landlord became less. Many of the outlying parishes would only rarely have been visited by Lord Leicester, although his agent was making regular inspections of the farms. Almost all the farmland was owned by Holkham in the 1850s, but usually less than half the cottages were estate property, and even these were often let to independent craftsmen rather than to agricultural labourers. The occupations within the village were varied and, except at Holkham, dependence on the landlord for employment was not marked.

The village school, however, was usually partly financed by the earl, so the spirit of obedience and deference towards him would be fostered there. At Tittleshall, the Cokes' family vault attached to the church would present a constant reminder of the existence of the landowning family.

One of the greatest problems for both town and country resulting from the population increase of the early 1800s was that of housing: Keary's description shows that conditions around Holkham were no better than on other estates. On this progressive estate, we might have expected the landlord to set an example in cottage building as he did in farm improvement, but until after 1860 this was not the case and both dilapidated and overcrowded cottages were usual. Although the Cokes could easily have afforded the relatively small-scale investment required for cottages, they held back. In this, the most important aspect of community welfare, they were found lacking. There was no pressure from tenant farmers for the building of cottages, as they were afraid of increasing the burden of the poor rates. After the Union Chargeability Act, interest in cottage building grew and, by the end of the century, landowners were by far the most important builders of agricultural housing and the proportion of cottages owned by the Holkham estate within Holkham villages increased.

By the 1870s the contrast between the living conditions on the large and small estates was often noted by observers. Great landowners had plenty of capital behind them and could afford to build cottages, which, although they did not provide an economic return, did make their farms more attractive to tenants. Holkham and Houghton were quoted as estates where great improvements had taken place.

The problem of tied cottages was one which the early agricultural unions had to face. Here, too, the cottage tenant on the large estate often fared best. The Earl of Leicester tried to provide greater security by letting most of his cottages directly rather than with his farms, in the hope that this strategy would prevent unfair eviction by farmers.

The role of the tenant in village life and in the improvement of farming at Holkham must not be underestimated. Estate correspondence and the wording of entries in the audit books make it clear that the initiative for many farm and village improvements came from tenant farmers. Men such as the Hudsons and the Overmans were forceful characters, famous nationally for their agricultural achievements through their work at Smithfield and the Royal Agricultural Society. The estate benefited from having them as tenants. All farmers would maintain a close contact with the hall. They would receive regular visits from the agent; they would attend the annual audit and, at an earlier date, the annual sheep shearings. They would be in correspondence with the estate whenever they wanted to modify their leases, or needed new buildings and repairs to old. They wrote requesting rent reductions, and notices to quit were also made in writing. Their lives and sometimes their very ability to remain solvent were in the hands of the estate.

The influence of Holkham through the farmsteads it erected was the most important that it exercised and it has been possible to follow both the type and the timing of this investment through the audit books and the buildings themselves. The timing is interesting as it suggests the motives, and the evidence for both Woburn and Holkham shows that giants such as these did not follow the timing or invest for the same reasons as the often smaller estates studied by Professor Thompson. Nationally, interest in farm buildings was probably influenced by the activities of the large estates. It has been shown that both the motives and the type of building erected changed through the nineteenth century, but that the standard of building was always high. By the 1850s the Holkham farms were among the best laid out in the country and the contrast between them and the nearby owner-occupier farms, or those on smaller estates, is often very noticeable.

The landlord–tenant system at Holkham was valuable in promoting good farming and also, by the end of the century, in improving housing conditions. There is far less evidence concerning the other activities of the estate, and it seems that educational and philanthropic duties of the landlord were performed to only a minimal extent. Visitors to Holkham saw only the cottages, schools and almshouses at the gate of the hall. Conditions on the rest of the estate were far lower.

Evidence for the financial affairs of Lord Leicester and his influence on the outside world was very difficult to come by. Dr Parker has shown that up to 1822, at least, the Cokes were borrowers and not lenders, so money from agriculture was not going to the new industries, but rather the reverse. However, after the financial crisis of 1822, there was a gradual building up and strengthening of the family's financial position and, by the 1870s, the flow had reversed and large sums were being invested, not in British industries, but overseas, mainly in railways.

The contrast between the effect of the depression on landlord and tenant is very great. In spite of declining rents there is no indication that Lord Leicester needed to change his life style. Shooting parties and the entertainment of royalty continued as before. Most of the great landowners held industrial or urban estates as well as agricultural land. In the mid-century Lord Leicester, however, relied entirely on farm rents for income. After 1880, although agricultural rents were declining, profits made in the boom years had been reinvested in stocks and shares and so economies were not necessary.

At Holkham we see a good landlord and able tenants working together to create an improved agriculture which was held up as an example in Britain, Europe and America. While conditions were favourable, the estate prospered. The effects of the post-1873 depression were delayed, but eventually Holkham suffered along with the rest of the arable areas of England. New men came in and the old traditions and ties came to an end.

The depression of the 1920s and death duties of the 1940s resulted in the selling of much of the estate's property and the tenant farmers often bought their own farms. Estate influence on farming practice is only a shadow of what it was a century ago. Since 1967 even the tenant's yearly agreement is a standard one drawn up by the Ministry of Agriculture. Now the European Common Agricultural Policy and government incentive programmes have far more impact on the tenant farmer than the agent or the landlord.

Appendix 1

Agricultural statistics for the county of Norfolk in 1854

IA. Acreages of land-uses in Norfolk Poor Law Unions in 1854

Union	Total acreage	Acreage under wheat	Acreage under barley	Acreage under oats	Acreage under rye	Acreage under peas and beans	Acreage under tares or vegetables	Acreage under potatoes	Acreage under turnips or rape	Acreage under carrots
Aylsham	67,665	11,531	11,575	784	46	337	65	50	11,049	16
Blofield	44,432	6,525	5,004	851	21	799	4	30	5,401	8
Docking	80,964	13,843	14,556	3,214	21	390	128	30	14,489	31
Erpingham	70,344	10,799	11,702	1,963	31	429	92	93	10,218	23
Forehoe	38,102	6,436	6,597	510	51	815	117	78	5,599	64
Henstead	41,722*	6,663	6,679	498	56	843	90	69	5,658	72
Loddon and Clavering	68,664	8,424	8,256	497	54	2,206	301	59	6,478	80
Mitford and Launditch	106,632	18,764	18,135	1,340	66	873	154	71	17,617	53
Swaffham	80,677	10,461	10,896	3,101	1,052	457	208	120	11,637	22
Walsingham	76,705	13,512	12,482	1,552	4	186	119	49	12,441	17
Wayland	49,863	7,113	7,499	1,681	481	526	120	12	7,095	63
St Faith's	48,953	7,866	8,014	644	144	181	182	138	7,670	36
East and West Flegg	26,408	4,602	3,600	1,009	8	848	87	150	3,326	15
Freebridge Lynn	71,324	9,705	8,914	3,199	94	835	30	275	9,912	75
Guiltcross	43,703	5,914	6,328	1,612	209	1,843	401	95	5,332	36
Tunstead and Happing	59,630	10,389	9,497	1,446	37	1,380	49	39	8,834	39
Depwade	72,681	11,302	11,507	875	53	4,033	752	63	7,685	13
Downham	83,687	22,203	5,711	10,049	141	4,576	206	1,324	8,955	208
Thetford	120,733	3,925	4,418	2,527	1,870	264	155	39	6,112	11

* This figure was obtained from W. White, *Norfolk Directory* (London, 1883), as the one given in the Parliamentary Papers appears to be wrong.

IA. *cont*.

Union	Acreage under mangolds or beetroot	Acreage under cabbages	Meadow and pasture	Acreage under lucerne or clover	Acreage under other crops	Fallow	Woods and plantations	Commons and wastes	Holdings of less than 1 acre	Land not accounted for
Aylsham	382	3	11,644	11,310	36	288	4,238	3,639	662	?
Blofield	854	—	11,242	5,554	—	51	1,275	508	665	1,837
Docking	587	31	9,534	14,831	5	103	3,033	3,778	509	2,064
Erpingham	550	1	6,400	10,704	21	961	5,107	4,389	562	6,225
Forehoe	937	21	6,588	5,927	1	158	1,161	860	360	1,572
Henstead	595	13	7,626	5,946	119	446	2,188	489	551	3,115
Loddon and Clavering	857	13	17,028	6,249	106	1,128	2,039	4,917	554	364
Mitford and Launditch	766	7	17,907	17,686	262	167	3,402	1,283	2,408	3,909
Swaffham	442	19	17,643	12,620	213	972	4,192	5,216	628	773
Walsingham	767	8	12,602	12,665	74	328	4,172	1,078	650	3,407
Wayland	628	12	11,125	7,094	133	869	1,675	2,433	530	499
St Faith's	294	—	5,736	7,857	130	279	3,389	1,340	239	1,901
East and West Flegg	284	28	3,581	3,370	154	168	326	840	247	1,272
Freebridge Lynn	513	16	14,343	9,900	77	1,379	2,715	2,644	738	5,768
Guiltcross	480	2	9,518	5,338	1,480	1,114	1,462	842	569	1,120
Tunstead and Happing	943	—	9,418	9,237	49	360	2,327	2,834	715	2,038
Depwade	1,647	52	11,281	7,420	177	2,049	1,244	1,050	1,040	8,422
Downham	1,942	260	24,103	7,308	284	4,282	1,589	1,719	1,206	1,229
Thetford	166	7	16,190	6,657	696	2,284	4,604	529	228	16,556

1B. *Number of animals in Norfolk Poor Law Unions in 1854*

Union	Horses	Dairy cattle	Other cattle	Sheep and lambs	Swine
Aylsham	3,308	1,496	6,238	31,560	6,687
Blofield	1,561	707	5,113	17,644	3,431
Docking	3,044	1,936	1,372	69,168	5,248
Erpingham	3,105	1,374	5,651	28,215	6,126
Forehoe	1,926	1,142	3,955	22,543	5,713
Henstead	2,125	895	2,632	21,732	4,733
Loddon and Clavering	2,803	1,732	4,271	26,661	6,878
Mitford and Launditch	4,505	2,724	6,683	62,203	9,396
Swaffham	2,174	1,107	3,721	60,836	4,991
Walsingham	3,168	1,594	3,344	57,279	6,450
Wayland	2,025	1,084	2,729	36,860	4,495
St Faith's	1,877	702	2,806	25,807	3,822
East and West Flegg	1,855	765	2,074	4,868	3,763
Freebridge Lynn	1,829	1,204	3,060	45,331	3,591
Guiltcross	1,610	1,025	2,601	22,870	4,543
Tunstead and Happing	2,952	1,410	5,124	18,310	5,896
Depwade	3,294	2,477	4,268	26,211	9,731
Downham	6,417	2,511	9,444	36,491	7,116
Thetford	1,317	515	1,508	29,279	4,828

2. *Percentage of land in Norfolk Poor Law Unions under crops of grain (wheat, oats, barley and rye), roots (peas, beans, turnips, carrots, beetroot and mangolds), clover and lucerne, meadow and pasture, commons and waste, and woods and plantations in 1854**

	Grain	Roots	Lucerne/ clover	Meadow/ pasture	Commons/ waste	Woods/ plantations
Aylsham	35.4	16.8	16.8	17.3	5.4	6.25
Blofield	28.1	15.9	12.0	25.0	1.1	2.9
Docking	39.2	18.6	18.4	11.7	4.2	3.4
Erpingham	34.9	16.0	15.2	13.6	5.9	6.95
Forehoe	35.6	20.0	15.5	17.3	2.6	3.2
Henstead	33.3	17.1	14.2	18.2	1.1	5.25
Loddon and Clavering	25.0	14.7	9.1	24.8	7.15	2.9
Mitford and Launditch	36.0	18.1	16.5	16.8	1.2	3.19
Swaffham	31.6	15.7	14.6	21.5	6.4	5.1
Walsingham	36.0	12.7	16.6	16.1	1.4	5.5
Wayland	33.25	16.7	14.1	22.1	4.9	3.3
St Faith's	34.0	16.7	13.8	11.8	2.73	7.0
East and West Flegg	34.4	17.6	12.8	13.3	3.6	1.2
Freebridge	30.3	15.8	13.9	20.0	3.12	3.8
Guiltcross	31.0	17.56	12.2	21.8	1.9	3.7
Tunstead and Happing	35.0	19.0	15.5	15.8	4.75	3.9
Depwade	32.5	18.4	11.2	15.5	1.2	1.7
Downham	45.6	18.7	8.4	29.0	2.3	1.8
Thetford	10.6	5.4	5.5	13.0	0.4	3.8

* Not including fallow, flax, cabbage and other crops, holdings of less than one acre or land not accounted for.

3. *Percentage of wheat, barley, oats and rye in the total grain crop for Norfolk Poor Law Unions in 1854*

	Wheat	Barley	Oats	Rye
Aylsham	48.2	48.3	3.2	0.2
Blofield	52.6	40.3	6.7	0.2
Docking	43.7	46.0	12.0	0.1
Erpingham	44.1	47.8	8.0	0.1
Forehoe	47.0	48.5	3.7	0.3
Henstead	48.0	48.3	3.6	0.4
Loddon and Clavering	48.7	47.7	2.99	0.3
Mitford and Launditch	48.5	47.0	3.49	0.3
Swaffham	41.0	42.7	12.1	4.1
Walsingham	49.0	45.0	5.65	0.3
Wayland	42.5	44.7	10.4	2.4
St Faith's	47.0	48.0	3.83	8.5
East and West Flegg	50.0	39.0	11.6	0.0
Freebridge	44.0	41.0	14.6	0.4
Guiltcross	39.8	46.0	11.8	1.5
Tunstead and Happing	48.0	43.0	6.65	1.7
Depwade	47.5	48.5	3.7	0.22
Downham	58.5	14.9	26.3	0.3
Thetford	30.6	34.5	20.1	14.6

4. *Percentage of peas and beans, turnips and rape, carrots, and mangolds and beetroot in the total root crop for Norfolk Poor Law Unions in 1854*

	Peas and beans	Turnips and rape	Carrots	Mangolds and beetroot
Aylsham	2.8	93.7	0.13	3.2
Blofield	11.3	76.0	0.4	12.0
Docking	2.5	93.5	0.2	3.7
Erpingham	3.8	91.0	0.2	4.9
Forehoe	11.0	75.5	0.86	12.6
Henstead	11.2	79.0	1.0	8.4
Loddon and Clavering	22.9	67.0	0.8	8.9
Mitford and Launditch	4.5	91.5	0.3	3.9
Swaffham	3.6	92.5	0.1	3.5
Walsingham	1.4	92.0	0.1	5.7
Wayland	6.3	85.2	0.7	7.5
St Faith's	2.2	94.0	0.3	3.6
East and West Flegg	18.4	75.0	0.6	6.3
Freebridge	7.3	87.0	0.4	4.5
Guiltcross	24.0	69.0	0.5	6.0
Tunstead and Happing	12.1	79.0	0.34	8.4
Depwade	30.0	57.5	0.0	12.3
Downham	29.0	57.5	1.3	12.4
Thetford	4.1	93.5	0.0	2.5

5. *Number of animals kept per 100 acres in Norfolk Poor Law Unions in 1854*

	Horses	Dairy cattle	Other cattle	Sheep	Swine
Aylsham	4.8	2.2	9.1	4.7	10.0
Blofield	4.0	1.6	11.6	40.0	7.6
Docking	3.7	1.3	5.5	83.0	6.4
Erpingham	4.4	1.9	8.3	40.0	8.6
Forehoe	5.0	3.0	8.3	62.0	15.1
Henstead	5.1	2.2	6.2	52.0	11.0
Loddon and Clavering	5.0	2.9	7.6	44.0	11.7
Mitford and Launditch	4.4	2.5	5.5	58.7	9.0
Swaffham	3.1	1.3	4.7	76.0	6.2
Walsingham	4.1	2.1	7.1	76.0	8.3
Wayland	4.0	2.2	2.4	76.0	9.0
St Faith's	4.1	1.5	6.2	58.7	8.3
East and West Flegg	5.2	2.9	7.9	18.0	15.1
Freebridge Lynn	2.6	1.6	4.4	66.0	5.0
Guiltcross	3.6	2.3	6.2	50.0	10.4
Tunstead and Happing	4.4	2.3	8.6	31.0	10.0
Depwade	4.6	3.5	6.2	38.0	13.0
Downham	4.5	2.6	9.3	58.7	7.2
Thetford	1.1	0.66	3.8	3.8	2.3

Source: Parliamentary Papers (1854), (1761), LXV, *The Agricultural Statistics for Norfolk and Hampshire*, Sir John Walsham and Mr Hawley.

Appendix 2

Investments of the first two Earls of Leicester, 1811–1891

	Value of shares £	Purchase price £	
1811	150	150	Lynn Theatre
	150	150	Reform Club
1846	150	150	Royal Agricultural College
1853	100	100	Fakenham Corn Exchange
1855	11,640	11,640	Wells and Fakenham Railway
1857	20	24	E. Dereham Corn Exchange
1866	2,628	2,628	W. Norfolk Junction Railway
1870	10,000	10,891	Gt Indian Peninsular Railway
	11,800	11,800	Gt Eastern Railway
1871	8,500	12,650	North Eastern Railway
1872	680	765	North Eastern Railway
1873	1,550	1,548	London and North-Western Railway
1874	1,000	1,000	Norfolk County School
1875	3,450	3,536	London and North-Western Railway
	10,000	12,055	Gt Western Railway
	680	1,020	North-Eastern Railway
	5,000	5,207	London and North Western Railway
1876	10,000	11,540	Madras Railway
	5,000	5,719	South Indian Railway
	1,182	1,182	North Eastern Railway
1877	5,000	5,719	South Indian Railway
	10,000	11,685	Sind, Delta and Punjab Railway
1878	5,000	5,871	Madras Railway
1880	5	5	Walsingham Coffee House
1881	600	600	Eastern and Midland Railway
	500	500	Norfolk and Norwich Agricultural Hall
	493	493	North Eastern Railway
1882	6,000	10,332	London and North-Western Railway
	7,000	9,986	Gt Western Railway
	30	30	Wells Harbour Bonds
1883	1,210	1,210	Midland Railway
	1,020	1,076	North-Eastern Railway

	Value of shares £	Purchase price £	
1884	10,000	14,380	Gt Western Railway
	4,000	5,439	Midland Railway
	7,500	10,463	Gt Western Railway
1885	6,000	5,999	Caledonian Railway
	6,300	6,029	North British Railway
	20	20	Farmers' Foundry Co. Ltd
	517	646	North-Eastern Railway
	600	600	Midland Railway
	2,800	4,231	North-Eastern Railway
	2,500	3,926	London, Southend and Tilbury Railway
	7,800	9,856	London and South-Western Railway
1886	3,157	4,017	New S. Wales 3½% stock
	2,900	3,093	Ontario and Quebec Railway
	3,700	3,996	Melbourne Harbour Bonds
	2,101	2,007	New S. Wales loan
	2,500	2,967	Gt Northern Railway
1887	1,500	1,490	Western Railway of Buenos Aires
	1,700	1,510	Argentine 5% 1886 issue
	2,000	1,265	Canadian Pacific rail shares
	1,758	1,999	Gt Northern Railway
	2,750	2,028	Australian Mortgage Land and Finance Co.
	2,000	2,206	The Nezams Railway
	1,000	1,027	The Smyrna Cassaba Railway
	2,000	2,125	Canadian Pacific Railway
	2,000	2,676	Guinness
1887	900	900	Wells Improvement bonds
	260	260	Caledonian Railway
	1,500	1,374	Argentine 5% stock
	1,149	1,499	Buenos Aires and Pacific Railway
	190	190	London, Tilbury and Southend Railway
	4,000	4,012	Allsop and Sons
	1,500	1,513	Buenos Aires and Western Railway
	3,000	3,000	Manitoba Mortgage and Investment Co.
	3,000	3,000	S. Australia Land Mortgage and Agency Co.
	2,800	3,031	Canada 4% Bonds
	2,800	2,985	Victoria Govt 4% Railway Loan
	2,500	2,578	Cape of Good Hope Stock
	22	25	Australia Mortgage Land Co.

Appendix 2

	Value of shares £	Purchase price £	
1888	5,000	5,312	City of Toronto 5% 1897 Bonds
	11,800	10,829	Great Eastern Railway
	2,200	3,513	Imperial Fire Insurance
	10,000	13,576	London and South-Western Railway
	1,632	1,638	North British Railway
	3,000	3,105	Illinois Central Railway
	1,000	1,035	Lawes Manure Co.
	2,600	2,876	Pennsylvania Railway
	3,600	5,046	London and South-Western Railway
1889	270	310	Caledonian Railway
	10,000	10,200	Truman, Stanbury and Co.
	13,700	10,007	Gt Eastern Railway
	1,000	1,020	Whitbreads
	5,000	4,994	Fifty Bank of Australia shares
1890	4,000	4,000	Buenos Aires Gt Southern Railway
	5,000	5,793	Railway shares
	800	2,853	London Westminster Bank
1890	250	248	Buenos Aires and Pacific Railway
	1,000	1,000	Peter Walker and Son
	1,200	1,204	Caledonian Railway
	11,400	9,918	Minneapolis Railway
	315	362	Caledonian Railway
	612	734	North British Railway
1891	1,330	1,330	Buenos Aires Gt Southern Railway
	4,800	5,417	National Provincial Bank
	1,425	3,763	London Joint Stock Bank
	1,395	3,820	Union Bank of London
	25	25	Cooperative Fish Company
	10,000	7,719	Canadian Pacific Railway
	2,000	2,034	Canadian Pacific Railway
	1,250	2,025	Buenos Aires Gt Southern Railway

Source: Holkham MSS, 'List of investments of Thomas William Coke 1811–'.

Appendix 3

The amount of rent collected, the sum in arrears and the amount spent on repairs on the Holkham estate, 1790–1900

	Rents £	Repairs £	Arrears £
1790	18,461	1,392	1,381
1791	18,907	1,810	2,136
1792	19,039	2,237	3,287
1793	19,039	6,036	4,349
1794	19,655	3,097	2,090
1795	19,763	4,835	4,084
1796	20,184	3,160	3,802
1797	20,244	7,084	6,105
1798	20,353	3,061	3,056
1799	20,373	3,141	3,054
1800	20,429	2,446	4,032
1801	20,507	5,712	1,359
1802	20,823	4,131	359
1803	20,880	5,959	1,194
1804	21,324	3,396	1,068
1805	21,322	3,079	1,195
1806	21,404	2,779	1,396
1807	21,839	2,080	1,484
1808	22,100	3,009	1,653
1809	23,188	3,338	1,769
1810	23,267	2,836	1,733
1811	24,203	4,956	1,784
1812	28,253	4,994	2,326
1813	27,736	5,461	1,672
1814	30,008	4,535	1,769
1815	30,833	6,156	3,168
1816	31,049	5,815	1,435
1817	31,037	5,078	1,202
1818	31,227	4,978	790
1819	31,651	3,577	1,571
1820	31,948	4,220	4,364
1821	32,186	2,794	7,584
1822	31,680	4,280	2,894
1823	30,990	5,505	2,088

Appendix 3

	Rents £	Repairs £	Arrears £
1824	30,950	4,270	1,597
1825	31,091	4,114	1,585
1826	31,134	5,371	1,831
1827	31,296	5,304	1,016
1828	31,469	4,350	995
1829	31,656	5,224	1,160
1830	31,789	3,456	979
1831	31,790	4,503	712
1832	31,861	2,957	800
1833	32,059	3,880	1,071
1834	32,265	3,531	1,516
1835	32,477	5,179	918
1836	32,528	7,310	816
1837	32,624	5,266	843
1838	33,168	4,836	843
1839	34,176	5,662	1,068
1840	35,000	4,375	683
1841	35,299	4,093	687
1842	35,805	2,964	734
1843	35,953	3,834	3,125
1844	39,265	2,606	1,437
1845	39,268	2,600	1,051
1846	39,231	2,941	1,105
1847	39,308	2,446	1,067
1848	40,072	625	1,391
1849	41,982	513	1,496
1850	42,309	527	2,300
1851	42,200	1,404	3,675
1852	42,709	8,848	2,438
1853	42,782	8,239	1,076
1854	43,420	9,854	1,020
1855	45,005	10,585	800
1856	48,315	14,343	669
1857	49,000	13,855	174
1858	48,765	6,623	459
1859	49,601	6,870	1,461
1860	49,897	8,287	2,490
1861	51,682	6,458	623
1862	51,004	7,773	1,617
1863	53,273	4,337	203
1864	52,949	5,091	200
1865	50,094	6,894	2,264
1866	51,304	5,964	2,166
1867	53,817	6,664	245

	Rents £	Repairs £	Arrears £
1868	53,588	9,897	370
1869	54,241	6,453	728
1870	55,107	8,933	1,334
1871	56,015	9,651	1,291
1872	55,828	7,806	1,571
1873	58,195	9,702	224
1874	57,624	8,407	205
1875	57,643	6,740	263
1876	57,563	6,937	860
1877	58,705	7,374	232
1878	58,051	7,741	10,357
1879	58,778	8,681	1,061
1880	51,908	9,719	7,169
1881	56,826	7,682	8,750
1882	59,709	8,836	6,545
1883	56,912	8,184	6,543
1884	51,157	7,739	3,156
1885	46,791	4,497	3,248
1886	47,196	2,731	3,574
1887	43,381	3,247	6,077
1888	43,208	3,558	6,698
1889	45,990	3,464	2,592
1890	45,569	4,605	1,792
1891	43,068	5,226	2,509
1892	43,174	4,623	3,126
1893	35,830	2,620	4,346
1894	33,479	3,378	6,403
1895	35,970	3,201	4,684
1896	34,299	3,313	2,545
1897	31,935	3,831	2,587
1898	33,368	3,788	871
1899	31,396	4,475	906
1900	31,393	4,111	1,179

Source: Holkham MSS, 'Audit books.'
Note: Some of these figures differ from those quoted by R. A. C. Parker, *Coke of Norfolk, a Financial and Agricultural Study, 1707–1842* (Oxford, 1975), tables M and N.

Appendix 4

Size of farms and expenditure on them, 1790–1900

	Acreage (1851)	Expenditure £
Longlands, Holkham	1,800	9,017
Leicester Square Farm, South Creake	865	6,221
Egmere Farm	1,122	6,121
Dunton Farm	1,144	5,709
Beck Hall, Billingford	653	5,480
Bintry Farm	750	5,094
Lodge Farm, Castle Acre	788	5,053
Longham Hall Farm	584	5,042
Burnham Sutton Farm	997	4,970
Panworth Hall, Ashill	556	4,901
West Lexham Farm	1,131	4,870
Wicken Farm, Castle Acre	1,209	4,656
Hall Farm, Flitcham	382	4,252
Brake Hall, Billingford	496	4,084
Wellingham Farm	1,000	3,827
Tithe Farm, Weasenham	498	3,719
Manor Farm, Fulmodeston	801	3,510
Kipton Ash Farm, Weasenham	733	3,493
Godwick Farm, Tittleshall	503	3,282
Warham Hall	559	3,227
Doughton Farm, Dunton	534	3,170
Warham Grove Farm	453	3,166
Abbey Farm, Flitcham	916	3,147
Harpley Dam Farm, Flitcham	1,101	3,147
North Hall Farm, Warham	1,428	3,026
Manor House Farm, Tittleshall	493	2,918
Lower Farm, Castle Acre	367	2,778
Massingham Farm	946	2,704
Manor Farm, Sparham	469	2,636
Quarles Farm	560	2,569
Sparham Hall Farm	636	2,390
Hall Farm, Wighton	413	2,169
Branthill Farm	928	2,150

	Acreage (1851)	Expenditure £
Grenstein Farm, Tittleshall	496	2,060
Dobbs Farm, Wighton	123	1,956
Kempstone Lodge Farm	438	1,837
High House Farm, Warham	349	1,722
Inn Farm, Holkham	120	1,655
Kempstone Manor Farm	291	1,532
Whitehall Farm, Flitcham	545	1,426
Weasenham Hall Farm	319	1,411
Weasenham Manor Farm	582	1,365
Manor House Farm, Wighton	218	1,330
Farm No. 2, Wells	87	1,319
Burghwood Hall Farm, Tittleshall	272	1,284
Farrer's Farm, Warham	836	1,271
Wheycurd Farm, Wighton	531	1,246
Waterden Farm	762	1,216
Crabbs Castle Farm, Wighton	595	1,126
Upper House Farm, Warham	495	1,105
Manor Farm, Billingford	232	1,074
Church Farm, Sparham	222	1,002
Lower Farm, Billingford	288	964
Farm No. 1, Wells	504	968
Cokesford Farm, Tittleshall	355	894
Wicken Farm, Tittleshall	140	804
Clipstone Farm, Fulmodeston	313	634
Farm No. 2, Longham	220	626
Peterstone Farm, Holkham	157	608
Abbey Farm, Castle Acre	367	507*
Farm No. 3, Longham	54	480
Croxtone Farm, Fulmodeston	247	478
Rose ? Farm, Tittleshall	?	334
Burnham Overy Farm	100	309
High House Farm, Tittleshall	389	270
Godwick Hall Farm, Tittleshall	234	211†

Source: Holkham MSS, 'Audit books'.
* Land dispersed among other Castle Acre farms in 1856.
† Amalgamated with Godwick Farm post 1900.

Appendix 5

Condition of cottages on the Holkman estates, 1851

Place	No. of bedrooms	No. of inhabitants	State of repair		Other remarks
			Good	Bad	
Flitcham	1	4	×		
	3	2		×	Good cottage
	1	7			A most wretched thatched cottage
	1	?			Ditto
	1	5			Small poor cottage
	1	7			Ditto
	2			×	Small but comfortable
	Two families in one house, five persons, in bad repair				
	2	9		×	
	2	5		×	
	1	3		×	
	1 small	7		×	
	2 very small				Unfit to live in
	2 ditto		×		
	2 ditto		×		
	2	5			In a very bad state
	1	4			Ditto
	2	6	×		
	2	10 One lodger			Rain comes in. Small bad cottage
	2	11			Very filthy and unwholesome
	2	2			Ditto
	1	6 Two families		×	
	1	5		×	Pigsty in a filthy state
	1	6		×	Very small
	2	7			Ditto
	1	4 Two lodgers		×	Small bad cottage
	1	4		×	Rain comes in
	1	4		×	Ditto
	1	9		×	Ditto
	2	7		×	Ditto
	1	8		×	No privy
	1	5 Two families	×		

Appendices

Place	No. of bedrooms	No. of inhabitants	State of repair Good	State of repair Bad	Other remarks
Flitcham (cont.)	1	6 Two families Three lodgers			Surprisingly clean and neat
	2	8	×		
	2	6			
	2	8 Two families	×		
	2	5			
	2	2	×		
	2	8			Small and poor
	1 small	10		×	Very wretched
	1	9 Five lodgers			
	1	3			A most wretched cottage unfit to be inhabited
	1 damp	2			Wretched, unwholesome
Tittleshall	1			×	Very bad
	1			×	Ditto
	0 (1 living room)				
	0 Ditto	5		×	Ditto
	0 Ditto			×	Ditto
	1	8		×	Ditto
	1	4		×	Ditto
	1	2	×		
	2	5	×		
		5		×	Very bad
	1	6			Small and wretched
	2	1		×	Very bad
	2	4	×		
	2	5 One lodger			
	2	8	×		
	2				
	1				
	2	10		×	Very bad state
	2	4			
	1	4			In which two married couples sleep
	1	5		×	Very bad
	2	6		×	Ditto
	2	1			Single storey
	1		×		
	1		×		
	1	4	×		
	1	4	×		
	2	6	×		
	2	4	×		
	2	3	×		Single storey
	1	6	×		
	1	2		×	Very bad

Appendix 5

Place	No. of bedrooms	No. of inhabitants	Good	Bad	Other remarks
Tittleshall (cont.)	1	7		×	Ditto
	2	7		×	Ditto
	1	1		×	Ditto
	1	7		×	
	1	4		×	
	1	4			
	1	5			
	1	3			
	1	3			
	1	3			
	1	7		×	Very bad, must come down
	2	6		×	Very bad and dirty
	1	9			
	2	8			
Weasenham	2	5	×		Good roomy cottages
	2	7	×		Ditto
	2	1	×		Ditto
	2	5	×		Ditto
	2	2	×		Ditto
	1	2			Very small, bad, dirty, slovenly
	1	6			Ditto
	1	6			Ditto
	1	6			Thatched, small bad cottage
	2	4		×	Small, poor
	1	9			Single storey, nine people in one room
	1	7			Very bad indeed
	2		×		
	2		×		
	2			×	Small, bad
	1	4		×	
	2	9		×	
	2	11		×	
	2	12		×	
	2	5 Two lodgers	×		
	2		×		
	1				Very small and bad
	2	8	×		
	1				Very small and bad
	2			×	Ditto
	2				Good roomy cottage in bad repair
	1				In very bad state, should be repaired immediately

Appendices

Place	No. of bedrooms	No. of inhabitants	State of repair Good	State of repair Bad	Other remarks
Weasenham (*cont.*)	1	3 grown-up persons, male and female sleep in a most disgraceful state			
	1	4			Small and bad
	1				Ditto
	2	5	×		
	2	5	×		
	1				Small and bad
	1				Ditto
	1				Ditto
Warham	2		×		Drains bad
	2	10 Two families, one lodger			
	1	4		×	
	2	5 One lodger			
	1	1			1 privy to 4 cottages
	2		×		
	2	3			
	2	5			
	1	6			
	2	4			
	2	8		×	
	6	8 Two families	×		
	3	8 Ditto	×		
	1				Poor bad cottage
	1 room, no pantry, very bad				
	2	4 Two families			
	2		×		
	2	6 Two families			
	2	2			
	2	5 Two families			
	2	3			
	2	4	×		
	2	9	×		
	2	7	×		
	2	5 One lodger			
	2	8 Two families			
	1	7 Two families			Very filthy state
	1	2		×	
	1	2		×	
	1	2		×	
	1	4		×	
	2			×	
	2	6			A good cottage

Appendix 5

Place	No. of bedrooms	No. of inhabitants	State of repair Good	State of repair Bad	Other remarks
Warham	2				A good cottage
(cont.)	3			×	
	2				Very good repair
	2				Ditto
Burnham	2	3		×	
	2	1		×	
	2	2	×		
	1	1	×		
Bintry	2	7	×		
	2	4	×		
	1	3			Small poor cottage
	2	6	×		
	1	6			Very small and bad
	1	7			Ditto
	1	3	×		
	2	5	×		
	2	4	×		Good cottage
	2	4	×		Ditto
	2	5	×		Ditto
Castle Acre	1	3			Very small, bad cottage
	3				Small but comfortable little house
	2	3			Very small
	3 cottages in the meadow by the river				Just rebuilt in good repair
	2	6			
	1	2			
	1	7	×		Bad cottage
	1	2	×		
	2		×		Very small
	2		×		Ditto
	1	6		×	Bad cottage
	1	2		×	
	3	3		×	
	1	7		×	
	2	5		×	Very dirty and bad
	2	9		×	Very old and bad
	2	1		×	Very dirty and bad
	2	4		×	Ditto
	2	2		×	Wretchedly bad
Wighton	2	3		×	
	1	2		×	
	2	4	×		Dirty
	1	10			Very clean and neat

			State of repair		
Place	No. of bedrooms	No. of inhabitants	Good	Bad	Other remarks
Wighton (cont.)	2	This cottage is occupied only by an old woman who should be removed to a smaller one			
	1 room	Two families living in a most disgraceful state			
	3	5			
	3	3			
	1 small room	5			A house quite unfit for a family to live in
	1 room	2			Quite unfit for anything but a single man or woman
	3	8 Three families		×	
	2	5			
	3	2			
	2	4		×	
	2	5			
	2	6 One lodger		×	A very comfortable cottage
	2	6			Ditto
	2	10 One lodger		×	
	2	7 One lodger			Not very clean
	3	4		×	Very clean and neat
	1	2		×	
	1			×	
	2	5 One lodger			Dust hole in a filthy state
	A very small room in which five persons sleep, and by no means fit to accommodate so many				It is very crowded. No privy
	2	5			Clean and neat
	2	5			Ditto
	1	5		×	Privy in bad state
	2	2			In a most dilapidated state. Unfit to live in and should be pulled down
	2	12		×	Very much crowded
	1	2		×	
	2	2	×		

Appendix 5

Cottages let with farms

Billingford	Two double cottages. 2 bedrooms each. Small and low. Good repair.
South Creake	Steward's house where servants boarded.
Massingham	Yardsman's and shepherd's cottages. Both comfortable. Two others in a dilapidated state and not fit to be repaired.
Kempstone	Bailiff's house now divided into two. Two sitting rooms, 4 bedrooms.
	Two cottages, 1 bedroom each, bad roofs, hardly worth repairing. Erect new and better ones in a few years.
	Three cottages. Sitting room, lean-to pantry and 2 bedrooms.
	Lodge from Litcham Common, low small thatched 2 rooms.
Holkham	One erected 1838 sitting room, back kitchen, pantry, 2 bedrooms, outhouse for oven and copper. In good repair.
	One needing new roof and windows.
Fulmodeston	One living room, scullery, 2 very small bedrooms, requires attention
Flitcham	Two mud with flat tile roofs. Built by tenant.
	Small and inconvenient cottage converted out of one end of a waggon lodge and granary.
Egmere	Two with 3 bedrooms. Could be comfortable but need repair.
	Three old bad cottages much out of repair.
	Two with 3 bedrooms. Could be comfortable but need repair.
Dunton	Double cottage 2 bedrooms each. Good repair.
	Seventeen others all old, many badly arranged. Most with 2 or 3 bedrooms.
	Four in tolerable repair.
Castle Acre	Three very small poor cottages, originally sheds, but turned into dwellings for which they are quite unfit.
	A new good house, 4 bedrooms, comfortable.
	A new good cottage let to steward.
	Good double cottage.
Burnham	One double cottage, two bedrooms in each. Good repair.
	Four more, two bedrooms, sitting room, scullery.
	Two more occupied as one by yardsman who lodges a teamsman, 3 bedrooms.
Bintree	One double cottage, 2 bedrooms each. Good repair.
	One single storey cottage, 1 sleeping room. Very dilapidated.
Wighton	Double cottage occupied by steward and shepherd, 1 storey, low and bad.
	Double cottage. Living room, scullery, two small bedrooms, good repair.
Wellingham	Two cottages, good repair.
West Lexham	Pub. and 8 cottages all with good gardens.
	Two bedrooms, 10 inhabitants, bad repair
	Two bedrooms, 7 inhabitants, bad repair.
	Two bedrooms, bad repair, rain comes in.
	Two bedrooms, fair repair.
	One bedroom, fair repair.
	Two bedrooms, 1 storey, fair repair.

Weasenham	Two bedrooms, small and poor, wretched state, rain comes in.
	Cottage and garden, a small poor cottage in bad repair.
	Two bedrooms, good repair.
	Two bedrooms, good repair.
	One bedroom, good repair.
	Two bedrooms, tolerable repair.
	Two bedrooms, tolerable repair.
	Two bedrooms, tolerable repair.
	Two cottages, comfortable dwellings, bad repair.
	Double cottage, yardsman and teamsmen, 1 living room, 3 bedrooms, roof leaks.
Tittleshall	Three cottages entirely rebuilt last summer. Small and inconvenient.
	One small living room, 1 bedroom and a sort of closet
	Two cottages, tiles need repairing. 1 storey, 2 rooms.
Sparham	One dilapidated and uninhabited.
	One very wretched. Quite unfit to be repaired.
	Double cottage, poor, wretched, 1 bedroom each.
	Two dilapidated and uninhabited.
	Two more, deteriorating.
	One recently built, should be comfortable but the rain comes in.
	Two bedrooms on the ground floor. Very damp.
	One dilapidated. Soon be unfit to be inhabited unless repaired, but would cost little more to build a new one.

Source: Holkham MSS, W. Keary, 'Description of the estates of the Earl of Leicester' (1851).

Select bibliography

Arch, J. *The Story of his Life, Told by Himself* (London, 1898)
Ashby, M. K. *Joseph Ashby of Tysoe, 1859–1919. A Study of English Village Life* (Cambridge, 1961)
Bacon, R. N. *A Report of the Transactions at the Annual Holkham Sheep Shearings* (Norwich, 1821)
   Agriculture of Norfolk (London, 1844)
Bateman, J. *The Great Landowners of Great Britain and Ireland* (London, 1883)
Bedford, Duke of. *The Story of a Great Estate* (London, 1897)
Caird, J. *English Agriculture in 1850–51* (London, 1851)
Cairncross, A. K. *Home and Foreign Investment* (London, 1953)
Chadwick, O. *A Victorian Miniature* (London, 1960)
Chambers, J. D. and Mingay, G. E. *The Agricultural Revolution, 1750–1880* (London, 1966)
Communications to the Board of Agriculture on Farm Buildings (London, 1796)
Dean, G. A. *The Land Steward* (London, 1851)
Denton, J. B. *The Farm Homesteads of England* (London, 1863)
Edwards, G. *From Crow-scaring to Westminster* (London, 1922)
Ernle, Lord. *English Farming, Past and Present* (6th edn, London, 1961)
Haggard, H. Rider. *Rural England*, 2 vols. (London, 1902)
Harvey, N. *A History of Farm Buildings in England and Wales* (Newton Abbot, 1970)
Havinden, M. A. *Estate Villages, a Study of the Berkshire Villages of Ardington and Lockinge* (Reading, 1966)
James, C. W. *Chief Justice Coke, his Family and Descendants at Holkham* (London, 1929)
Jeffries, R. *Hodge and his Masters* (London, 1890)
Jenks, L. H. *The Migration of English Capital* (London, 1927)
Kent, N. *Hints to Gentlemen of Landed Property* (London, 1775)
   A General Survey of the Agriculture of the County of Norfolk (London, 1796)
Marshall, W. *Rural Economy of Norfolk*, 2 vols. (London, 1787)
Mingay, G. E. *English Landed Society in the Eighteenth Century* (London, 1963)
Orwin, C. S. and Whetham, E. W. *A History of British Agriculture, 1846–1914* (London, 1964)
Parker, R. A. C. *Coke of Norfolk, a Financial and Agricultural Study, 1707–1842* (Oxford, 1975)
Perry, P. J. (ed.) *British Agriculture, 1875–1914* (Newton Abbot, 1973)
Peters, J. E. C. *The Development of Farm Buildings in East Lowland Staffordshire* (Manchester, 1969)
Read, C. S. 'Agriculture of Norfolk', in W. White, *Norfolk Directory* (London, 1883)
Riches, N. *The Agricultural Revolution in Norfolk* (London, 1967 reprint)

Rigby, E. *Holkham and its Agriculture* (3rd edn, Norwich, 1817)
Spring, D. *The English Landed Estate in the Nineteenth Century* (Baltimore, 1963)
Springall, L. Marion. *Labouring Life in Norfolk Villages, 1834–1914* (London, 1936)
Stirling, A. M. W. *Coke of Norfolk and his Friends*, 2 vols. (London, 1908)
    The Letter Bags of Lady Elizabeth Spencer Stanhope, 2 vols. (London, 1913)
Stephens, H. and Burns, R. S. *The Book of Farm Buildings* (Edinburgh, 1891)
Thompson, F. M. L. *English Landed Society in the Nineteenth Century* (London, 1963)
Trow-Smith, R. *History of British Livestock Husbandry, 1700–1900* (London, 1959)
Waistell, C. *Designs for Agricultural Buildings* (London, 1827)
Young, A. *A General View of the Agriculture of the County of Norfolk* (London, 1804)

Index

afforestation of the dunes, 131
agent (*see also under individual agents*), 51, 67–73
agricultural machinery, 6, 110, 116, 120
Albemarle, William Charles Keppel, 4th Earl of, 41, 45, 77, 78
allotments, 192
almshouses, Holkham, 204; Longham, 122
American War of Independence, Coke's attitude to, 40
Anmer (Norfolk), 240
Arch, Joseph, 206, 243
Ashill (Norfolk), Panworth Hall Farm, buildings 143, 146–7, 157, 178; enclosure, 127; tenants, 110, 112

Bacon, R. N. (journalist), 16, 110, 218
bakehouses, 221
Baker, William (agent 1832–51), 71
barns, eighteenth-century importance, 137, 138; nineteenth-century importance, 143, 158, 160, 174, 178; simple barns, 156; Wyatt barns, 130–3; *see also* field barns
Bawdeswell and Foxley school, 195
Beauchamp, Sir Proctor, 222
Beck, Mr (tenant, Mileham), 110, 147
Bedford, Francis Russell, 5th Duke of, 77, 89 90
Bedford, John Russell, 6th Duke of, building activities, 169; cottage improvements, 221, 242, 244, 246; pensions, 205; philanthropy, 188–9; rents, 92, 93; school building, 196
Belcham, Mr (tenant, Tittleshall), 107
Bell, Mary (tenant, Tittleshall), 107
Betts, Mr (tenant, Ashill), 112
Billingford (Norfolk), 2; Beck Hall Farm, 113; church, patronage of, 201; enclosure, 127; school, 195, 106, 200; woodland, 83
Bintree (Norfolk), enclosure, 127; school, 200; woodland, 83
Birchams, the (Norfolk), 200, 224
blacksmiths' and carpenters' shops, 158, 160, 176, 177, 178
Blaikie, Francis (agent, 1816–32), 52, 67, 71; and building schemes, criticism of elaborateness, 69, 70, 155; approval of Waterden, 143; and Coke family affairs, 59, 70–1; farming, influence on, 68, 109, 165; leases, 75; and tenants, 69–70
Bloomfield, Mr (tenant, Flitcham), 109
Bloomfield, Mr (tenant, Warham), 110
Blyth, Mr (farmer, Sussex Farm, Burnham), 89, 240
Boileau, Sir John (Ketteringham), 187, 202
Branford, Mr (tenant, Godwick), 69, 107
Brereton, Mr (tenant, Flitcham), 69, 74
breweries, 63
brick kilns, Holkham, 4, 58, 84, 187; Tittleshall, 84
Brown, 'Capability', 252
bullocks, as draught animals, 116, 120
Burke, Edmund, 44
Burnhams, the (Norfolk), 3, 12, 240; Burnham Market, 107; Burnham Sutton Farm, 109, 110, 118; Burnham Thorpe school, 196; enclosure, 127; Sussex Farm, 88
Burrell brothers (tenants, Flitcham), 69

Caird, James (agricultural writer), 81, 108
carpenters, 177; shops, *see* blacksmiths
Castle Acre (Norfolk), 2, 3, 4, 107; Abbey Farm, 112, 155; church, patronage of, 201; restoration of, 202; closed village, 238; cottages, 217; gang system, 239, 240; Lodge Farm, 83, 114; employment of gangs, 241; expenditure on house and farm buildings, 101, 150, 154, 175, 177, 180; 'high' farming techniques, 110, 114–17; mechanisation, 6; Manor Farm, 88, 114, 116, 117; school, 195, 197–8; soup kitchen, 203; Wicken Farm, 101, 150–1, 163, 180
carstone, 208, 222
carthorse stables, *see* stables
Caterham Farm (Surrey), 141
cattle (*see also* livestock), 13, 16; sheds and yards, *see* livestock accommodation
cereal crops, 22, 80
Chesterfield, Lord, 67
child labour, *see* gang system
Cholmondeley estates (Norfolk), 163, 224, 242

285

churches, patronage of, 201; restoration of, 114, 187, 248
clay lump building, 208, 222
closed parishes, 236–7, 240
coal, 176
Coke, Ann Margaret (b. 1779, m. 1794), 42
Coke, Lady Anne Amelia (née Keppel), Countess of Leicester, 2nd wife of Thomas William, 1st Earl (m. 1822, d. 1884), 46
Coke, Anne (b. 1845, m. 1874), 55
Coke, Sir Edward (Lord Chief Justice) (1552–1634), 2, 3
Coke, Edward Keppel (b. 1824), 54
Coke, Elizabeth (b. 1795), see Stanhope
Coke, Georgina (née Cavendish), Countess of Leicester, 2nd wife of 2nd Earl (m. 1875), 55, 56
Coke, Gertrude (b. 1847, m. 1866), 55
Coke, Jane (née Dutton), 1st wife of Thomas William, 1st Earl (m. 1775, d. 1800), 39, 42, 45
Coke, Jane Elizabeth (b. 1777, m. 1796), 42
Coke, John (1590–1661), 3
Coke, Julia (b. 1844, m. 1864), 55
Coke, Juliana (née Whitbread), Countess of Leicester, 1st wife of 2nd Earl (m. 1843, d. 1870), 52, 56
Coke, Thomas, Earl of Leicester, 1744 (1697–1759), 3, 39
Coke, Thomas William, 1st Earl of Leicester of Holkham, 1837 (1754–1842), 39, 42–4, 45–6, 49–50; agricultural improvements, 1, 49, 89–90, 256; parliamentary career, 40, 42–5, 46; sheep shearings, 48; sport, 47
Coke, Thomas William, nephew of 1st Earl (b. 1793), 42, 46, 59
Coke, Thomas William, 2nd Earl of Leicester of Holkham (1822–1909), 52, 55–7; Cottage building, 18, 217, 224, 241; financial affairs, 58–60; hospitals, support of, 65–6; investments outside the estate, 61–5, 257; political interests, 53; reading room, 194; tenants, concern for, 111, 118, 181
Coke, Thomas William (b. 1848), 55
Coke, Wenman (1717–70), 39, 40
concrete, 182, 228–9, 235
county council, 193
corn rents, 86
Cottages, 206–48; building, 212, 214–16, 224–5, 228–9, 255; concrete, use of, 228–9; condition, 207, 217–18, 221–4, 226–8, 230–2; cost, 216, 225, 235, 245; improvements, 232–3; letting, 188; model, 212, 218–20; overcrowding, 235, 237–8, 247; rents, 192; size, 211; tenure, types of, 243–4; at Woburn, 221
Crick, Francis, 51
Cromer convalescent home, 65

crop rotations, see 'Norfolk husbandry'
crops, see cereal crops, root crops

dairying, 25, 118, 158
Davy, John (agent, 1888–95), 72
Dean, G. A. (agricultural engineer), 169–72, 185
Docking, 240
drainage, land, 75, 96–7, 100, 103, 108, 131; of the marshes, 131
Dungeness lighthouse, 58, 69
Dunham (Norfolk), 107
Dunton (Norfolk), cottages, 216, 217, 228, 229, 237; enclosure, 127; farm, 157; school, 200

education, estate expenditure on, 200–1; expansion (1850–80), 195, 196, 200; log books, 199; school boards, 196, encouragement of, 197, tenants' interest in, 197–8; school plans, 200; schools, at Castle Acre, 196, charity, 193, 'dame', 193, at Holkham, 194, Sunday, 194, at Tittleshall, 195, at Wighton, endowed, 193
Edwards, George, M.P., 188
Egmere Farm (Norfolk), 3; cottage building, 241; cottages, 229, 237; farming methods, mid nineteenth century, 118, late nineteenth century, 83, 113, 184; rebuilding, 72, 169, 171–4, 176; woodland, 83
Elmham (Norfolk), 2
emigration, 205
enclosure, commons and wastes, 127, 236; Longham, 101, 119, 127; rents affected by, 87, 104, 127; Tittleshall, 130; Wellingham and Weasenham, 129
England, Mr (tenant), 69
Everett, Mr (tenant), 110
Everington, Mr (tenant), 113

Fakenham, Nurses' Home, 66
farm buildings, 131–86; at Castle Acre, 121; concrete, 181–3; financial aspects, 95, 96, 98–104, 161–3; improvements, 85, 93, 97, 135, 143, 156–60, 164–8, 175, 176; at Longham, 120, 122; at Longlands, 96, 173
farm houses, 113, 114; designed by S. Wyatt, 149, 160
farm machinery, see agricultural machinery
Farmers' Foundry Co. (Great Ryburgh, Norfolk), 63
farmers' wives, 106, 113
farms, size of, 8–9, 107
female labour, 191, see also gang system
fencing, see hedging
fertilisers, 75–6, 110, 120, 121; bone dust, 14; farmyard manure, 16, 110, 116, 165, 176;

fertilisers (cont.)
  guano, 116; rape cake, 14; superphosphates, 116
field barns, 165, 175
flint, 222
Flitcham (Norfolk), 4; church, patronage of, 201; cottages, 208, 215, 226, 227, 228, 238; Harpley Dam Farm, 158, 200, cottages, 215, 216; school, 196, 200
Forbes, Mr (agent, 1885-8), 72
Forby family (tenants, Tittleshall), 107, 114
Fountaine's estate, Norfolk, 197
four-course system, see 'Norfolk husbandry'
Fox, Charles James, 40, 42, 44, 45
fox hunting, 72
French revolution, 44, 45
Fulmodestone (Norfolk), 205; cottages, 232; Croxton Farm, 108; enclosure, 127; woodland, 83

game, effect of depression on, 36-7, 60-1, 257; game keeping, 37, 187; larder, 48; shooting parties, 42, 47, 51, 55
gang system of labour, 18, 191, 239, 240, 241
Garwood, Mr (tenant, Billingford), 109; (tenant, West Lexham), 14, 70
Gayford, Mr (tenant), 110
George III, 40, 42
gig house, 160, 175
Gloucester, Duke of, 47
grain prices, at mid century, 91-2; during Napoleonic Wars, 11-12; post Napoleonic Wars, 14, 91; post-1870 slump, 27-8, 34, 96
granaries, 174
Grey, John, 219
Grimston (Norfolk), 114
guano, see fertilisers
Gurdon, Brampton, 222
Gurney, J. 220

Haegren, Mr (tenant, Quarles), 69
Hare family of Stow Bardolph, 6
Hart, Mr (tenant, Billingford), 110
harvest, 17
Hastings, J. S. (tenant, Longham Hall Farm, 1816-69), 16, 75, 119-22, 198, 202
Hastings, J. (tenant, Longham Hall Farm, 1869-84), 122
Hastings, J. (tenant, Longham Hall Farm, 1884-1907), 125
hedging, 97, 131
Helhoughton (Norfolk), 201
'high' farming, 15, 76, 116
Hill, Rev. Copinger, 219
Hill, Money (tenant, Waterden), 12, 110, 147
Hillesden estate (Buckinghamshire), 59
hiring fairs, 190

Holkham estate, purchase of, 2; size of, 4
Holkham park, 48, 202, 251-4; gates, 254; gardens, 187, 254; Great Barn, 48, 150, 153; home farm, see Longlands; Honcklecronkdale Farm, 253; lake, 253; lodge houses, 254; monument, 254; New Holkham, 212; vinery, 253; wall, 253
Holkham parish, church, patronage of, 201, restoration of, 203; clothing club, 203; cottages, 211, 214, 232, Rose Cottages, 212, 217, 218; Inn Farm, 173; Peterstone Farm, 160; reading room, 194; school, 194, 200; Staithe Farm, 204; woodland, 83; workhouse, 205
Holkham sheep shearings, 1, 48, 49, 52, 104, 108, 126, 254
horses, 25, 116, 120
horse paths, 143
Houghton estates, 11, 136, 210, 255
Hudson, John (tenant, Castle Acre), 15, 17, 18, 73, 88, 106, 110, 198, 202; as designer of farm buildings, 166-7, 178; intensive methods, 14, 16, 76, 116, 117
Hudson, Peter (tenant, Wighton), 183
Hudson, Thomas (tenant, Castle Acre), 116, 117, 256
Hunstanton convalescent home, 65

implement sheds, 176-8
implements, see agricultural machinery
Iveagh, Lord, 37

Jenny Lind Hospital, 65
Justices of Peace, 114

Keary, H. W. (agent 1851-63), 71-2; cottage survey, 217, 224, 243, 244, 246; erection of new buildings, 96, 163; farm survey, 109, 144-5, 146, 158, 174; manager of home farm, 81; report on Duke of Norfolk's estates, 162
Keith, Mr (tenant, Egmere), 83, 113
Kempstone (Norfolk), 3; cottages, 215, 237, 242; enclosure, 127; Lodge Farm, 149-50; woodland, 83
Kendle, Mr (tenant, Weasenham), 69, 110
Kent, N. (surveyor and agricultural writer), 73, 136
Kent, W. (architect), 253
Ketteringham (Norfolk), 202
Kings Lynn Theatre, 62

labour supply, 18, 190, 199, 206, 238-42
landed classes, 8, 36-7
leases, 11, 52, 77, 104, 164, 165
Leeds, Mr (tenant, Castle Acre), 112, 198, 202
Leicester nurses' home, Norwich, 66

288 Index

livestock; 116, 120; importance, in farming system, 15; increase of, after 1850, 81, 166, 176, 178; number in 1854, 24–5; *see also* cattle, sheep
livestock accommodation, 138–40, 143, 157, 160, 175; covered yards, 166, 183; loose boxes for cattle, 147, 157, 172, 175
lodgers, 238, 241
Longford (Derbyshire), 39, 42, 47, 51, 71
Longham (Norfolk), 2, 101; church, 122, 202; enclosure, 88, 119, 127; Hall Farm, 88, 119; school, 122, 195, 200; woodland, 83
Longlands, 77–81; Dean, G. A., work of, 169, 173; rebuilding, 72, 82, 96, 161, 169, 173; steam engine, 175; Wyatt, S., work of, 154
Lowestoft convalescent home, 65

manure, *see* fertilisers
marling, 14, 70, 108
Massingham, (Norfolk), 200; Hall Farm, 136
Middleton family (tenants), 112
Mileham (Norfolk), Burghwood Hall, 2, 112, 130, 155; enclosure, 127; Grenstein Farm, 130, 143, 145, 147, 155, 180
Minster Lovell (Oxfordshire), 59

Napoleon, 45
National Society for the Promotion of Christian Knowledge, 193
Nelson family (tenants, Sparham), 69
Newton (Norfolk), 197
non-conformity, 187
Norfolk, Duke of, 162
Norfolk and Norwich Hospital, 65, 206
'Norfolk husbandry', four-course system, criticisms, 13; in practice, 19–22, 72, 109, 110, 116, 118, 120; leases, 73–4; origin, 10; self-sufficiency, 15; Young's definition of, 10
North, Lord, 40, 42
North Creake, school, 196, 200
Norwich Blind School, 65
Norwich inundation fund, 203

office management, 73
open villages, 236, 238–9
open field, *see* enclosure
Overman, H. (tenant, Burnham), 12, 105, 109, 110, 118, 256; dairy cattle, 118, 175; leases, 76
Overman, R. (tenant, Egmere), 118, 173
Overman, R. (tenant, Weasenham), 118, 218

Parliament, 40, 46, 47, 54
Penrhyn, Earl of, 84
pensions, 204
pheasant shooting, *see* game
piggeries, 158, 174
Plowright (tenant, Wighton), 109

population, growth, 206, 236; decline, 206
primogeniture, 189
purchases of land, 2–3, 87

Quarles (Norfolk), cottages, 215; farm, 3

railways, 4, 5, 15, 176; shares, 62–3
Raynham (Norfolk), 163, 184, 201
reading room (Holkham), 194
Reform Bill (1832), 46
religion, 201–4
rents, arrears, 85, 87; on Bedford estate, 90–1; decline, post-1870, 36, 86, 93; of individual farms, Lodge Farm, Castle Acre, 101, Longham Hall Farm, 101, 123–4, North Hall Farm, Warham, 103, Wicken Farm, Castle Acre, 117, Wicken Farm, Tittleshall, 101; and investment, 104; rise, in Napoleonic Wars, 12, 85, 87–8, post-1830, 86, 91–2, 111; stagnation 1816–30, 85–6, 88–9, 90, 91
Riches, Isaac (tenant), 107
Rix (tenant), 69, 107
road and bridge improvement, 114
Rockingham Whigs, 40
root crops, 14, 24
rotations, *see* 'Norfolk husbandry'
Roxburgh, Duke of, 163
Royal Agricultural Society, 71, 72, 81, 114, 165, 218

Sandringham (Norfolk), 232, 245
Saxham (Suffolk), 140
Saxmundham (Suffolk), Hurts Hall, 155
Sayer family (tenants, Sparham), 106, 112
schools, 114, 187, 222, 255; boards, 72, 194, 196, 197, 200; fees, 199; subscriptions, 200; *see also* education
servants, 49, 55, 61, 113, 187
settlement laws, 225, 236, 240
Seyer brothers (tenants, Longham), 69
sheep, feeding, 16, 78; importance in 1854, 25; numbers, fluctuation in, 1860–90, 32, increase in, at end of century, 83, at Longlands, 81; Southdowns introduced, 13
sheep shearings, *see* Holkham sheep shearings
Shelburne, Lord, 42
Shellabear, Samuel (agent 1863–85), 73, 198, 224
Smallborough (Norfolk), 207
Smithfield show, 118
South Acre (Norfolk), 197
South Creake (Norfolk), enclosure, 127; Leicester Square Farm, 150–3, 161, 163, 180, 240; school, 196; woodland, 83
Sparham (Norfolk), 2, 106; Church Farm, 180; cottages, 215, 217, 228; enclosure, 126; Hall Farm, 111; woodland, 83

Index

Sporle school, 196
stables, 158, 160, 174
Stafford estates (Sunderland), 140, 161
Stanhope, Lady Elizabeth, née Coke (b. 1795, m. 1822), 45, 46, 48, 50–1, 54, 55, 70
Stanhope, John, 70
steam engines, 167, 168, 173, 175
Stow Bardolph (Norfolk), 6
Suffield, Lord, 58
Sunday schools, 194, 222
Sussex, Duke of, 47, 51, 56
Swaffham, 241
Sykes, Sir Tatton, 202

tenants, 105–14; capital needed by, 107–8; character of, 108–9, 110; duration of occupation, 106–7, 111–12; intermarriage, 106; new, post-1870, 112–13; role in village community, 114, 256; value of, 7, 48, 105–6
Thorney (Cambridgeshire), 205
threshing machines, 177
Tittleshall (Norfolk), 2, 3, 4; brick kiln, 84; cholera at, 217; church, patronage of, 201; Coke, family vault, 47, 225; Cokesford Farm, 130; cottages, 217, 238; enclosure, 129; endowment for almshouses, 204; Godwick Farm, 2, 107, 157, 182; occupations of cottagers, 190; origins of tenants, 107; poor, 203, Mrs Forby's fund for, 114; Rose Farm, 157, 177; school, 195, 196, 199, 200; Wicken Farm, 101, 108, 181; woodland, 83
Townshend, Marquis of, 11, 40, 184
trade unions, 188
Turner estate (Warham), 136
turnpikes, 59
Tuttell-Moore (tenant, Warham), 69, 110

union chargeability, 240, 246, 255
United States of America, 109

Victoria, Queen, 47

wages, agents', 73; labourers', 191–2, 240; teachers', 194, 197
waggon lodges, 158, 160, 174, 178
Wales, Prince of (George IV), 42, 47; (Edward VII), 55, 57, 60

Walpole, Sir Robert, 11
Walsham, Sir John, 19
Walsingham, Lord, 58, 222
Ward, Mr (tenant, Warham), 69
Warham (Norfolk), 3, 136, 190, 205; enclosure, 127; Grove Farm cottages, 215; Hall Farm, 110, 155; North Hall Farm, 103, 110; school, 200; woodlands, 83
Waterden Farm, 3, 12, 237, 240, 242; rebuilding of, 143–4, 155, 157, 180; woodland, 83, 110
Weasenham (Norfolk), 2, 110, 190, 242, 243; cottages, 218; enclosure, 129; Friendly Society, 203; High House Farm, 129, 155; Kipton Ash Farm, 164, 183; school, 195, 200, 204; Tithe Farm, 129, 155, 158, 178; Weasenham Friendly Society, 203; woodland, 83
Wellingham (Norfolk), enclosure, 129; Manor Farm, 2; school, 195
Wells (Norfolk), benevolent society, 203; clothing club, 203; enclosure, 127; Leicester Lodge of Oddfellows, 203; lifeboat catastrophe, 203; railway, 5, 62; school, 200; school board, 197; turnpike, 59
West Lexham (Norfolk), 240, 242, 244; church, 203; enclosure, 127; Farm, 14, 112, 176, 237
West Norfolk and Lynn Hospital, 65
wheelwrights, 177
Whissonsett (Norfolk), 206
Whiteman, Mr (tenant, Billingford), 69
Wighton (Norfolk), 3, 109, 155, 190; cottages, 205, 229; Hall Farm, 180; school, 193, 196; workhouse, 205
Windham, Lord (Felbrigg), 44
Winter family (tenants, Sparham), 106
Woburn, 173, 256
woodlands, 58, 83
Wright, Mr (tenant, Wighton), 69
Wrightup, Mr (Ashill), 110, 147
Wrott, John (agent to Walpole), 11
Wyatt, Samuel (architect), 84, 149, 154, 160, 212, 253

Young, Arthur (agricultural writer), 1, 8, 10, 12–13, 14, 139, 143, 146, 207